Phillip Edmonds

Phillip Edmonds lectures in Australian Literature and Creative Writing at the University of Adelaide. He has also taught at the Victorian College of the Arts and Griffith University. His PhD, from Deakin University in 1997, is a study of the short story in Australia during the 1970s and 80s. In the 1970s he edited *Contempa*, and more recently, *Wet Ink: The Magazine of New Writing* between 2005 and 2012. Phillip is also the author of eight books, including the novella *Leaving Home with Henry* (2010) and a collection of short stories *Don't Let me Fall* (1989).

This book is available as a free fully-searchable ebook from
www.adelaide.edu.au/press

Tilting at Windmills

The Literary Magazine in Australia 1968-2012

by

Phillip Edmonds

Department of English and Creative Writing, Faculty of Arts
The University of Adelaide

UNIVERSITY OF
ADELAIDE PRESS

Published in Adelaide by

University of Adelaide Press
The University of Adelaide
Level 14, 115 Grenfell Street
South Australia 5005
press@adelaide.edu.au
www.adelaide.edu.au/press

The University of Adelaide Press publishes externally refereed scholarly books by staff of the University of Adelaide. It aims to maximise access to the University's best research by publishing works through the internet as free downloads and for sale as high quality printed volumes.

© 2015 Phillip Edmonds

This work is licenced under the Creative Commons Attribution-NonCommercial-NoDerivatives 4.0 International (CC BY-NC-ND 4.0) License. To view a copy of this licence, visit http://creativecommons.org/licenses/by-nc-nd/4.0 or send a letter to Creative Commons, 444 Castro Street, Suite 900, Mountain View, California, 94041, USA. This licence allows for the copying, distribution, display and performance of this work for non-commercial purposes providing the work is clearly attributed to the copyright holders. Address all inquiries to the Director at the above address.

For the full Cataloguing-in-Publication data please contact the National Library of Australia: cip@nla.gov.au

ISBN (paperback) 978-1-925261-04-2
ISBN (ebook: pdf) 978-1-925261-05-9
ISBN (ebook: epub) 978-1-925261-06-6
ISBN (ebook: kindle) 978-1-925261-07-3

Editor: Rebecca Burton
Editorial support: Julia Keller
Book design: Zoë Stokes
Cover design: Emma Spoehr
Cover image: Alan Benge, source — 123rf.com

Contents

	Graph of literary magazines in Australia from 1880 to 2012	viii
1	Introduction	1
2	Setting out	9
3	Definitions	13
4	Some background	25
5	The sixties and all that	33
6	A major expansion	39
7	Academic developments and other problems	83
8	A more 'realistic' decade	103
9	New editors	119
10	Changes among the established magazines	139
11	A magazine apart	149
12	Whither the universities	153
13	A brave new world	155
14	Everything that is solid melts	157
15	New magazines	165
16	The problem of poetry again	181
17	A new demographic?	189

18	Away from Sydney and Melbourne	203
19	Some of the same old problems	209
20	A case in point — *Heat*	219
21	Anti-democratic tendencies	227
22	An unreliable commodity	237
23	Complications and conclusions	253
Postscript		275
Works cited		279

Graph of literary magazines in

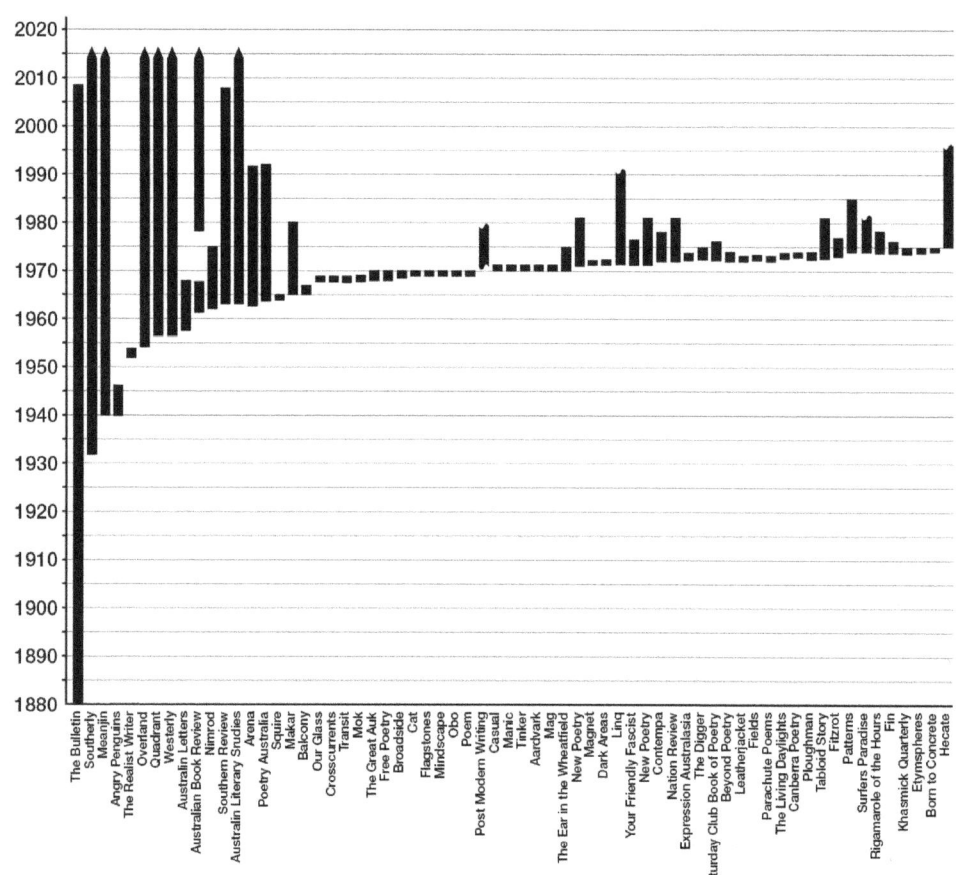

Australia from 1880 to 2012

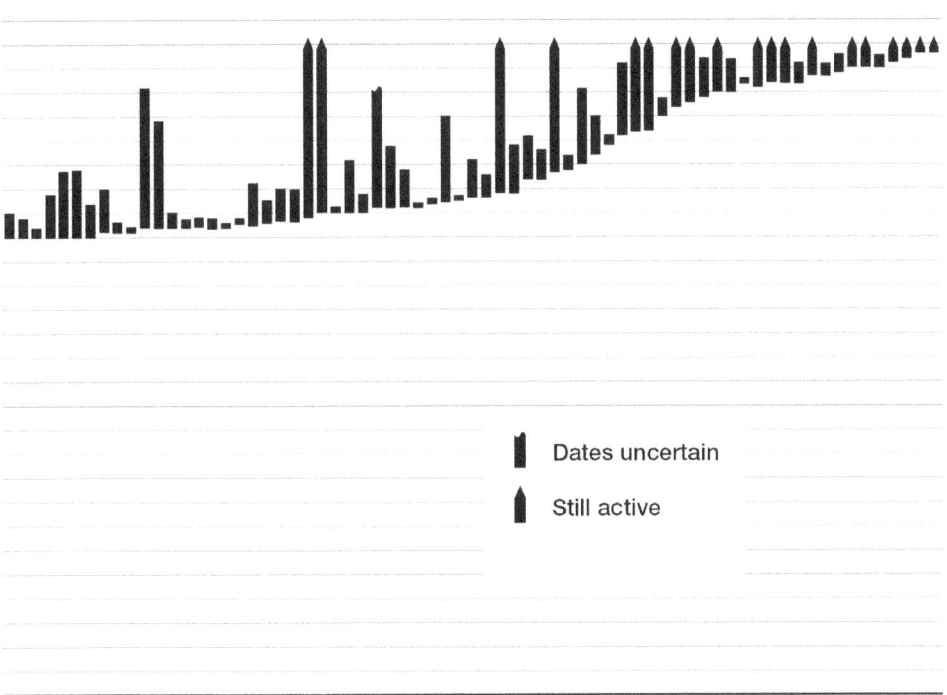

1. Introduction

Up until the late 1960s the story of Australian literary magazines was one of continuing struggle against the odds, and of the efforts of individuals, such as Clem Christesen, Stephen Murray-Smith and Max Harris. During that time, the magazines played the role of 'enfant terrible', creating a space where unpopular opinions and writers were allowed a voice. The magazines have very often been ahead of their time and some of the agendas they have pursued have become central to representations, where once they were marginal. Broadly, 'little' magazines have often been more influential than their small circulations would first indicate, and my argument here is that they have played a valuable role in the promotion of Australian literature.

After I completed this study, Robyn Annear, writing in the *Monthly*, suggested that the

> conventional wisdom is that journals are a hatchery for new talent. That partly explains the rationale for government support, as does the view that the genre is a 'worthy' one, in the sense of being non-commercial. (n.p.)

But after examining ten magazines, she was not convinced of the argument, and concluded:

> My hunch is that the absence of ... literary magazines, full stop[,] would discommode contributors, and potential contributors, far more than it would readers ... Are they really all that stands between us and philistinism? In a word, no. (n.p.)

While raising good points such as a lack of readers and uneven quality, she misses the central point that hatcheries are necessary — something I will demonstrate here.

So as to make this as multifaceted as possible, I intend a history informed by political economy because often discussions of cultural moments and movements have been marked by a largely individualistic story. This, I believe, has at times prepared the very ground for the eventual fragility of the literary magazines I will be discussing. By this I mean that the scholarly and public reaction to the journals has tended to float across a fault line of ideological difference in the cases of *Meanjin* and *Overland* (a Left perspective), and *Quadrant* (a Right oppositional stance). Of the remaining magazines, reactions have largely consisted of responses to individual pieces of creative writing and articles, and have been, as has been the way in Australia, generally insular and self-perpetuating. As far back as 1975, Thomas Shapcott prefigured as much in a review of several new poetry anthologies by wondering whether anyone could step outside their 'coteries' in Melbourne to provide an informed survey of events ('Poetry' 78). Because many of the little magazines have been, and are, springboards for self-promotion, writers have often been contrary in their support in that the reputation of particular publications has been all about perception and, as we will see, the ability to mythologise. In other words, the history of literary magazines is broader than anecdotal evidence and needs to be framed in social ways that are larger than individualised agendas.

It is simplistic, then, to discuss such a complex range of cultural activity without taking into account the multifarious nature of all factors in cultural creation, including the economic variables of publication and therefore the ways in which idealism mediates its own determinants. Although I am detailing the efforts of many individuals between 1968 and 2012, I do not dwell on conflicts and disputes, because that kind of discussion is, as I have suggested, insular and ultimately parochial.

A new study of the journals is required because they are intricate microevidence of social and cultural change and can be better understood in a framing informed by the very nature of their commodification over time. Issues surrounding commodification, I argue, have impacted on the marketability and longevity of journals, and on their public reception. This study offers new insights as a history because there has been little overview discussion of the journals other than a fistful of articles and Michael Denholm's pioneering and largely bibliographical work, which details the journals of the 1970s and early 1980s. I have endeavoured to place much of the journal activity during the late 1960s and 1970s, plus the subsequent decades, within an economic and cultural framework.

My first consideration has been to define my terms. Therefore in the next chapter, Chapter Two, 'Setting out', and in Chapter Three, 'Definitions', I discuss the ways in which the literary magazine has been framed historically in Australia and overseas, and my subsequent usage of the terms 'literary' and 'little' magazines. As the body of the book is basically a history of the magazines arranged chronologically, I follow this with several chapters giving a brief history of the magazines in Australia prior to the 1960s, after which Chapter Six, 'A major expansion', details the extensive developments during the 1970s.

After such a definitive decade, I then move on to explore the changing social and cultural landscape of the more pragmatic decade of the 1980s in Chapter Eight. In this chapter, entitled 'A more "realistic" decade', I discuss the fact that there were fewer magazines and more hierarchical expectations among writers and readers. By the 1990s, the editorial personnel were beginning to change and the magazines largely reflected seismic shifts in the social landscape, which I discuss in Chapters Nine ('New editors'), Ten ('Changes among the established magazines'), Eleven ('A magazine apart') and Twelve ('Whither the universities'). The year 2000 marked the onset of the internet's deconstruction of print, and I have therefore devoted a number of chapters to this topic. Chapters Thirteen ('A brave new world'), Fourteen ('Everything that is solid melts') and Seventeen ('A new demographic?')

explore the massive change that the internet has had on the means of production, the subsequent birth of new magazines, the contradictory role of the universities in cultural production, the continuing marginalisation of poetry in publishing terms and the generational changes impacting on the magazines. A central point that I hope to demonstrate is the cyclical nature of many of the problems of publishing in a small country: distribution (even with the internet) and visibility in the broader culture. I discuss this issue in particular in Chapter Nineteen, 'Some of the same old problems' and Chapter Twenty, 'A case in point — *Heat*', as well as in other chapters. I return to my central point that the literary magazine is a slippery commodity in Chapter Twenty-Two, 'An unreliable commodity', and I conclude the study with consideration of the period 2010 to 2012, in which some magazines survived in print form, and others ceased to exist. The 'Postscript' gestures towards possible shapes for the literary magazine.

Broadly, I am informed by the question: 'To what extent and in what ways is the literary imagination conditioned by its social contexts?' (Reid 1). I am further informed by Raymond Williams's statements that 'a lived hegemony is always a process' (112) and that in cultural analysis in complex societies 'works of art, by their substantial and general character, are often especially important as sources of this complex evidence' (113). Furthermore, as Gelder and Salzman have put it, (paraphrasing Williams),

> the freedom to write freely can only be 'guaranteed' by providing a material (some would say institutional) base; and for readings to be possible after this, further material conditions must also be created. Producing a text 'freely' is one thing, entering that text into the marketplace is quite another. And the ways in which a text enters that marketplace influence its reception — the readings it is given — in the *first* place. (1, emphasis in original)

In a sense, then, I hope I have written a social and cultural history in microcosm of the four decades in Australia from 1968 until 2012.

I have been inspired to write this story because, in the 2000s, we seem to me to be in stasis, overpowered by a past that it is too big and a present that is too quick. I simply want to identify markers. Although I will privilege political economy, by invoking patterns of commodification, I do not see culture as merely reflective of changes in the economic base. I am persuaded by the suggestion that

> works of art, depending as they do upon their special circumstances of production and of reproduction — will represent themselves, or be made to represent through our criticism, the widest possible variety of ideological positions. Furthermore, the ideology of a given work will assume various forms, and these will be ranged at different points on a scale of social consciousness. (McGann 156)

So, too, with the literary magazine, in that it has represented and reflected the mediating role culture has performed in the evolution of contemporary Australia.

The little magazine is often constructed as a high cultural manifestation, but it has significance as cultural evidence through its contradictory characteristics and precursive capabilities. Geordie Williamson has called little magazines 'gaudy democracies', and has stated that 'the variousness of writing on display in their pages defeats the instinct, common to bureaucrats and critics, to pigeonhole' ('Journal' 20). This history over four decades will demonstrate, I believe, how literary/small magazines in Australia are, despite their sometimes aristocratic tendencies, democratic moments in an ongoing tradition. In the late 1960s, and into the 1970s, and more recently in the 2000s, the birth of new publications has often coincided and articulated cultural and ideological upsurges. More to the point, a varied and vibrant magazine culture has meant that there has been (for better and for worse) a wider range of places to publish and a wider range of editorial gatekeepers. Cultures are like rivers: they need a steady flow of people and ideas to revitalise their ecosystems. It could be argued that the literary magazines, in the West at least, have been the vital tributaries to what we see in the broader stream.

Little, or literary, magazines have often captured a particular cultural moment in Australian history — such as Max Harris's *Angry Penguins* during the 1940s, the intent of which was to pursue Australian literary modernism

— to then disappear after their work was done. Others, like *Overland* and *Meanjin*, have struggled across generations due to the demands of broader ideas, and when some magazines have closed down, there has been a ritualistic wailing at their loss, such as with the recent demise of *Heat* in hard copy at the start of 2011. In contemporary 'post-modern' Australia it also can take the form of a type of 'recreational grieving' (Ruthven 31-3), which the small and isolated intellectual class engage in to mask a powerlessness they often refuse to confront.

The literary magazine, then, is often constructed as a charity worthy of support — almost the ethical, romantic 'other' to the inevitable business of corporate education and the inevitability of market forces — thus conveniently diminishing its role and potential power. In researching this book, I came to realise that I would also be investigating the almost sacrificial role performed by some of the magazines in a country that prides itself on its heroic failures: a place that is still in love with indifference, and that is nervous as to its inability to promote its own. In Australia, a lack of passion and discord (except for sport) is often culturally perceived as attractive, so we really do not care all that much about our achievements. This in a way is also the story of the literary magazine in Australia. Discussions of general directions and critiques of existing literary structures in Australia have also been fraught because of their isolated and under-resourced nature, so that any debates have remained insular and overly polite — often knee-jerk and opportunistic. I desire to stand sideways to that frame.

I also find useful Fredric Jameson's notion of cognitive mapping in this history because it is, in effect, what the literary magazine also sets out to achieve: a way of thinking through contemporary discontinuity, and a stance that strikes 'a situational representation on the part of the individual subject to that vaster and properly unrepresentable totality which is the ensemble of society's structures as a whole' (51). Put another way, literary magazines are complex and detailed evidence of the social and cultural changes in any society.

I have chosen to bookend this study with two major changes to the means of production as they have impacted on publishing, both in Australia and elsewhere: firstly, the advent of offset printing in the late 1960s, and secondly, the internet's ongoing deconstruction of physical books and magazines leading up to and around 2000.

I will attempt a discussion of small magazines between 1968 and 2012 in a framework that speaks of the ways in which the idealism of individuals and groups has negotiated changing economic and political landscapes, and I will discuss, in turn, class as a social determinant.

Fredric Jameson claimed in 1991 that, in our stage of late capitalist development, on all levels, there was evidence of 'the utter eradication of all forms of what used to be called idealism, in bourgeois or even capitalist societies' (387). While such a prescription might seem rather totalising and depressing, the period of my study demonstrates that commodification in all areas of social life intensified during the 1980s, 1990s and into the new millennium, and affected the nature of literary publications over that time — but commodification is a process and is never complete. Therefore the role of individuals who can identify moments of political and cultural agency is important. But we are living in an age where the theory and practice of capitalist modes of production have entered another period of crisis. In cultural spheres in Australia, rhetoric is dominating action, and bureaucracy appears to be mystifying the creation of real value. This situation was exposed, for example, in the global financial crisis of 2008, where the apparatus of the means of production were shown to have been poised on a shaky, unproductive pile of credit and 'spin'.

Moreover, we live in a time where intellectual property rights are ubiquitous as objects of trade, and the new technologies make ideas into commodities like never before. The irony of that is (as I will explore in the latter chapters discussing the advent of online publishing) that these new technologies are frenetically creating — and deconstructing — the exchange value (and commodification potential) of the very commodities they create.

This suggests that the modernisation of the means of production is resulting in pre-emptively declining rates of profit rather than accretion over time, as was Marx's prediction. Leaving that aside, small magazines currently are simultaneously 'in' and 'out' of social frames and as such are unreliable commodities.

2.   Setting out

Traditionally, literary/little magazines have been 'communities' of interest, encouraging ideas and conducting unencumbered conversations. Habermas's notion of the 'public sphere' (8) is a useful correlative here, because to embark on a history of literary magazines invokes a past that sights developments fertilised within the frame of his idea. David Carter usefully poses a central statement: 'We might, then, describe the history of modern periodicals as a history of attempts to re-invent the public sphere but in times, "when its material conditions had definitely passed"'('Magazine culture' 71).[1]

It is also helpful to note the connections between broader ideas of public space and the ways in which we have constructed the idea of the literary magazine. Currently, due to the advances of commodification into most areas of social life, public spaces are increasingly becoming regulated, and with that, people are being moved on who are not seen to be conducting useful 'business'. For example, universities are no longer relatively carefree debating sites; supermarkets offer us soundtracks and advertisements in case we forget why we went there in the first place; and — of direct relevance to this discussion — the advent of book chains has mitigated against the desire to wander and ruminate in over-organised shops. Since the mid-1990s the shopping mall has been the predominant public space.

---

[1] Carter is here quoting from Eagleton, Terry. *The function of criticism: From the spectator to post-structuralism*. London: Verso, 1984. Print.

Many of the bookshops of the 1970s were community meeting places as much as they were retail outlets, but over the period 1968 to 2012, cost pressures in publishing, as they in turn impacted on bookselling, broadly replicated the inexorable move in all retailing towards the supermarket as opposed to local corner stores, leading to (with some exceptions) the relative homogenisation of cultural products through mass-marketing. Concurrently, the impact on the literary magazines during the decades after the 1960s and 1970s was profound and contradictory, in that literary magazines are, by their very nature, an expression of the local and the ephemeral. In spite of this, during the 1980s and 1990s — in Australia, at least — a 'coffee culture' has sprung up in most cities and towns, offering people, on a superficial level, the chance to meet and chat. Meanwhile, on the literary level, community outbreaks have occurred, firstly in the form of writers' centres, and lately in mainstream writers' festivals, where public conversation is encouraged. However, such festivals have only existed due to government support and the charging of entrance fees.

Even using the most idealistic construction of the elusive public sphere, it is clear that literary magazines have been, and are, cheap and personal forms of debate. Currently, though, it appears that, because of their limited (and sometimes unjust) elitist profile, they could fall from consciousness, not unlike the traditional notion of politics, which was once seen to be relatively free of 'spin', stylisation, and management practices. I hope to look at the trends that led us to this, and, as I have argued elsewhere, (Edmonds, 'More than a mere story' 217) if 'post-moderns' are repressed romantics then it is worth investigating their contradictory impulses. On one level, post-modernists speak in progressive languages within institutional frameworks, while eschewing action outside their personal lives. The symptoms of this were evident as far back as the so called revolution of the 1960s and 1970s.

When it comes to literary magazines, the evidence of the past forty years is fascinating and contrary. Many trends would coalesce and reappear over the forty years, including attempts by the magazines at collective action, both in the 1970s and more recently in the 2000s, in a literary sphere that has always rewarded self-interest over co-operation.

Generally, writers are not corporate or collectivist by nature and I argue that some magazines found it difficult to organise as a result. The magazines that have survived the last forty years, such as *Overland*, *Meanjin*, *Southerly* and *Quadrant*, have for all their differences and problems published many writers, whereas the occasional publications of the 1970s in particular may have harmed the cause of new writers in the ensuing decades by creating an overly bohemian, insubstantial landscape where future ventures were easily seen as utopian and impractical. Overall, though, irrespective of the differing levels of market penetration, the magazines listed above have relied on government subsidies to survive. Most of the publications I will discuss here have received some form of assistance from the Federal Government, firstly through the Commonwealth Literary Fund, the Literature Board, and the Literature Panel of the Australia Council. The assistance has always been specifically to pay contributors, not editors. Thus, in most cases, editing the publications has been a voluntary and part-time commitment, which has often worked against longevity and sustainability.

3. DEFINITIONS

My working definition of 'literary magazine', then, for this study, is a publication that devotes a significant proportion of its pages to original fiction, poetry, essays, creative non-fiction, interviews and reviews, and is a periodical that publishes up to six times a year. I have not included little magazines that only publish socio-political content, commentary and articles, of which there were many in Australia between 1968-2012. In saying that, I am aware that some magazines — in particular *Meanjin*, the *Griffith Review* and *Overland* — have, and have had, a good proportion of their pages devoted to political issues. Even so, they have been constructed as literary publications in cultural discourse and have published a considerable amount of original creative writing over that period.

The story of the literary magazine in Australia, in particular, is one of persistence, obsession and — at times — cultural opportunity. Unlike in Europe or the United States, the potential for mass distribution is limited by a smallish population, and there has been little tradition of serious publications of substantial circulation, such as the *New York Review of Books*, the *New Yorker*, *Esquire*, or indeed the lesser circulations of the *Paris Review* or *Granta*, to nourish endangered literary genres such as poetry, the short story or the lengthy essay.

Unlike in the United States, journalism in Australia has not been sufficiently diversified and resourced to support the early careers of fiction writers. Laurenson has suggested that in the United States, 'throughout the nineteenth century the consolidation of the reading public by journals slowly enabled the writer to become more self-supporting' (162). As she has further suggested,

> many members of the reading public were first generation immigrants trying to learn English. The short story and light magazine article met their needs and increased further demand for magazine reading. (162)

In the United States, she claims, 'there was little leisure time for book-reading and so the periodical press became dominant, supplemented by the public library'. The magazine became 'the characteristic expression of American Democracy' (162). Australia has had few examples of such active commercial support in the literary arts, apart from the brief flowering of the *Bulletin* in Sydney during the 1890s, which made household names of Henry Lawson and Banjo Paterson. A further point is that since then, mass-circulation newspapers and magazines have constructed (with few exceptions) the arts as peripheral to their gatekeeping role of creating popular culture, a development that accelerated in the years after World War II, as Carter and Osborne have noted:

> In the decades after the end of the war, the magazine scene changed fundamentally. The independent commercial magazines and general reviews of culture and entertainment — weeklies and monthlies — had all but disappeared. (255)

Prior to that, Carter claims, 'general magazines in the twenties occupied the same cultural space as the theatre, which they reviewed extensively, forms that mixed popular and literary modes, art and commerce, art and entertainment' ('Magazine culture' 70).

As a result, the small or literary magazine in Australia has occupied an alternative space to the discourse of newspapers and popular magazines, in effect occupying an underground rarely noticed by the above-ground media. Prior to the onset of the new millennium the literary magazines in Australia provided places for writers to slowly build up their reputations. But over the period of this study, as different medias proliferated and the celebrity moment dominated popular culture, there was pressure on some magazines to be relevant, in tune, and above all noticed (as I will demonstrate in later chapters) when, in fact, the role of the small magazine is often to go against the prevailing tide. More to the point, publishers were under increasing pressure to promote the 'next big thing' in an impatient age.

Even so, literary (little) magazines in Australia have attracted followers because they have not been seen to be 'commercial'. Followers see them as being more precious than the stringencies of everyday commerce; but their very non-commercial nature has prevented many of their publishers from putting in place survival structures. In fact, the magazines I will be discussing broadly occupy a space between commercial publishing and self-publication, in that during the late 1960s and the early 1970s, new magazines appeared which were the creation of individual writers. In some cases, these writers achieved literary status due to whom they published in their magazines, and who their friends were, in contrast to self-published authors outside metropolitan areas and established networks.

The little magazine has always had a precarious future anywhere in the world, but more so in Australia, where prior to the 1970s the arts were considered marginal and/or esoteric to the concerns of a pragmatic culture. Local excellence, to an extent, has only ever been embraced in bursts in Australia, yet literary magazines here have discovered writers who would go on to accumulate substantial audiences, and in some cases magazines such as *Meanjin* and *Overland* were the lonely standard-bearers of the need for an Australian literature during the 1940s, 1950s and 1960s. Generally speaking, despite the difficulties I have alluded to above, Australia has supported a good number of literary magazines of differing configurations.

John Freeman, the editor of *Granta* (UK), has suggested that the primary function of journals is to 'promote ... messiness, conflict and disorder: to subvert the market; and to place writers in unexpected places, where they can create an unlikely community of readers' (18). But it is this very messiness and market subversion which can create a community and which can also be the reason a literary magazine might fail to find an instant 'market' due to its transgressive nature. Furthermore, in broad terms, as Carter suggests of the Australian situation,

> [m]agazines today are forced to define themselves in the cultural space of the media. Unlike the twenties, most literature in cultural magazines today, the ones we don't buy in the newsagent's, can't help but look like the residue of book publication. Those we do buy in the newsagent's belong wholly to the realm of the media. ('Magazine culture' 70)

In other words, literary magazines have increasingly occupied a segmented, subcultural space over the past forty years which is almost subeconomic, in defence of endangered genres. They have asserted themselves almost in opposition to 'popular' fiction and to journalism that has fractured and become a simulacrum of itself.

Despite such difficulties, they provide (according to the *Paris Review* editor, Phillip Gourevitch) 'that extra layer of depth and reflection' to the mass media and the newly fashionable blogs and online news (qtd. in Gruber 13), yet their positives and negatives are in constant debate. According to Gruber,

> [t]he positive view is that they are the literary lifeblood of the nation … The negative view is that literary magazines have small circulations, pay writers appallingly and are sometimes unreadable. For the majority of the population, they are invisible, a blur of titles in a dim corner of an independent bookshop, where hairy poets and English teachers flick through the pages, too poor or mean to purchase the journals they like to read. The little magazine probably has the most balanced ratio of readers to contributors. (13)

The literary/small magazine then, as far as we know what it is, is both in and out of any market, attracting and resisting instant commodification, depending on its formatting. David Sornig has stressed its innovation:

> Innovation … doesn't come out freshly hatched. It begins outside the market. This is probably the most important function literary magazines serve. They allow for safe experimentation, providing a means for testing experiments in public. (37)

The magazines are a form of research and development, in other words: something regarded as essential in science and business. So, then, questions as to the literary magazine's 'use value' are highly subjective, and the literary magazine — like the book — is subject to discretionary spending, as it does not have any irrefutable use value like 'useful' commodities such as food items. Yet the literary magazine possesses use value over time, in that it is often sold on and becomes second-hand, passing through the hands of many readers, as well as being stored in libraries. But that very use value in turn undercuts the 'exchange value'. In other words, most other commodities are destroyed in the act of consumption. By way of contrast, the little magazine often has an even more unreliable exchange value than a book due to the magazine's periodic nature, which dates it, unlike the potential timeless nature of a book.

The literary magazine then (in Australia, at least) sits in an exchange economy in a similar (but not identical) way to the book. Writing in the late 1970s of France, which has sustained a more central role to the literary arts than Australia, Debray has noted that

> a book is not a commodity like other commodities … [E]very book is unique in two ways. First, it is the irreplaceable product of an irreplaceable worker; and second, it gives rise to a single act of consumption (even if it is mass consumption). Its singularity defies planning. (211)

The literary magazine, then, can be a compilation of singularities in ways that are distinct from most other magazines, particularly those promoted to a mass market. As Marx pointed out, 'when commodities are in the relation of exchange, their exchange-value manifests itself as something totally independent of their use-value' (128). Furthermore, as Nelson and Timmerman point out, 'discussions about use values often reach vastly different conclusions than discussions based on exchange values' (77) — a statement that prefigures much of the following analysis in this book. My argument will be that to talk of literary magazines one has to speak of the intersection of such values, not in an overly idealised fashion but rather in a revolving historical frame, which places some weight on political economy. Marx's definition of use value was that of its intrinsic value to human beings over and above any price differential, so in that way, the little/literary magazine has a value suspended between the past and the future. It may have a sustainable price in the interim, or it may develop that over time through scarcity and/or its own notoriety, or the fame of some of its contributors.

My further argument is that the literary magazine is an example of a positive externality, something that benefits society but in ways that any publisher cannot fully profit from because unlike most commodities it is not destroyed by consumption. A community investment in a magazine is similar to that in national parks and environmental spaces, something which Cornes and Sandler have discussed in their *The Theory of Externalities, Public Goods & Club Goods*. It could be argued, then, that the value of the magazines is immeasurable. There are also interesting connotations of commodity fetishism in that, as Marx suggested, commodities are social by nature and can develop individual powers between people, becoming objects of mystification, and therefore reified. I will argue that magazines such as *Heat*, *Scripsi*, *New Poetry* and the *Ear in the Wheatfield*, although cheaply produced, set out to become, and did become, fetishised over time through their book-like formats and relative contentment with limited-edition circulation.

In publishing terms the literary/small magazine is, then, a 'problem child', unable, like a limited-edition book, to attract a deliberately inflated price because of its periodic nature, as it is caught between ambitions of community and the need to be itself. Yet ironically, years after ceasing to publish, many magazines become scarce commodities and their exchange value increases, especially if they have published writers who have become well-known and to an extent commodified. Some magazines are also ahead of their time, and never receive promotion from wider cultural forces to gain enough momentum for long-term survival. Between 1968 and 2012 in Australia there have been several magazines that fall into that category.

Any history of literary magazines is also a study in how cultural hegemony is achieved, and the subsequent dance of mystification and commodity fetishism. Although relatively obscure in social terms, literary magazines have played a vital role in discovering and privileging certain writers, have set intellectual agendas and, by publishing some academics, have been partly responsible for their promotion within their respective universities. A history, of course, reveals trends, so it is fascinating to observe how certain magazines achieve status and bestow cultural credibility in a similar way to the symbolic capital resting in an author's name, becoming, as Bourdieu suggests, a '"capital of consecration"' which 'implies a power to consecrate objects and make profits from this operation' (qtd. in Galligan 153). However, for the literary magazine this may work in ways that eulogise the publication without adding to its immediate exchange value, unlike the use of names by book publishers.

The history of Australian magazines demonstrates that an association with a university (traditionally a site of credentialing and prestige) is a signifier and place of consecration. *Southerly*, for example, has been connected to the University of Sydney all its life, and *Meanjin* to the University of Melbourne, albeit it in frustrating circumstances, thus giving them an assurance of 'quality' and reliability. Outside the universities, in the period of 1968-2012, there were hegemonic challenges to any canon of preferred publication outlets, some of which were successful, others not. But the imprimatur of support from the Literature Board of the Australia Council has been a defining mark of approval for all the magazines during a period of chaotic change and hierarchical confusion.

As the universities gradually withdrew from the public sphere over the time of this study, I will discuss some of the other factors that came into play in the pursuit of cultural hegemony. Prestige, I will argue, is the direct result of some magazines looking 'important', with expensive paper and colour inserts. Furthermore, the role of key literary figures should not be underestimated, such as Professor GA Wilkes in Sydney. What is intriguing is that ongoing involvement with literary magazines that became established has helped to create literary figures, such as Clem Christesen and Stephen Murray-Smith, James McAuley and Laurie Hergenhan, and those associated with the magazines as poetry editors. The case of *Meanjin*'s poetry editors is useful; Kris Hemensley, Judith Rodriguez, Philip Mead, Laurie Duggan and Judith Beveridge gained a broader cultural profile through their involvement.

Also intriguing is the way in which, as some magazines have gained longevity over the years, authors have become well-known, acquiring the potential for their work to become commodified. In strict terms, magazines add value to the work of writers by establishing a list of credits they can quote in grant applications, requests to publishers, scholarships and prizes, and in general visibility for their work. In effect the magazines give cultural credibility to larger structures. Economically, in a small way, they provide work for printers, post offices and envelope manufacturers among others, creating a multiplier effect. The literary magazine then, in this context, is the midwife, a catalyst that largely retains its marginal status while, on occasions, hastening exchange value. But an association with well-known authors can retrospectively boost a magazine's profile and, in some cases, lead to future increased sales. Each magazine is an attempt at establishing a consensus around a notion of potential cultural authenticity.

As we will see, relations between universities and literary magazines in Australia have been fraught and unpredictable because the former are usually concerned with the creation of prestige, and new magazines, in particular, are feral beasts which need time to establish notoriety and status. Thus in broad terms the social role of the literary magazine has often been understated, and considerations as to the literary magazine's influence have often been restricted to discussions about its initial limited circulation.

In this study of magazines from 1968-2012, I will be discussing the aesthetic precursors and urgencies behind the magazines, but also the ways in which their survival has been mediated by the political and economic changes over the four decades. I am particularly interested in the little magazine as a problematic commodity in late capitalism in Australia.

Little magazines everywhere, and particularly in Australia, have had to contend with adverse trading conditions compared with most other areas of publishing. Unlike large book publishers who establish broad lists of fiction and non-fiction titles (some of which have large print runs and thus economies of scale), small magazines have generally been printed in short runs at a higher unit cost for printing. Furthermore, due to the periodical nature of a magazine, backlist sales are not potentially as lucrative as some books. But it almost goes without saying that publishing in general, and literary publishing in particular, involves a combination of commercial and aesthetic considerations — and therefore, as commodities, both the book and, to a lesser extent, the literary magazine have slippery use value and marginal exchange value when compared in the first instance with, for example, a refrigerator or a car. Yet over time the perverse nature of books and literary magazines can invest them with other uses.

Literary works such as novels and some poetry have been published by large publishers such as Penguin because, even if they do not make any money, they add cultural capital to the overall list, thus giving the publisher cachet at the top end of the market, and invoking Bourdieu's notion of 'capital of consecration' ('Rule of art' 148). Such titles are subsidised in effect, but the literary magazine has rarely been supported by a large publisher as it would in most cases be too much of a major commitment and potentially a drain on overall cash flows, particularly in Australia. Most small magazines, then, have been started by individuals and not by companies with financial backing and sales support, and it can take several years for a new publication to assemble a subscriber base. Furthermore, I will argue that although the formatting of magazines has altered over the period of this study (due to changes in the means of production), most little magazines have survived on the unpaid surplus value of committed groups and individuals in a cash economy. During the 1970s, the then editor of *Overland*, Stephen Murray-Smith, spoke of the reality for most editors of literary magazines at that time:

> The magazines and their editors represent the best and cheapest form of government patronage of the writer and artist ... [A] major review, covering many fields of literary interest and publishing hundreds of thousands of words a year, cannot be produced by voluntary labour. (Qtd. in University of Adelaide 4)

Over the past three decades this situation has changed at least on one level, as the magazines have become more professional in their appearance and ambition. Most of the major magazines under discussion currently have paid editors on various levels of remuneration; even so, some undertake their tasks in addition to employment in universities, and others are effectively paid due to the higher levels of state and federal support for magazines than was the case in Stephen Murray-Smith's time. But compared to remuneration in other areas of publishing and in the burgeoning field of creative writing in the universities (for full-time academics), the editors of literary magazines are still largely unpaid and their creative role unrecognised. They still perform, as Murray-Smith suggested in the 1970s, a role that is contingent on the surplus value of largely voluntary work, at a time when creative writing courses are encouraging their many students to send work to the magazines.

Of those magazines in Australia which have survived into the new millennium, all have had generous assistance from the Australia Council and some form of institutional support from universities. But the institutional support has at times been fraught and inconsistent and concentrated on major universities. Universities in Australia, although benefiting from having articles and creative writing published in the journals, have had, with a few notable exceptions, a 'sniffy' attitude. Certainly, when the role of the public intellectual was recognised as worthy during the 1960s and 1970s, magazines like *Meanjin* were more central to the broader culture, but on the whole, universities played it safe and by the birth of the new millennium were retreating into competitive enclaves. Yet it must be said that on occasions university hosts have sometimes provided free postage (a useful subsidy) to the journals they have supported, such as *Makar* (University of Queensland), *Australian Literary Studies* (University of Tasmania and later University of Queensland), *Meanjin* (University of Melbourne), *Westerly* (University of Western Australia), *Southerly* (University of Sydney) and currently the *Griffith Review* (Griffith University) and *Island* (University of Tasmania). *Overland* has also received in-kind support in terms of offices and some infrastructure from Victoria University in Melbourne.

The literary magazine in Australia has been the worthy, poor cousin of publishing, acknowledged for the role it has played in discovering and promoting new writers, but ultimately it has been unrecognised in the past in the traffic of myth-making and currently in the urgent business of celebrity creation.

4. SOME BACKGROUND

Meanjin was founded in 1940 in Brisbane as *Meanjin Papers* by Clem Christesen, the name (pronounced as *Mee-An-Jin*) derived from the Aboriginal word for the land where the city of Brisbane is located. From 1947 to 1960 it was called *Meanjin*, from 1961 to 1976 *Meanjin Quarterly*, and again *Meanjin* from 1976 to the present day. Christesen pursued a nationalist agenda, an attempt at claiming a space for Australian literature in an environment where there were no courses in Australian literature in universities and the great majority of books published and sold came from the United Kingdom. He assembled around him a group of like-minded intellectuals such as Geoffrey Serle, Vance Palmer and AA Phillips. Phillips's famous essay, 'The Cultural Cringe', first published in *Meanjin* in 1950, persuasively argued that 'we' were still cringing in the face of our British forebears: that the centre of culture is ingrained in our psyche as being somewhere else. *Meanjin*'s relationship with the University of Melbourne was often fraught, yet Christesen forged on, as detailed by Lynne Strahan in *Just City and the Mirrors: Meanjin Quarterly and the Intellectual Front, 1940-1965*. Christesen established the magazine as Australia's pre-eminent literary publication by the close of the 1960s.

The *Realist Writer*, a cultural offshoot of the Communist Party of Australia, was the precursor to *Overland*. From 1954 it was titled *Overland: Incorporating the Realist Writer*, but after 1956, Murray-Smith, along with other intellectuals such as Ian Turner, resigned from the party after Khrushchev exposed the crimes of Stalin, and it became purely *Overland* in 1956, attracting

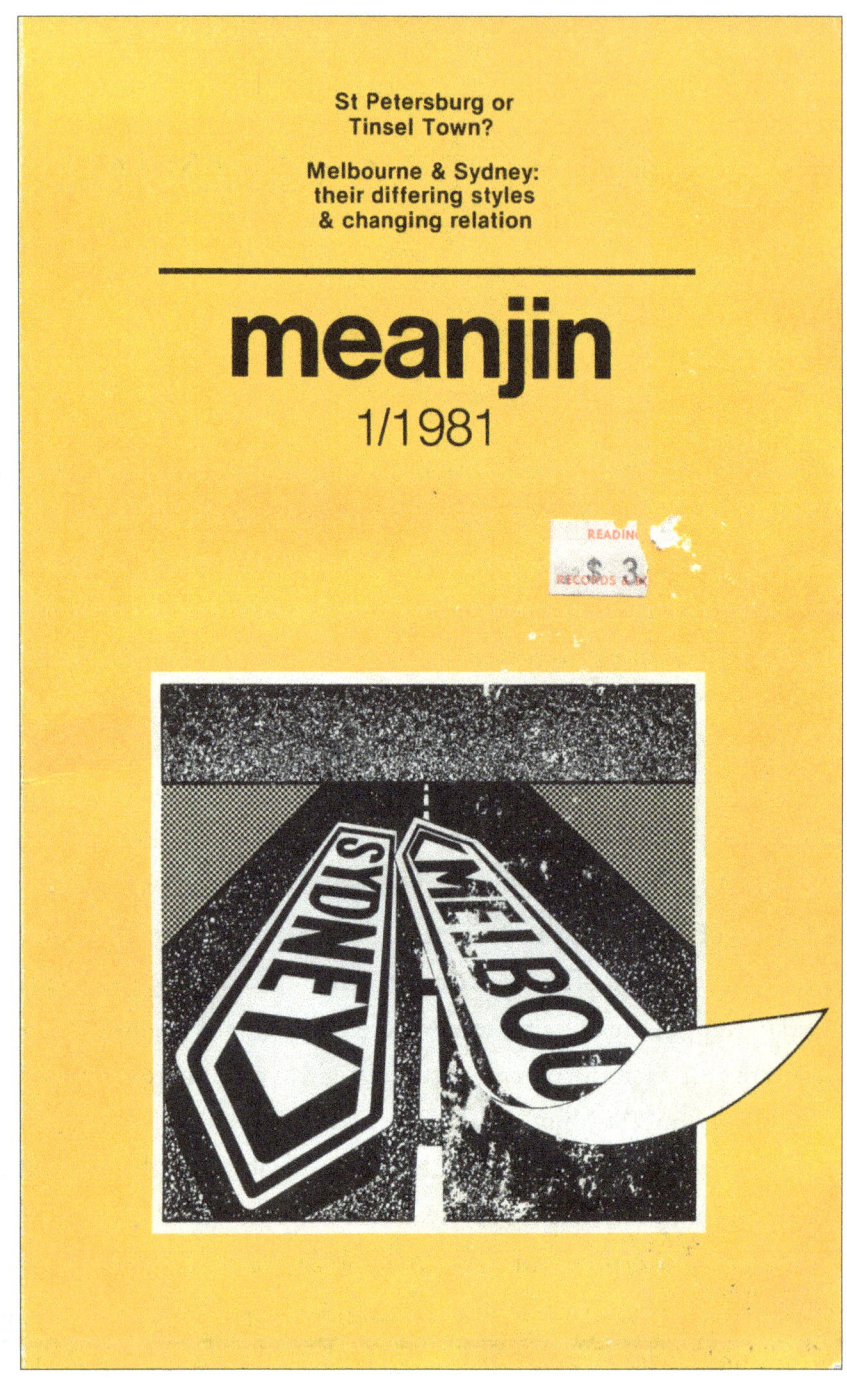

Figure 1: Cover of Meanjin, *no 1 (1981)*

artists and designers such as Vane Lindesay and Noel Counihan (who designed the first cover, depicting gold-diggers). *Overland*, then, grew out of a strong left-wing and working-class tradition of economic and cultural mobilisation prior to, and including, the Great Depression of the 1930s and the Second World War through organisations such as the Australasian Book Society, Worker's Educational Associations and radical newspapers, establishing as it were the magazine's ongoing agenda to develop a radical community of ideas.

That first issue in Spring 1954 (*Overland: Incorporating the Realist Writer*) published a rollcall of left-wing writers, among others Nettie Palmer, the short-story writer, John Morrison, Katharine Susannah Prichard, John Manifold, David Martin, the historian Brian Fitzpatrick and Eric Lambert. After 1956, the by-line on each magazine became 'temper democratic, bias Australian', a phrase taken from Joseph Furphy's classic novel, *Such is Life*, an iconic evocation of perceived linguistic larrikinism. As with *Meanjin*, *Overland* was also nationalistic in that it published a long line of authors who could loosely be described as belonging to the Lawson tradition. In broad terms, during the early twentieth century, Australian literature was characterised by writing that could be called social realist in terms of its narrative sites and typical characters. Bush settings predominated, especially before World War II, as Australia had not been industrialised.

The early editions of the magazine were broadly concerned with the local, and particularly with some socialist realist issues (as opposed to the social realist issues I alluded to above), which came out of overt ideological agendas during the Depression of the 1930s and the protracted violence of World War II. Creative writing in particular should have a political stance, the *Overland* group argued, through a stable of writers such as Alan Marshall, Gavin Casey, Frank Hardy and Dorothy Hewett, among others. Funding for the early issues was inherently fragile and reliant on donations, as Nita Murray-Smith recalls: 'We couldn't get grants because the government regarded it as a Communist front magazine' (Edgar & Geddes 23). She added:

Figure 2: Cover of Overland, *no 195 (2009)*

> Stephen [Murray-Smith] and Ian Turner felt that Australian culture had a lot to offer and wanted to try and revive the early Australian writers. Not so much republish them, but publish profiles and criticism of those writers. (23)

Murray-Smith and his group of true believers battled on during the end of the 1950s and into the 1960s, by which time the magazine had become established, if only in the sense that it had achieved consistency and was one of the few continuous literary publications in the country.

The period prior to the late 1960s was then characterised by the continuing presence of *Meanjin*, *Quadrant*, *Overland* and *Southerly*. *Southerly* was founded in 1939 by RG Howarth at the University of Sydney, and although initially it did not have any official university support, it gained some secretarial assistance through the editor's university position, especially when the later editor, GA Wilkes, became Professor of Australian literature. There were also *Westerly* in Perth, *Poetry Australia* from New South Wales and *Australian Letters* from South Australia, and a number of occasional publications, but in broad terms, the number of publications reflected the stringencies of World War II and the broadly social conservative 1950s, in that experimentation was not encouraged. *Meanjin* and *Overland* in contrast were products of the great social upheavals of the 1930s and 1940s, and proceeded to crystallise their ideological agendas. They were printed by letterpress, which was relatively expensive, and the publications were all dependent on taxpayer subsidies and in some cases also on universities: *Meanjin* (University of Melbourne), *Southerly* (University of Sydney), and *Westerly* (University of Western Australia). *Overland* from the beginning relied on its committed band of left-wing supporters to create a community of support.

Of the group, *Southerly* is Australia's oldest literary magazine, one year older than *Meanjin*. The first issue, calling itself the 'magazine of the Sydney Branch of the English Association', appeared in September 1939, the editor, RG Howarth, writing: 'No literary journal, no literary review of any scope, standing and influence, at present exists in Australia' (4). According to John Tregenza, it sought to 'maintain its character as a catholic medium and critical review by publishing work by a wide range of writers and encouraged academic criticism of Australian writing' (94). Its regularity was under threat during the war years, but it has had regular in-kind assistance over the years from the University of Sydney. Editors have either been prominent figures in Australian Letters, such as Kenneth Slessor (1956-61), or senior academics in the English Department at the university, including for many years Professor GA Wilkes, who single-handedly produced four issues a year for twenty years. Elizabeth McMahon, writing on the occasion of the magazine's seventieth birthday in 2009, noted the times when it experienced financial difficulties, such as when Kenneth Slessor resigned in frustration in 1960 after Angus and Robertson withdrew their support, and when Elizabeth Webby (editor from 1987-99) experienced continual battles with the Literature Board over funding (7).

In 1999 the editors became David Brooks and Noel Rowe. *Southerly* has published a representative sample of the breadth of Australian poetry and performed a strong role in advancing academic discussion of Australian literature alongside *Australian Literary Studies*. Richard Nile claims that *Southerly* 'helped to legitimise poetry within the academy, which in a sense was already predisposed, certainly more so than towards any other genre in Australia' (113). In the early 2000s, it went from publishing four times a year to twice a year in two big, book-length editions. It is still obviously a periodical, given the nature of its contents, but in marketing terms, it is now commodified as a book. But compared to the high profile (and sometimes controversial nature) of *Meanjin* and *Overland*, particularly in the immediate post-war years, *Southerly* has effectively stayed under any ideological radar, as it is notable for measured, serious and considered scholarship rather than agenda-setting. During the 1960s and 1970s, *Southerly* was a significant presence among the magazines. *Overland*, *Meanjin* and *Quadrant* usually evoked political positions of one type or another, but *Southerly* brought forward earnest, neutral scholarship during a polarising decade.

It also needs to be said that the 1950s and 1960s witnessed a staunch ideological Cold War battle in all areas of Australian life, and, in particular, between *Meanjin* and *Overland* (on the Left) and *Quadrant* (on the Right). Under Christesen's editorship, *Meanjin* had advanced what broadly could be described as a Left nationalist line from the end of the war into the 1950s and then into the 1960s, when Australia was asked once again to support the United States in a foreign war. But the West's honeymoon with the Soviet Union during World War II in opposition to Germany and Japan eroded after 1949 into the onset of militant McCarthyism in the United States and Australia. The Liberal Government under Robert Menzies employed security agencies to spy on a range of Australian writers for two decades at least. Writers who had been members of the Communist Party, including Gavin Casey, John Morrison, Ian Turner, Stephen Murray-Smith and Dorothy Hewett, were under surveillance as Australians in concert with a foreign power, and by implication so were Left nationalists such as Vance and Nettie Palmer, as Fiona Capp has explained in *Writers Defiled*. In such an environment, *Meanjin* could be constructed as a fellow traveller but *Overland* could be more rigidly stereotyped. *Quadrant*, first published in the summer of 1956-57 in Hobart by the poet and academic James McAuley, was a general literary magazine containing political essays, creative prose and poetry, and it always delineated itself from the literary magazines of the Left, which it would claim were harbingers of 'fashion' and of, at times, out-and-out ideological warfare against Australia. While its political and philosophical contributions often tended to attack such positions on the Left, the literary content tended to be apolitical to the extent that what was published occupied the presumed ground of literary merit. Even so, none of the left-wing writers promoted in the pages of *Overland* were published in *Quadrant*, and this coincided with a broader general rejection of these writers' work as vulgar realism, particularly authors such as Judah Waten, who were influenced by the socialist realism of the 1930s and 1940s.

Quadrant created a clear line in the sand in cultural terms and continued such a position into the 1960s. Published by the Australian branch of the Congress for Cultural Freedom, the magazine, it has been suggested, received indirect funding from the US Central Intelligence Agency in the

1960s. During that decade it published and promoted a group of Australian intellectuals such as Patrick O'Brien, Hal Colebatch and Owen Harries — a group who became a minority in academic circles over their support for the Vietnam War.

5. THE SIXTIES AND ALL THAT

> *Mutual aid and support cannot be limited to a small association, they must spread to its surroundings, or else the surroundings will absorb the association.*
> (Kropotkin 164)

The intellectual wars prior to the 1950s were to be intensified and complicated by social and cultural changes of the 1960s while Australia had become a close military partner of the United States of America in Southeast Asia; sections of its population were calling for an independent foreign policy. An anti-disciplinary New Left was rejecting both state control in the USSR and US imperialism in the Third World. In the cultural sphere of the little magazine, roneoed broadsheets appeared, such as *Our Glass* in 1969, edited by Kris Hemensley in Melbourne, who began organising poetry readings around the city. McLaren claims that Hemensley's editorial rationale was to 'create a free area around himself which he could fill with new talent outside the control of the established media and the academies' (180).

As I have already suggested, the journals that were to survive the timeframe of this study relied on the support of outside organisations. The 1960s highlighted what McKernan later characterised in 1991 as an acceptance of literary journals as unquestioned 'good things', which were created outside existing ideological and publishing structures, and which were evidence of

> a rather idealised notion of the literary journal as the nurturer of literature and a place where writers may test new ideas and approaches. This notion of the literary journal has its base in the reality of the ephemeral magazine which springs from a group of writers and critics, flourishes for a time and then is heard no more. (165)

One of the first little magazines in the 1960s (which flourished for a time) was Michael Dugan's *Crosscurrents* Magazine, an ultra-thin journal of poetry of less than twenty pages: evidence of a nascent reading culture around the La Mama Theatre in Carlton. Dugan was an organiser and facilitator of other such magazines well into the 1970s, as he encouraged other writers and anyone interested in starting a new magazine. Through family connections at the *Age* he also linked up the small-press activity into wider networks.

Poetry Australia was publishing through the decade, along with *Quadrant*, *Overland*, *Meanjin* and *Westerly*, but there were relatively few journals in the early years of the decade apart from the odd eccentrically designed and letterpress-printed magazine such as *Expression Australasia*, which began in Brisbane in 1962. Its early manifestations, as *Expression*, were as the newsletter of the Writers Guild of Queensland. In 1966, *Expression Australasia* became a quarterly with the stated aim to 'do its bit for the Literature of Queensland', although it called itself a national magazine for the first time (Denholm 1: 135). It struggled financially through its life, and in 1969 it moved to Quorn in South Australia with Peter Bladen as editor and publisher. Increasingly its contributors were from other states, many from South Australia, including Ian Mudie and Graham Rowlands. In 1972 Alan Osterstock became the editor, but it ceased publication in early 1974. An eclectic journal, it was outside the literary networks of the cities.

Poets were prominent in producing magazines in the late 1960s, a situation that was a precursor of what was to follow in the 1970s — examples being Michael Dugan (*Crosscurrents*), Charles Buckmaster (the *Great Auk*), Nigel Roberts and John Goodall in Sydney (*Free Poetry*) and Richard Tipping and Rob Tillett in Adelaide (*Mok*). The magazines of the late 1960s were fitful moments in many ways, as they were under-resourced and reliant on one or two individuals. *Crosscurrents* had six issues, *Mok* five, *Our Glass* seven, the *Great Auk* eleven, *Free Poetry* eight. Then there was a list of even more peripatetic publications — *Cat* (one issue), *Flagstones* (five), *Mindscape* (one), *Obo* (one), *Poem* (two), *Manic* (one), *Tinker* (two), *Aardvark* (one), *Mag* (one), *Magnet* (one), *Transit* (two), *Riverrun* (four) and *Dark Areas* (five) — all of which were typical of the rebellious times, as some were roneoed and most were published in cheap offset formats (Dugan 223).

Mok, from Adelaide, foregrounded innovative layout and integrated graphics into the overall look, unlike many of the others, which basically contained printed poetry, black on white, on opposite pages. *Mok* 5 (Spring 1969), was deliberately political, publishing Richard Tipping's poem 'Soft Riots/TV News', one of the most powerful anti-war poems in Australian poetry. *Mok* also contained concrete poetry. Issue 5 had work by Vicki Viidikas, Nigel Roberts, Bill Beard, Terry Gillmore and Charles Buckmaster among others, plus an article by Peter Ward, the then poetry reviewer at the *Australian Book Review*, who fired a shot across the bows of the new generation of poets:

> The trouble with so many young contemporary poets is that they lack ideas. They have a new way of saying very little. In ideology the new poets are as poverty stricken as the old. There may be a great deal of self-conscious talk about sexual and political revolt and alienation, but there's rarely, hard-edged commitment to specific, comprehensive ideas and values, intelligently thought out, cleanly argued or crisply expressed. (3)

Ward was also concerned that the new generation appeared to privilege protest and politics over beauty in rejecting 'even the most basic poetic techniques. Things like assonance, rhythm ... [T]here's little thinking and not much singing'. For better or worse, aesthetic battlelines were being exposed in the upsurge.

Michael Wilding claimed in 1977 that

> something happened in Australian writing around 1968-69. Some time then a huge gulf opened between what had been appearing before and the new writing that has appeared since. ('A survey' 117)

He cited the considerable influence of the new international war in Vietnam, in that 'even those writers who were not and are not conscious of political issues were caught up in the frenzy of activity, the enthusiasm, the surge of creativity'. Inherent in such questioning, he wrote, was a re-evaluation of 'Australianness'. Of the writers, he said, 'some would conceive of themselves as "writers", as supra-nationals, the context in which they worked was Australian'. Yet in a cautionary note he added, 'even at their most imitatively American, they demonstrated their Australianness in revealing the new domination of all areas of Australian cultural and economic life by the USA' (117).

David Malouf, returning to Australia in 1968, noted a similar vibrancy in the poetry scene:

> Almost any night of the week in Sydney there was a reading, either formal or informal — a good many of them, in those days of intense political activity, protest readings against the war in Vietnam. (Qtd. in Nile 113)

Richard Nile claims that 'poetry had achieved an almost cult status within the counter culture movement of the sixties and seventies' (113). Writing in 1977, Robert Kenny, who was a small-press activist during the 1970s, further suggested that

> the late 60s broke down the confines of the old ... [T]he little magazines then saw their job as destroying the idea of a literary establishment ... not just a particular literary establishment, but the *very* concept, the fraudulent concept, of a conscious opinion of what was good or bad. I think they succeeded. (202, emphasis in original)

In Sydney, up-and-coming prose writers such as Frank Moorhouse and Michael Wilding were stressing the value of taking a libertarian line in such complicating times — an idea that Moorhouse would characterise and develop in his publications of the 1970s (*Futility and Other Animals*; *The*

Americans Baby; and *Tales of Mystery and Romance*), with a concentration on individual consciousness and a tone that was sceptical of group allegiances. The early careers of Moorhouse and Wilding were facilitated by the upsurge of the small press in Sydney. Libertarianism had taken a foothold there unlike in Melbourne, where the Left and the Right seemed to battle along more rigid lines of determination. Poets such as Robert Adamson, Nigel Roberts and Vicki Viidikas predominated in the scene around the inner Sydney suburb of Balmain. Nigel Roberts, Johnny Goodall and Terry Gillmore published the occasional issue of *Free Poetry*, which was foolscap-size and made from pages stitched together on a sewing machine.

In a letter dated 24 September 2011, Wilding claims that the 'new poetry' was influenced by the Beat movement in the United States, the hedonism of the counter-culture, drugs and sexual experimentation ('Letter to the author'). He claims, years after the event, that '[i]t was the victory of the postmodern, the art of self-referentialism, the construct, the con, the illusion, the imagination, the glorious lie', something he had come to revise over the course of his study through his interest in class and politics. Reflecting on that time, he suggests that 'with the poets who had no market presence, it was all about the art of self-advertising and accessing the public purse'. Wilding, in the 1960s an academic at the University of Sydney, was also involved in academic politics through producing the magazine *Balcony*, with Stephen Knight among others, for six issues from 1964-66, which apart from being a forum for battling Leavisite-critical positions at the University, published some new writing by Rodney Hall, John Tranter and Antigone Kefala (Denholm 2: 245). Attacks on Leavisite-critical positions in the universities in Australia during the 1960s were an early salvo in what was to lead to the onset of cultural studies, deconstruction and post-modernism. In this sense the decade was a precursor to the battles and agendas of the 1970s, and became a mythical site for further conflict and intrigue.

6. A MAJOR EXPANSION

The little magazine blossomed in Australia during the 1970s. In the checklist of the special 1977 issue of *Australian Literary Studies* entitled 'New Writing in Australia', there were over forty magazines of one variety or another. Peter Pierce has noted of the period that '[one of] many of the magazine's reasons for being is the notion that they are part of a decisive moment of change within Australian literature and publishing' (219); and he identified that much of the upsurge was driven by a militant attitude among poets towards recognition. But poetry was only a part of a larger story of increasing cultural confidence and experimentation. The early 1970s, in particular, were a period where the belief in an effective 'avant-garde' became evident.

Despite such idealism and passion, it needs to be said that the elements already existed to make the upsurge a bubble rather than a long-term tangential shift, in that (unlike the established magazines) the great majority of the forty publications were initially under-resourced and lacked sustainable organisational structures. To establish a new magazine of ambition requires waiting for receipts from the distributor for ninety days (in the first instance), and setting up a subscriber base from scratch, let alone dealing with the realisation that advertisers generally do not see promotional potential because of low circulation. It has always been difficult placing such products before potential readers, unlike pop culture publications which have been (since then) increasingly backed by large media organisations.

In contrast, little magazines have traditionally been the idealistic passions of key individuals, and in the 1970s many considered themselves as part of an 'alternative' scene, where marketing was seen as capitalist. Furthermore, as Debray suggested of the changing nature of publishing in France after the 'revolution' of the 1960s (in a situation which became relatively typical of other Western countries such as Australia), one inheritance was the growth of a mass market for cultural products where 'the distributors of thought become separated from the producers, [and] the distributors now determined not only the volume but the nature of production' (91). Hamilton has also noted how the period was a turning point away from publishing as a 'gentlemanly' business:

> [T]he model was accepted as a happy marriage between art and commerce. But something happened in the 1960s that began a transformation ... [T]he industry was bought up bit-by-bit by conglomerate media corporations ... ('Sympathy' 88)

In Australia, this resulted in further structural difficulties for literary magazines, in that they could not market themselves to a lower population base in competition with a mass media 'run on personality, not the collective, the sensational, not the intelligible and the singular, not the universal' (Debray 82). Broadly, the marketplace became more crowded and prone to the effects of new marketing techniques.

The decade also saw an interrogation of the very idea of the literary (or small) magazine in terms of size and formatting, such as changes to the means of production including the choice of offset printing over the labour-intensive letterpress, a variation on the theme of small-scale craft production. The small magazine (in those terms) in Britain, at least, had always been a moveable feast of sizes and expectation, particularly during the 1920s. In the late 1960s and 1970s, offset printing (or camera-ready copy) meant that most people could become small publishers if they had a light table, layout and Letraset sheets, and glue to stick down the strips of type. Such a development was arguably as significant a change to the means of production as the invention of the paperback book and its later marketing promotion by Allen

Lane when he formed Penguin books in 1935, which opened up a market for cheaper books for an expanding readership. As Jim Hart, who worked for the then fledgling travel publisher Lonely Planet in the 1970s, has explained:

> The growth in publishing — especially the number of new publishers — was helped by changes in book production. The use of 'cold' type and offset printing, which had already started to replace letterpress in the 1960s, allowed a much higher illustrative content and greater flexibility in design. (54)

Type could then be photographed from existing formats without having to be reset, and

> the flexibility of offset production helped lower the entry cost for young publishers. As typesetting and layout became almost kitchen-table operations, it wasn't too hard for ideas-rich but cash-poor entrepreneurs to finance a short print run. (55)

As he has pointed out, in Australia at least, other realities remain fixed: 'Sadly there was no new technology to change other economic realities of the book trade, such as distribution to a relatively small readership scattered across a large continent' (55). As John Tranter would years later put it, 'You can solve all the other problems, but that one is intractable. Or it was, until the internet' ('The elephant' n.p.).

The paperback revolution really did not hit Australia until the 1970s, in the years between 1972 and 1975, through at first Penguin Australia, then the University of Queensland Press, small presses such as Fremantle Arts Centre Press, and McPhee Gribble in 1975. Indeed, the 1975 Working Party into the Australian Book Trade concluded:

> The most visible trend in the demand for book trade products is the steady growth in sales of mass-market paperbacks ... The growth of paperbacks has certainly played a very significant part in extending the reading habit. (Qtd. in Nile 95)

According to Nile, 'by the 1980s paperbacks were the norm and the vast majority of Australian titles continue to be produced in this way'. So the paperback, riding on the back of offset printing, resulted in a democratisation and availability of reading. The election of the Whitlam Labor Government in 1972 also saw the acceleration of the rapidly growing tertiary sector, which had begun in the 1960s. This resulted in an expansion of potential readers (of paperbacks, and perhaps, literary magazines) and writers, facilitated to an extent by increased educational spending by the Federal Government.

The university student newspaper was revolutionalised by the new technology, in that quick publication could respond almost overnight to issues such as the growing war in Vietnam. Newspapers such as *Honi Soit* (University of Sydney), *On Dit* (University of Adelaide), *Farrago* (University of Melbourne) and *Lot's Wife* (Monash University) demonstrated that the printed word was no longer cumbersome. Underground publications of different shapes proliferated and the student press, particularly at Monash, saw itself as part of a developing alternative media. Interestingly, some of the literary publications appeared within such an environment and were started by students and ex-students at universities. The commercially conservative Melbourne *Age*, for example, was persuaded in the early 1970s to venture into the stirrings of countercultural politics by creating *Broadside*, edited by Pete Steedman (the former editor of *Lot's Wife*), containing stories, poetry, cartoons and opinion pieces within a cheap, accessible format.

Allowing for changes to the means of production, the election of the Whitlam Government in 1972 heralded an intense period of cultural nationalism, the creation of the Australia Council (loosely modelled on the Canada Council) and a renaissance in the film industry. In terms of political economy, the legitimisation of increased government spending for the arts by the incumbent government made it easier for books from new authors to be published, through schemes such as the Book Bounty, a payment of 25 per cent of the invoiced price to printers for printing local books, and a publishing subsidy scheme under the auspices of the Australia Council. Such fundamental changes helped to create a plethora of small literary and political journals — so much so that two Sydney librarians, Tom and Wendy Whitton, established the *Australasian Small Press Review* in 1975, modelled on the Californian magazine *Small Press Review*, to review and notice the expanding range of publications. They would go on to form a small press of their own, Second Back Row Press, which published books on alternative lifestyles and some new local fiction as well as importing for local distribution a range of titles from independent presses in the United States and the United Kingdom.

As I have suggested, Michael Wilding, a notable figure in the upsurge of small-press publishing and the 'new writing' during the late 1960s and into the 1970s, identified another important moment in Australia which unlocked creative potential: the dropping of censorship of books and magazines in 1972. Prior to that, he noted, 'you were constantly in censorship hassles — which were not enjoyable, were a nuisance, and took time from writing and just living … ' ('A survey' 115). Along with Moorhouse, he had published largely in risqué magazines, such as *Squire*, *Casual* and *Chance*, which were not beholden to censorship rules. Gareth Powell, the 'girlie' publisher, had first published Moorhouse's *Futility and Other Animals* in 1969. Wilding said of the time, speaking in effect for himself and other writers such as Frank Moorhouse, 'to us at that time the girlie magazines provided the only outlets for works that dealt with sexuality, for works that weren't committed to the old outback tale and other formulae that the established literary magazines ran' (121). Wilding was interested in a strand of new writing that he admired

> in that Kosinki-Warhol alienated world — Colin Talbot's work for instance. But that, too, has required further changes in the modes of literary production — that has required new presses, new magazines, to cater for it: its message is too extreme for the overground media … (116)

His view was that a 'new writing' was required and the apparatuses to publish it needed to be set in place, so with Pat Woolley he set up Wild & Woolley in 1973. Colin Talbot was part of a group including Morry Schwartz which set up Outback Press in Melbourne. The new writing, he felt, would be a fabulist tradition, tracing back to Marcus Clarke in Australia, and the then more contemporary models of Borges, Calvino, Barthelme, and Cortazar, yet astute to the fact that 'the small press movement has its huge variety of politics and aesthetics: and a lot of the movement is very politically unaware'

(125). Yet he was relatively utopian then, something fairly typical of the time, stating:

> [T]he international small press movement offers a grouping in opposition to the multi-national domination of publishing ... A new literary culture is emerging separate from the commercial overground. (125)

The upsurge in small-press literary publishing, then, was reflecting, and in a small way implicated within, broader changes in the print media and in the wider culture. By the late 1960s and early 1970s, the New Left had not only thrown off the model of state-centred socialism epitomised by the Soviet Union. It also advocated libertarianism in most things, and was implicated in the broader countercultural movement taking root particularly in the United States. Later in the decade, small-press publishers such as Wild & Woolley spoke of their debt to imported countercultural titles from California, where there was a lively small-press scene around San Francisco. In the spirit of *Rolling Stone*, alternative papers such as the *Digger* and the *Living Daylights* appeared and promoted the notion that culture could be more persuasive than the 'high cultural' frames promoted by late capitalism. The first rock newspaper in Australia, *Go-Set*, like the *Digger*, promoted a form of New Journalism that blurred to an extent the line between fact and fiction. The advent of the weekly paper *Nation Review* and the eventual birth of the *National Times* promoted a new writing that encouraged journalists to be writers of opinion. Both publications had an interest in the literary, which helped to create an idealistic environment where, for better or worse, change was possible and attempts were made to break down the barriers between high and popular culture.

Compared with the restricted review space for books available in the major newspapers and even in literary magazines in the early years of the new millennium, papers such as the *Age* in Melbourne and the *Sydney Morning Herald* in the 1970s devoted a large proportion of their arts pages to regular reviewing of new publications. It was therefore much easier for titles from small presses to gain exposure. Literary editors such as Stuart Sayers at the *Age*, albeit conservative in much of his taste, would regularly interview up-

and-coming writers and the editors of some of the new little magazines. Presses such as Outback Press and Wild & Woolley were given prominence as the 'new' was still considered newsworthy and, compared with three decades later, fewer new titles were being published.

There had been talk of 'media monopolies' in terms of popular culture, but also of the need to create small book presses to cater for the new, younger voices and to counter the role of a few large multinational book publishers. The Whitlam Labor government had reinstated nationalism as a progressive and relatively trendy new direction, and the opposition to the war in Vietnam was a demonstration of a desire for political independence, by a minority of the population at least. Critiques of the mass media predominated, such as Humphrey McQueen's *Australia's Media Monopolies*, which took aim at the subservient nature of the Australian press. McQueen, a Maoist historian, among others, argued for the promotion of a distinctive Australian nationalism. In terms of book publishing, Michael Wilding lamented an industry largely controlled by overseas firms ('A random house' 106).

The opposition to the war had crystallised a broad alliance of opposition, including the New Left radicals (some Maoist), the ALP (by the early 1970s), churches, young people, most trade unions and the old Communist Party, which had been in the process of splitting from the Soviet Union. The Communist Party of Australia had promoted Australian left-wing culture, evidenced by its involvement in the *Realist Writer* years before. Although it was beginning to be seen as 'old' and perhaps irrelevant to the many social changes taking place, its bookshops, such as Intervention in Sydney, International in Melbourne, and the People's Bookshop in Brisbane, had always stocked new Australian writers and magazines. The mass media, it was suggested, rather than telling us what to think, set agendas, and told us what to think about. In such an environment, small magazines and underground publications were battling against incredible odds, the least of which was lack of finance. For example, literary magazines always had problems with distribution to bookshops and newsagents. Very few of them had the backing of a large book publisher with sales departments and representatives on the road, and freight was expensive on orders for small quantities in a large country. With the exception of *Quadrant*, which was able to be distributed through Gordon and Gotch as the result of connection to the Packer family, none of the magazines had newsagent distribution.

Such anti-disciplinary gestures were also evidence of an expanding youth market for rock and roll music. The deconstruction of boundaries between high and popular culture outside of the music area — for example, whether there would be an expanding book and magazine market — was another question, as its commodification potential was limited to the extent that major transnational corporations found music easier to promote and sell and to create a mass market for. Books (and to an extent literary magazines, which often looked like books and contained perceived esoteric content and therefore were not easily suited to mass-market penetration), would continue, though, to be a problem. Even so, after the innovations of the 1970s, marketers would identify niche areas in an environment where stable centres of representation were being interrogated by fashionable marginality.

For every change to the means of production, then, such as in this instance offset printing (which facilitated a further push towards mass production and a reduction in labour costs), there were countervailing tendencies towards small-scale, 'organic' products working their way through the upsurge of the countercultural explosion of the late 1960s and 1970s in Western capitalism — tendencies which were, on the surface at least, a reaction to mass culture and increasingly impersonal and industrialised societies. Such contradictions were inscribed in the little magazines of the late 1960s, and early 1970s. If the movement of the 1960s was anything, it contained both a desire for modernisation and a resistance to accelerating changes in the means of production in Western capitalism. Enzensberger has claimed that during that period the old bourgeois fear of 'the masses' reappeared as a longing for pre-industrial times dressed up in progressive clothing:

> At the very beginning of the student revolt, during the Free Speech
> Movement at Berkeley, the computer was a favourite target for aggression

> ... During the May events in Paris the reversion to archaic forms of production was particularly characteristic. Instead of carrying out agitation among the workers with a modern offset press, the students printed posters on the hand presses of the École des Beaux Arts ... It was not the radio headquarters that were seized by the rebels, but the Odeon Theatre, steeped in tradition. (27-8)

Were the 1960s, then, (among many questions) a revolutionary moment or an attempt to halt the speed of encroaching commodification into all areas of daily life? Part of that question has been obscured by four generations of nostalgic mystification, and the answer involves the positives and negatives in the very contradiction that is the decade, something which DeKoven wrestles with (from her United States experience) in an attempt to reconcile the anti-disciplinary nature of the period into its post-modern inheritance. She seems to argue that the decade was totalising within its utopian rhetoric, and also formative of subsequent local and personal politics (139). But her argument seems tentative as to the contradiction of eventual co-option and subversive otherness, which she categorises as post-modernity. In any case, were some of the cultural manifestations an insistence on 'acting out' the contradictions of powerlessness as much as they were direct action on the streets? (Bell 52) Stephens puts it another way, suggesting in her summation of that time that

> [a] new language of protest was developed which aimed to transgress the boundaries between the political and the aesthetic. This new politics was a playful and self-referential celebration of ambiguity, where the theatrical and the spectacle were privileged ... [I]t was a politics which drew more on the themes of popular culture than on the heritage of the Left for its language of protest. (22)

Such tensions would be played out in the ongoing story of the literary magazine in Australia, and possibly in the plethora of performance poetry events since the 1960s. That is, was there a masking of the realisation that oppositional culture (including poetry) has been continually marginalised inside Western capitalism since the 1960s, along with a belated recognition that the cultural means of production are notoriously difficult to change? I should at this point suggest that many of the little magazines of the period were interested in changing at least the literary means of production, but not all were concerned to pursue it. Some were, in fact, seduced by the existing contradictory structures, as Foucault has suggested: 'If power had a solely repressive function it would be much more easily overthrown' (qtd. in Stephens 87).

A poetry performance is largely an uncommodified form of publication, albeit to a small number of people, so it is not uneventful, and is not necessarily a withdrawal from public space. Poetry performances seem to invoke a notion of utopian defiance, yet they can be uncritical of the status quo, because over the forty years of this study, the major tangential shift to bear witness to, in the changing nature of the cultural means of production, is the almost total domination of market forces, mediated by utopian moves by individuals and groups. As Doyle has perhaps pessimistically suggested,

> the market simply is deemed to operate on 'natural' properties and truths...
> [C]itizens are now individualized consumers and individually consumed, with any notion of society as a composite entity now gone. (196)

Many of the poetry readings of the late 1960s and 1970s were, I dare to say, attempts at recapturing public space, but given the individualised agendas of most writers, their influence raises further questions. Magazines, by contrast, have been in Australia small public spaces, bringing together the previously disparate into an idea of community: an 'acting out' on one level, but also, aspiring to a readership, at least a symbolic political act.

As we have seen, at the level of the physical means of production, though, offset printing was implicated in forces that would go on to revolutionise the look of publications and allow for expressive, experimental formats. The contradictory indications of change had already been percolating, however, in a number of roneoed (almost pre-industrial) journals such as the *Ear in the Wheatfield* and *Our Glass*, both edited by Kris Hemensley, and the *Great Auk*, edited by Charles Buckmaster in Melbourne for several years. They expressed a desire, if you like, for swift, uncomplicated communication free of the august constraints of the established magazines. They were an expression of demystification against the establishment, something which

Stephen Murray-Smith at *Overland* would have found strange, as he and his publication had always been marginal to the largely conservative mainstream representations of Australian politics. Kris Hemensley spoke of the time as 'a wild assertion of vitality' (226-39), the backdrop being what Michael Wilding regarded as a 'new writing' which brought forth new formats.

The decade was dotted with examples of little magazines that existed for several issues and disappeared with little or no ambition for longevity or commercial survival. *Dharma*, co-edited by Larry Buttrose from Adelaide, lasted three years. *Mok*, edited by Richard Tipping and Rob Tillett, survived for two years, and at the end of the decade, *Post-Modern Writing*, edited by Michael Wilding and Nigel Roberts, published three issues between 1979 and 1981, in a format that was designed to resist easy commodification. It was printed on a duplicator and stitched by sewing machine, in a similar foolscap-size to *Free Poetry* of the late 1960s. *Post-Modern Writing* was distributed largely through the mail, in fact surreptitiously through the departmental mail, of the University of Sydney's English Department.

The social landscape was anti-disciplinary and increasingly discontinuous, and to survive it — to become organised and institutionalised — was anathema to the anarchic spirit inherited from the 1960s. Performance poetry became almost a norm, providing poets both with a venue to read and another form of publication. This was seemingly democratic, but in essence it meant that living in the inner city was advantageous to participation. Meanwhile, publications were more often than not stapled, resisting easy commodification and setting them apart from the established literary magazines, which had perfect binding. The irony was that, broadly speaking, the little magazine was considered (and up to a point considered itself) as marginal in the broader culture, so that popular magazines, such as the glossy *Australian Women's Weekly*, could have staples and get away with it so long as they sold well.

Seemingly, all cultural, political and social assumptions were under review, and also the largely marginalised left-wing agendas were being described as narrowly masculine. A list of magazines reveals publications of every size and description. *Fitzrot, Dodo, Saturday Club Book of Poetry, Born to Concrete, Free Poetry, Real Poetry, Makar, Mok* and *Your Friendly Fascist* were all stapled and already rougher in design than other magazines. Even so, offset printing gave their editors the ability to experiment with layout, and in the case of *Born to Concrete*, to be devoted to 'concrete poetry' (essentially a visual play on words, a deconstruction of traditional notions of the poem, and most certainly, any idea of rhyme and meter). Letterpress printing could have made some of those experiments problematic.

Born to Concrete first appeared in February 1975 with Pi O as the general editor and Rosemary Edwards, Jas H Duke and Chris Croft as contributing editors. It was a statement of belief in the notion of concrete poetry and for several years Pi O and Jas Duke actively promoted the form around student newspapers and on radio with 'sound' poetry. The publication was cheaply produced and occasional, which worked against bookshop sales. I recall Jas Duke saying that the *Age* never reviewed him, or magazines he was associated with, because his publications were stapled ('Respectable or risqué' n.p.). The freewheeling nature of the decade was a moment in which small publications could experimentally resist commodification.

In comparison, some little magazines, perhaps foolishly, eschewed more ambition and opted to focus on presentation and therefore audience. *Aspect*, edited by Rudi Krausmann from Sydney, the later *Contempa*, edited by myself from Melbourne, *Canberra Poetry*, *Helix*, *Luna* and *New Poetry* presented 'professional' formats (with perfect binding and colour covers), and often expressed a desire to have respectable bookshop sales and to be taken seriously by the literary establishment. How was it possible to attract reasonable sales and sponsorship from the Australia Council without presenting a professional face? Given the tiny market for the literary magazine, it could be argued in retrospect that the editors were fighting over slim pickings and to spend considerable money on glossy production would endanger long-term sustainability, even if it impressed people such as grant-funding bodies. *Meanjin, Overland, Southerly* and *Quadrant* all had established subscribers and communities of interest, whereas *New Poetry*, *Contempa*, *Aspect*, *Luna*, *Helix* and *Canberra Poetry* could not survive for very long into the 1980s and in a sense did not have much of a chance at establishing respective constituencies.

Helix, which first appeared in the late 1970s, was expensively produced and perfect-bound like a book. Edited by Les Harrop, it published a range of well-known Australians and a sprinkling of international authors, giving the magazine a distinctly 'important' look, something which was a feature of the decade in that, although there was an upsurge of the local, underneath, the 'cultural cringe' lurked. *Helix* was once described as 'being comparable with the most attractive literary publications to be found anywhere in the world' (Denholm 2: 153). Later published by Poetry Helix in association with Victoria College in Melbourne, it continued into the early 1980s, publishing a number of double issues containing a sprinkling of locals and internationals with a positive emphasis on serious literary discussion. In 1984 the editorship passed to David Brooks at the University of Western Australia, and its Australian contributors included Les Murray, Kevin Hart, David Carter and Roger McDonald. It had editorial addresses in Melbourne and in California. Like the *Ear in the Wheatfield*, *Helix* made much of the need for our literature to open out and dispense with the time-worn themes of the past. External validation was a major theme. *Helix*, in its short life, was heavily supported by the Literature Board of the Australia Council, perhaps since the Board may have been impressed by the range of international names displayed in its pages.

Another magazine that was supported for most of its life — a fact which paradoxically could have made it more vulnerable — was *Compass* from Sydney. Its first editor, Chris Mansell, claimed it was 'started because there seemed to be room and as a reaction to other magazines' (qtd. in Denholm 2: 136). This was shorthand, perhaps, for the idea that different writers needed showcasing. It was first published in July 1978, publishing with colour covers, and lasted until spring 1985. In 1980 it received support from the Literature Board, which was discontinued in 1983. *Compass* during its lifespan featured poetry and the work of Susan Hampton, and Judith

Beveridge, and in one volume, the work of women writers. Issues showed a distinct number of Sydney-based writers and poets including Dorothy Porter, Kate Lilley, Christopher Kelen and Keith Shadwick. The second issue of Volume 5 was edited from the Western Australian Institute of Technology by Brian Dibble, Elizabeth Jolley and Ross Bennett, the first in a number of issues from that state.

While Australia had always found it difficult supporting a fistful of literary magazines up until the 1970s, this group of diverse newcomers were looking for support from arts bodies and, hopefully, literary consumers. Whether they would survive was another question. A rollcall at the conclusion of the decade would tell a salutary story, as we will see below.

Aspect (Art & Literature) from Sydney was deliberately ambitious in its format and had links to the art scene in that city. *New Poetry*, which had come about as a result of a coup in the Poetry Society of Australia by Robert Adamson, set about promoting the 'new poetry' influenced by then luminaries such as John Ashbery and Robert Duncan in marked contrast to the more formalist tradition exemplified by Les Murray and his contemporaries. It was beautifully produced on expensive paper, with ambitious colour artwork, and it threw down a challenge to the design standards of *Meanjin*, *Overland*, *Southerly* and particularly *Quadrant*.

Makar was a persistent stayer in the magazine pack of the 1970s. Started in 1960 in the English Department of the University of Queensland on the suggestion of the then head of the English Department, Professor AC Cawley, (a noted mediaevalist), it concentrated on publishing poetry during a period of poetic experimentation. After 1968, a member of the English Department, Martin Duwell, became editor and literally the mainstay of the publication. The magazine was instrumental in devoting an individual issue each year to single poets, with an eclectic editorial line which refrained from taking sides in the poetry wars. Poets whose first book was published by *Makar* include Alan Wearne, Antigone Kefala and Graham Rowlands. The format of *Makar* was saddle-stitch (stapled) but the issues of Gargoyle Poets, a series which it also published as books by individual poets, had attractive gloss covers.

Most of the activity, though, took place in Melbourne and Sydney, the largest two cities. Melbourne is in my opinion a major home of the little magazine, as it has always been a place of ideas, producing, in political terms, ideologically committed politicians such as the late Jim Cairns, Deputy Prime Minister in the Whitlam Labor government, and RG (Robert) Menzies, the first theoretician and leader of the Liberal Party. The city has always had the advantages, like Sydney, of a large population base. Melbourne, by the 1970s, hosted *Meanjin* and *Overland*, and a plethora of little magazines, so that criticism of 'Melbourne cliques' emerged.

Even so, other states have published magazines, such as *Westerly* in Western Australia, about which Jim Davidson, the former editor of *Meanjin*, wrote: 'It is *Westerly* more than anything else that keeps the image of the West alive in quality bookshops' (qtd. in Bennett & Cowan 202). The praise continued for *Westerly*: it 'is a national magazine centred in Perth rather than Melbourne or Sydney'. It commenced in 1956 as a student production, and in 1975 Peter Cowan and Bruce Bennett became joint editors from the English Department of the University of Western Australia. Over the years it has been a 'forum' publication, promoting Western Australian writers such as Tom Hungerford, Fay Zwicky and Dorothy Hewett to a national audience, while at the same time keeping an eye out for new writing from other states. Indeed, in the 1970s, it welcomed contributions from a number of relatively unpublished writers such as Vicki Viidikas, as well as new fiction from up-and-comers like Peter Goldsworthy, James McQueen and Wendy Jenkins. By this stage the magazine was quarto-size on glossy paper and open to experimental poetry. As with most of the other magazines, its history is dotted with financial ups and downs and dedicated individuals. In 1975, its circulation was only 1000 copies (Bennett & Cowan 209); even so, it continued to publish into the 1990s.

Phillip Edmonds

The 1970s, as elsewhere, had seen an upsurge in activity in Western Australia, and the appearance of new magazines was usually evidence of this. Fremantle Arts Centre Press, established by Ian Templeman, began publishing individual volumes of fiction and poetry in Perth, including the first published work of Elizabeth Jolley, and the centre became a creative hub for readings and workshops, leading to the establishment in 1974 of a poetry magazine, *Patterns*, edited by Fay Zwicky, Nicholas Hasluck and Ian Templeman. It was the only literary publication other than *Westerly* coming out of Western Australia, and in a largely broadsheet format it published from 1974 until 1985.

Because most of the magazines came from Sydney and Melbourne, as did most of their readers, it was often a case of 'out of sight, out of mind' for writers in the west, let alone those in the Northern Territory and North Queensland. As I have previously suggested, the bohemian and 'grub street' characteristics of the small magazine revival in Sydney and Melbourne were well-documented and privileged in the 'New Writing' issue of *Australian Literary Studies* in 1977. The issue contained contributions that spoke of the ways in which magazines sparred with each other and fed off one another, the implication being that the scene was dynamic, almost as though the rest of the country hardly existed. Yet break-outs such as *Westerly* occurred elsewhere, too: *Canberra Poetry*, *Dharma* from Adelaide, *Inprint* from Bathurst, *Riverrun* from Newcastle and *Linq* from Townsville.

Linq was published by James Cook University, and the title is an acronym from 'literature in North Queensland'. The first issue appeared in 1971, with an editorial committee comprising David Foott, Gordon Inskip and Elizabeth Perkins. Townsville had been officially a centre for Australian literature after Colin Roderick (formerly of the publisher Angus and Robertson and later the biographer of Henry Lawson), took up the first foundation Chair in Australian Literature at James Cook University in 1966. In the 1970s, though, *Linq*'s visibility was limited outside its region, while in the other states, the new little magazines chattered away, largely among themselves. Even so, *Linq* continued publishing in varying frequency through to the 1990s.

Out of Newcastle in New South Wales, meanwhile, came *Riverrun*, which had only four issues from 1976 to 1978. Originally an idea of Keith Russell and Brian Musgrove, it intended to replace *Nimrod*, which had come out of the University Student Council at Newcastle University. Their stated intentions were to publish more locals from the Hunter Valley region, but the magazine would be a 'meeting place for locals and outsiders, unknowns and "names"' (Denholm 2: 191). Contributors included Rae Desmond Jones, Tom Thompson, Ross Bennett and Robert Adamson.

Adelaide had been quite a centre of literary activity prior to the 1970s, largely through the efforts of Max Harris and Geoffrey Dutton. Harris had published his notorious *Angry Penguins* in the 1940s, which became the object of probably Australia's most notable 'cause célèbre' in the Ern Malley hoax, a reaction by James McAuley and Harold Stewart to Harris's championing of modernism in Australian art and letters. With Dutton, Harris founded and edited *Australian Letters* from 1957-68, an expensive-looking journal of creative writing and review articles, supported by some advertising in its pages — a rare objective for a literary publication to pursue.

Harris and Dutton were also involved in the first incarnation of the *Australian Book Review* between 1961 and 1974. *Southern Review* was established in 1962 by Kevin Magarey, an academic in the English Department at the University of Adelaide who formed a committee to obtain finance from the university for the early publications. It was to continue as an overly academic journal, with small amounts of creative writing, through the 1970s, published by the English Department at Adelaide and its equivalent at Macquarie University in Sydney. Although originally subtitled 'An Australian Journal of Literary Studies' in 1964, *Southern Review* never took on the role of promoting Australian writing, unlike *Australian Literary Studies*. It was clearly internationalist in focus, and as the 1980s and 1990s progressed the published material increasingly took on the flavour of literary theory, as was the trend with other academic journals. Eventually, the University of Adelaide dropped its subsidy and the journal moved to Monash University, proving the case that publications with an over-reliance on one large funding base are always vulnerable.

Adelaide established the first writers' festival in Australia in 1960 — Writers Week at the Adelaide Festival — but there had not been any other journals to speak of in Adelaide until the 1970s, when a poetry-reading culture started to develop, eventually culminating in the Friendly Street Poets readings, which have persisted to this day. *Dharma* was first published by the Dharma Poetry Society in March 1971, and, according to Michael Denholm, 'it was an outlet for mystical poetry, and encouraged writers concerned with the quest for knowledge' (1: 81) — although it also pursued a political social realist agenda (its title certainly suggested something along those lines). The inspiration came from a line in Jack Kerouac's *Dharma Bums*, where some of the characters decide to set up their own press. It was a cheaply produced, stapled publication, not unlike similar magazines in Melbourne and Sydney of the day, whose editors thought nothing of their magazines appearing portable and grungy. In February 1975 its editors were Larry Buttrose, Donna Maegraith and Stephen Measday, and it received some funding from the Literature Board of the Australia Council and from the University of Adelaide to encourage student readings. Later changing its name to *Real Poetry* in 1976, it published two issues, one of which was handset. Contributors included Rae Desmond Jones, Graham Rowlands, Joanne Burns and Peter Murphy.

Another One for Mary was started in 1976 and was pretty typical of literary/alternative publications coming out of Adelaide over the period, in that it was unsustainable for reasons including a small population home-base and a general conservatism despite a longish history of literary activity — something which would plague the city for years to come. *Another One for Mary* was portable, laid out and designed like a pop magazine with funky graphics. It was edited by John Kingsmill and involved Paul Kelly, then a very young up-and-coming writer/songwriter. Kinsgsmill said that it was born 'out of dissatisfaction and boredom with what constituted "alternative" publishing in Adelaide at that time' (qtd. in Denholm 2: 102). He wanted to create a 'literature that had the smell of life about it', but it didn't last longer than a few issues. Yet Kingsmill was involved again in publishing, along with Rosemary Jones, in *Ash*, which first appeared in 1979 and lasted for sixteen issues. Contributors included John Emery, Mike Ladd, Anne Brewster and Rory Harris, young writers around Adelaide at the time. Typical of the time, poetry dominated in Adelaide and elsewhere. *Dark Areas* (edited by Jane Donald and Sandy Clark) came out in 1971, and it published five cheaply produced issues until 1972. *Fields*, loosely associated with Flinders University, published a number of interstate authors including Michael Dransfield, Bill Beard and Philip Hammial. Editors over that time included Steve Evans and Adrian Flavell.

Another feature of the 1970s was the diversity and extravagance of the magazines' titles. *Your Friendly Fascist*, a poetry journal published between 1971-76, probably had the craziest name of the decade, yet it had a strong contender in *Predator of the Marvellous*, which came out of Sydney for one issue in 1977 (Denholm 2: 206) thanks to Te-Rea Nolan. It proclaimed that it was not associated with any literary factions and published Tom Thompson, Robert Harris and David Malouf, among others. Founded by Rae Desmond Jones in Sydney, meanwhile, *Your Friendly Fascist* was noted for its feral editorials and unpredictable contents. Contributors included Eric Beach, Joanne Burns and Stefanie Bennett. Desmond Jones and the then co-editor, John Edwards, said of its birth: 'The primary reason for this mag's existence when there must be a dozen other equally crazy such mags in Australia at the moment, is because none of them consistently publish US' (qtd. in Denholm 1: 130). Desmond Jones, when reflecting on his editorial line, did reveal the differences between the magazines:

> [I]t is necessary for magazines and writers not to take themselves so seriously, not to be fucking pompous ... [W]e have sought to restore something of the anarchic delight which should be in poetry, but which is frequently nullified by a serious and heavy magazine or book format. (213)

It was certainly true at that time that some magazines, such as the *Ear in the Wheatfield* and *Etymspheres*, took their pursuit of poetic aesthetics very seriously. Even so, Desmond Jones went further in his attack on the romantic image of the artist. Of his editorial mission, he added:

> I think the best way to do this (whatever else one is doing) is to stimulate writers not to be introverted wankers wilting in corners, or extroverted self-indulgent beautiful people ... to be passive in one's perceptions but active in the assertion of them. (214)

Going by the evidence of *Your Friendly Fascist*, Desmond Jones saw himself as a gadfly, something the decade encouraged, alongside the myth-making behind new movements and the reputation-building.

There were some other great names for magazines. *Surfers Paradise* was edited by John Forbes (probably the most talented new poet of the time) and Laurie Duggan in Sydney, with four occasional issues over nearly ten years. *Ploughman* (edited by Gary Oliver), which was another poetry publication, originating in Sydney in 1973, had a few manifestations, its first title being *Ploughman's Lunch* and later *Ploughman*. It had seven issues and ceased publication in 1974; contributors included Carol Novack, Mal Morgan, Richard Tipping and Joanne Burns.

Luna, produced by a feminist collective led by Barbara Giles in Melbourne in 1975, set out to delineate a space for itself. The editors stated, 'We are, apparently, the only group of women producing a literary magazine which is neither pedantic, polemic nor political in bias', (qtd. in Denholm 2: 225), thus making a claim that they would also publish male contributors unlike the more militant *Hecate*. *Luna* was very much a forum publication in terms of the styles and variety of the authors represented, such as Judith Rodriguez, Maria Lewitt, Gig Ryan, Gwen Harwood and some males, and its appearance became graphically predictable and relatively staid in comparison to many of the other journals, even though it published prints and drawings on occasions. For all of this, *Luna* represented a moment when women were beginning to organise in the small-press movement after years of largely male networking and relative posturing. It published on a semi-annual basis between 1975 and 1986, and annually from 1987-89. Over its life, it mainly used the same cover graphic, featuring the moon for all issues with colour changes.

Figure 3: Cover of Luna, *vol 2, no 4 (1979)*

Canberra Poetry, edited by Alan Gould, Philip Mead and Kevin Hart, was distinctly non-bohemian in appearance, which suited the aesthetics of the editors and their cautiousness about poetic experimentation. This group of Canberra poets were open as to their suspicion of the fashionability of the 'new poetry' (owing a debt to AD Hope), and to an extent sided with Les Murray in subsequent poetry wars. Like *Luna*, it was a perfect-bound, paperback-size journal that stressed a desire for permanence. It was originally published with the assistance of the Australian National University Students Association; its first issue was in 1973, and its aim was to provide for writers living in, and connected with, Canberra. According to Denholm, its editors believed 'that Canberra suffered from the absence of a recognizable landscape, a frame of reference ... ' (1: 76). *Canberra Poetry* was notable for the conservative range of writers and poets it published, such as David Campbell, Grace Perry and Geoff Page. This was a clear statement of the editorial predilection, and in Kevin Hart and Alan Gould's particular case, a desire not to be associated with the bohemian impulses coming out of Balmain in Sydney and Carlton in Melbourne. Kevin Hart and Philip Mead would, after moving to Melbourne in the late 1970s, go on to establish very successful academic careers in Australia and abroad.

Contempa was founded in Melbourne by Robert Kenny and myself in 1972, the year of the election of the Whitlam Labor government, as a result of a chance meeting between the two of us in Carlton at La Mama. The magazine received positive support from local poets Michael Dugan and Judith Rodriguez, among others, who saw a need to represent the creative upsurge at the time. The magazine's first four issues were rough and stapled, representing as it were, financial sense; but due to Robert Kenny's design skills, the magazine always looked attractive in its first few years. Kenny saw the birth of *Contempa* as part of a vacuum:

> When Phillip Edmonds and I began *Contempa* in late '71 all the magazines of the late sixties were dead ... [I]t was a magazine that grew out of a lack of activity rather than an activity; it wanted, I suppose, to create its own activity. (203)

In its early years, it published the work of Walter Billeter, Pi O, Robert Harris, Michael Dugan, John Jenkins and Ken Taylor (some also in book form), but by 1974, according to Kenny, 'the problem was, Mr Edmonds and Mr Kenny had their heads in different clouds'. Kenny was moving in the direction of the aesthetics of Hemensley, Billeter and Jenkins: 'an interest in writing being "self-conscious", aware of its own processes' (204):

> And so I kissed *Contempa* goodbye. In many ways it would have been best if *Contempa* had stopped there … Now, I think, it has attempted to become an institution: it's no accident the last issue looked like *Overland*. In its paranoia to not be associated with any 'group', or 'ideology', it is simply irrelevant. (204)

After Robert Kenny left, and in receipt of Literature Board support, I made the magazine perfect-bound with some striking covers. Peter Pierce commented on an editorial split (220), after which I struggled towards making the magazine more of a forum publication containing a wide range of prose and poetry. I resisted the idea that such a magazine should be overly self-conscious. But *Contempa*'s later history, although it occasionally became as good-looking as *Meanjin* and *Overland*, was cut short by a lack of financial support and limited distribution and subscriptions. Like most magazines on the list quoted above, it was a one-man/one-woman band which could not compete with the established networks of the magazines which had survived World War II and the Cold War. By the evidence of *Contempa* and others which did not survive the decade, some little magazines were individual dreams nurtured in the idealism of the 1970s. In the case of Kris Hemensley's publications, they were at the crest of ideological waves that were not sustainable or had become co-opted in a general intellectual move towards deconstruction and post-structuralism.

The paradox was that the initial sales for even the rougher manifestations of *Contempa* and others were healthy, as many booksellers saw their role as creating social and cultural space, in contrast to the 1990s and early 2000s, when bookselling became increasingly corporate and bestseller-driven. Little magazines of the time, broadly speaking, could afford to resist commodification

Figure 4: Cover of Contempa

and homogenisation. In other words, the little/literary magazine existed as it always had, simultaneously in and out of the marketplace, but in an environment where there was less conceptual and informational traffic than currently and more acceptance of unprofessional formats.

If one moment represented the deconstruction, or indeed the renovation, of the very idea of the literary magazine, it was the advent of *Tabloid Story* in the early 1970s. Created by Frank Moorhouse, Michael Wilding, Carmel Kelly and Pat Woolley, it was, in a sense, a magazine you had when you did not have a magazine — in that it was a supplement to existing mass-market publications containing short fiction. Moorhouse and Wilding had been concerned that the short story had disappeared almost altogether into the small circulation which came with the established magazines. *Tabloid Story* could be viewed as a form of lateral thinking in response to sheer frustration at the inability of any Australian literary magazine to break out from the ghetto of limited circulation and marginalisation. Michael Wilding described it as

> an entire packaged magazine, already edited, typeset, designed and camera-ready. The host magazine taking *Tabloid Story* would give us a run-on of 2,000 copies of the supplement to distribute to subscribers, contributors, bookshops … This way we got access to the host paper's circulation — without having to build up sales ourselves, without having to sell distribution, or arrange printing. ('Tabloid story' 299)

The proposal met with enthusiastic support from the Literature Board, the members of which possibly saw it as a chance to escape the confines of the literary arts; and its subsidy meant that *Tabloid Story* could pay authors in excess of established Australian Society of Authors rates. Not having any printing, postage and administrative expenses also helped. Between 1973-84, *Tabloid Story* received $41 155 in subsidy from the Australia Council, pretty well all of that sum going to authors (Shapcott, *The Literature Board* 258).

The first edition of *Tabloid Story* appeared in 1972 in *National U* — the paper of the National Union of Students distributed free on every Australian university campus, and it paid its authors from a grant from the then Commonwealth Literary Fund (later renamed the Literature Board of the Australia Council). Wilding has explained that the editorial ideology was very much a reaction to the nationalist tradition of the 1890s, propagated by critics such as PR Stephensen and the Palmers, which some claimed had begun with Henry Lawson's 'realistic, up-country, outback, bush stories' ('Tabloid Story' 304). Furthermore, Wilding wanted to recreate a more varied and cosmopolitan Australian tradition, and the cultural changes of the late 1960s effectively fertilised the cultural ground for *Tabloid Story*: '*Tabloid Story* was committed to the variety of the new prose' (304). This new prose — for example, work by Peter Carey and Dal Stivens — was influenced and inspired by the fabulists and by overseas writers such as Borges, Cortázar and Calvino. It was a literature influenced by the Beat Generation, Fielding Dawson, Jack Kerouac and others. As Wilding put it: 'then there is a literature of process, fiction interested in, self-conscious of, its own evolution, aware of its generative process…' (305).

Tabloid Story would later appear in a broad range of host journals, including *Nation Review*, the *National Times*, *Education*, *Honi Soit*, *Living Daylights*, *Qantas Flight Magazine*, the *Melbourne Times*, *On Dit* and the *Bulletin*. Its perceived influence was such that critics like Clunies-Ross claimed that the 'role of *Tabloid Story* in reinvigorating Australian short fiction was as important as that of the *Bulletin* in inaugurating it' (174). After nineteen issues it continued into the early 1980s in Melbourne under a variety of new editors. After arriving in Melbourne, it retained its shape and intention, but slightly changed its editorial orientation with a floating group on the editorial committee, including Laurie Clancy, Caroline Lurie, Susan McCulloch, myself, David Kerr and John Timlin. It published inserts in the *National Times*, the *Melbourne Times*, the *Australian Book Review* and *Nation Review*, and an inaugural short story competition in conjunction with the *Age* newspaper. Contributors included a somewhat less experimental batch of authors (probably because the editors did not commission work as actively as had Moorhouse and Wilding in Sydney), such as Morris Lurie, Nicholas Hasluck, Helen Garner and James McQueen, and the first story or early stories by writers who would become well-known: John Bryson, Beverley Farmer, Judith Woodfall, Marion Halligan, Tim Winton and Garry Disher.

Laurie Clancy wrote of the difference between the Sydney and Melbourne orientations. He explained, 'Michael Wilding makes much in his afterword to the *Tabloid Story Pocket Book* of the claim that "*Tabloid Story* was committed to the variety of the new prose" … the fabulists, the literature of process, fiction interested in, self-conscious, of its own evolution' (247). Clancy questioned the radical nature of the authors published, aside from Peter Carey and Murray Bail, and wondered whether the definition used to describe social realism was accurate. His point was demonstrated in that the Melbourne group published more naturalistic and realist authors on the whole. In any case, by the early 1980s the group were running out of host journals and newspapers, and it subsequently lost its Literature Board subsidy (and only source of income), and the mantle for the promotion of the short story fell to Bruce Pascoe's *Australian Short Stories* during the remainder of the decade.

Tabloid Story's moment had really been a reaction to the marginalisation of the short story as a previously popular literary form in Australia after its heady days in the 1890s under Lawson and Steele Rudd. Moorhouse, as a nascent writer of short fictions, had been concerned to reactivate the literary form and *Tabloid Story* was one initiative. In 'What Happened to the Short Story' in the October 1977 edition of *Australian Literary Studies* he charted out the declining number of short fiction anthologies and popular outlets and called for action.

Tabloid Story had rescued the short story from the ghetto assigned for it by publishers, and therefore the reading public after World War II, but as I explained above, it was purely subsidised. Sadly, after its demise, the newspapers and journals that hosted it did not continue the idea by regularly publishing short fiction and thereby popularising the form. The *Age* in Melbourne began its permanent short story competition as a result, but generally newspapers saw their function in Australia as reporting the news, and were not prepared to invest in short fiction writers, unlike a long tradition in the United States and Europe where journalism had a literary side. The *Sun-News Pictorial* was an exception in the 1970s when it published a long shortlist of short stories during each January stimulated by a competition, an interesting development for Melbourne's tabloid alternative to the *Age*. Meanwhile, although it hosted the *Age/Tabloid Story Short Story Competition* in 1982 (supported by the Literature Board), the *Age*, through its then editor, Creighton Burns, was alarmed that the judges insisted on three joint winners, which would have been a departure from a one-winner mentality that would permeate short story promotion in later decades. Competitions would continue, whereas regular publication in mass outlets would remain a dream.

Despite the frustrations, *Tabloid Story* was not the only new initiative. The many, largely peripatetic journals always published short fiction. From Bathurst in New South Wales *Inprint*, edited by Nigel Krauth, Bill Turner, Jan Woolley and W Franks, declared itself, 'the short story magazine'. Its format articulated the varied nature of the changes to printing in the 1970s in that, like with some of the chapbooks produced by small presses (for example, *Rigmarole of the Hours*), its format was such that the text was printed on cheap stock inside and the covers were well-designed on thick card, the magazine itself stapled together. Some of Tim Winton's early short stories were published by *Inprint*, and the early work of Brian Castro was also printed in the magazine, demonstrating that most authors never achieve instant exposure and recognition. The magazine was formed in response to frustration by some short story writers at having work accepted by established magazines, only to have to wait up to a year before they were printed. Because *Inprint* devoted most of its pages to short fiction it could achieve speedier publication (Krauth, 'Interview with the author').

Figure 5: Cover of Inprint, *vol 3 (1979)*

Phillip Edmonds

Writing in 1981 (on behalf of the other editors), Nigel Krauth said that *Inprint*'s policy 'has always been to publish quality stories that give a good read. This evoked criticisms early on from those who wanted the magazine to define its interests more narrowly'. He then went on, 'The editorial policy was to encourage the short story's development without changing the direction of such development' ('Editor's statements' 259). There were other considerations as well, including an interest in ethnic writing in English, and stories from New Zealand, New Guinea and Fiji were published in several issues.

Inprint's birth in Bathurst, in the central west of New South Wales, was an exception for little magazines, and Krauth felt that it was a tolerant place for the birth of the magazine in 1977, resulting in *Inprint* being 'something of a pioneer and a mild rebel. It was a small-town publication with a large vision' (259). Among the newer Australians it published were Serge Liberman, James McQueen, Gabrielle Lord and Tim Winton. But as the 1980s arrived, costs increased and the magazine moved from its original stapled look into a perfect-bound, paperback size. 'It's getting more difficult to produce something attractive and reasonably priced', Krauth wrote (260); and with that, the manuscript critique service that the editors had been offering lapsed. In any case, 'in terms of quantity, during the last four years *Inprint* has published more stories than the major magazines combined (some 130 pieces)' (260). But there was frustration that the magazine could not find more of an audience. It was the same issue that bedevilled all Australian literary magazines, no matter of what persuasion and ambition, caught between ambition and financial reality. Krauth thought that *Inprint* had already achieved a great deal in its four-year history until 1981, and speaking of the editors, he added, 'however, their intrepidity presently urges them to lift *Inprint* out of its apprenticeship phase and make it known to a wider audience. How should we do this?' (260)

Inprint became a useful outlet for new authors and it was published for nine years from 1977 to 1986. Its formatting resisted any respectable commodification in the book trade, but it was attractive without looking cheap, and it sold (as with most of the newer small magazines) almost exclusively by subscription, as well as in 'alternative' inner suburban bookshops. Flashier formats required capital injection and newsagent distribution, something which editors of small magazines rarely had at their disposal. According to Krauth, the magazine's later move into a perfect-bound format was unsustainable, yet this was adapted by the editors of the new *Australian Short Stories* when they started publishing during the early 1980s, using a small paperback-size booklet format of approximately eighty to ninety pages ('Interview with the author'). During the mid 1980s *Inprint* had adopted a similar format after it moved to Sydney with issues such as 'Bite a Short Story' edited by Bill Turner. *Inprint* is a case in point of a small magazine that achieved a great deal in its short life and was another attempt at breaking the short story out of the ghetto assigned for it by a culture which had anointed the novel as the pre-eminent literary form.

As I suggested in my introduction, the story of the Australian literary/little magazine has often been that of passionate individuals. Stephen Murray-Smith's persistence and vision was the stable reason behind *Overland*'s survival through the Cold War and into the late 1900s, in that the magazine did not have the type of institutional support given to *Meanjin* or *Southerly*, due perhaps to its political connotations. In 1976 Murray-Smith was interviewed (on the occasion of *Overland*'s twenty-first birthday) and invited to look back over *Overland*'s establishment and the then current state of small magazine publishing. He spoke of the difficulties of wresting the magazine from the Communist Party of Australia in the 1950s, and he was not all that charitable about the newer crop of magazines. Yet he inadvertently exposed some of the contradictions of the decade:

> The desire to reach out to a mass audience and a common culture are seemingly not interests which are shared by the young, by and large ... Young people it seems are interested in doing their own thing and realizing their personalities. ('*Overland* is twenty-one' 4)

The interview went on to expose how Murray-Smith felt frustrated that *Overland* was perceived as being an establishment structure in the 1970s:

> The younger editors and writers don't seem to have the generosity to try and see what we are trying to do, in the same way we try to understand what they are trying to do ... In an important sense *Overland* is less 'establishment' than some of the smaller magazines, in the sense that they are looking up their own arse-holes. (5)

He also repeated the *Overland* project he had fought for during the height of the Cold War: 'We are still trying to reach out to people, to touch their hearts and minds. We are still interested in this. This seems to me the mark of non self-satisfaction'. Of the new poets, 'they are radical in themselves and about themselves ... [T]hey are only interested in circulating to a coterie group or amongst themselves'. In contrast, he thought that *Overland*'s audience 'largely consists of non-intellectuals: trade unionists, pensioners and housewives, for instance' (4). In 1976, he explained that *Overland*'s circulation was, '2000 which is still very poor. Of this 1400 are subscribers and the remainder are sold in bookshops'. His comments were a mixture of pride and frustration:

> Most of what passes for radicalism in contemporary Australian magazine publishing is simply petit-bourgeois fundamentalism, not hard to distinguish if you've been through it all before ... Australia is a pretty gutless country and even the literary editors are a pretty gutless lot. (6)

Clem Christesen had also taken *Meanjin* through many battles from 1940 until the 1970s. The magazines of the 1970s, many of which lasted only a year or two, were often the creation of one or two individuals without any organisation behind them. They would not have existed but for those people, but they folded when the passion waned. Although charming in their eccentricity and freshness, it could be said that they did not have to face the responsibility of pursuing a particular political agenda, unlike *Quadrant* and *Overland*, so they could remain coquettish.

A significant number of the new magazines (many of which I have referred to above) were devoted to poetry, as it remained in a permanent crisis of perceived obscurity in the 1970s. For a multitude of reasons, the genre had almost disappeared from popular consciousness since Banjo Paterson and the bush ballardists. Poetry publications had been kept alive by relatively obscure, university-backed little magazines such as *Southerly*. There had always been 'poetry wars', but in the 1970s passions boiled over in such things as competing reviews and the enunciation of different aesthetics. Poets who actively participated in such disputation and dialogue were Robert Adamson in Sydney and Kris Hemensley in Melbourne.

Adamson, in fact, was involved in forming a number of different magazines including *Beyond Poetry* and *Leatherjacket*. *Beyond Poetry* was a well-produced fold-out pamphlet that appeared at irregular intervals as often as finances permitted, beginning publication in 1974. From 1975 its only charge was fifty cents in stamps for the cost of postage. The editors were Cheryl Adamson and Chris Edwards, with Robert Adamson doing the layout and artwork. By August 1975 there had been eight issues, including the work of the US poet Robert Duncan, as well as locals Max Williams, Chris Edwards, Leith Morton and Pi O. Both Cheryl and Robert Adamson were also involved in *Leatherjacket*, which first appeared in 1972. In June 1973 it had a print run of 100 copies, but only two issues were published.

Adamson clearly regarded himself as an activist in the poetry scene and would continue to be involved in a number of publications over the remainder of the decade. In terms of the sometimes passionate debate, one example was the poet and budding critic Jamie Grant, who would often take pleasure in attempting to flail what he saw as the 'new poetry' school of Adamson, Hemensley and Robert Harris in the pages of *Contempa* (after 1974) and *Poetry Australia*, and on occasions in *Quadrant*. As Peter Pierce noted:

> Some of the magazines were created in order to compete with others, for instance in attracting certain schools of poets to publish with them. One effect of this competition is visible in the slanging matches disguised as reviews and interviews ... (226)

In any case, for many years the Poetry Society of Australia had provided a focus in the under-populated poetry market and spawned a number of publications. *Poetry Australia* first appeared in December 1964, when Grace

Perry (a Sydney general practitioner) broke away from the Poetry Society, who were the publishers of *Poetry Magazine* (Denholm 1: 111). *Poetry Magazine* later became *New Poetry* under the editorship of Robert Adamson. Under Perry, it was to continue into the 1970s, persisting with a letterpress format, and publishing a catholic selection of largely non-experimental work under its poetry editor, Les Murray.

In contrast, *New Poetry* became in the 1970s one of the most avant-garde magazines alongside the Melbourne-based the *Ear in the Wheatfield*. Heavily influenced by contemporary United States poets such as John Ashbery and Frank O'Hara, *New Poetry* published an occasional series called 'Prism', and an almost exclusively experimental set of poets, including Jennifer Maiden, Tim Thorne, Richard Tipping and a younger Thomas Shapcott, one of the early enthusiasts for the 'New American Poetry' and 'new' Australian poetry through his anthology *Australian Poetry Now*. Under Adamson's influence, with the considerable assistance from his then wife Cheryl, *New Poetry* set itself up as the place to publish if one was a new poet looking for recognition. A number of its editions were expensively produced with glossy colour covers and thick paper stock, something that was relatively unsustainable after several years of publication. Even so, Michael Wilding claims that Adamson edited *New Poetry*

> with a commitment unequalled in any other poetry magazine. He lived poetry, his entire working day ... [O]f how many magazines could it be said that every issue was eagerly awaited? His lack of commitment to political positions or social issues or any known value schemes or morality other than poetry made him a unique poetry editor and he had a profound effect on encouraging and fostering the creativity of the seventies and eighties. ('Letter to the author')

When it came to poetry in Australia, it was always a case of revolving 'elites' gaining access to publication and exposure in a small space. In fact, Rae Desmond Jones in 1982 would claim that 'almost immediately Adamson, Dransfield, Tranter, Tim Thorne, and so on and so forth, they became the establishment; they became people with access to power ... ' (qtd. in

McLaren 185). Later in the 1970s, Adamson would concentrate on what he termed his 'New Romanticism'. During the 1970s, *New Poetry* would be seen as the trendiest place to publish poetry. The magazine was beautiful and produced on some of the most expensive paper stock available: an artefact in its own right, a form of commodification in a deliberately small print run, an irony within an irony.

After Robert Kenny, looking for a new direction, left *Contempa* in 1974, he founded his own magazine and press, *Rigmarole of the Hours*. Denholm described *Rigmarole* as 'a series of publications of poetry, prose and criticism that appears irregularly, between five and eight times a year' (1: 116). The first issue appeared in August 1974 in a magazine format and later issues were devoted to the work of single authors or translations. Magazine issues contained the work of Finola Moorhead, Colin Talbot, Robert Harris and John Anderson whereas booklet-size editions were published including works by Katherine Gallagher, Paul Celan (translated by Walter Billeter), Ken Bolton, Gerard Lee, Kris Hemensley and Kenny himself. A number of the volumes were subsidised by the Literature Board of the Australia Council under their book-publishing subsidy program. Some single-author editions were numbered and signed by the authors, with print runs of 250-300 copies, distinguished by beautiful design and wraparound covers, which were similar to that of some of the Californian presses of the time. Leaving aside the quality of the contents, they looked too good to be marketable in traditional terms at the time. Of the design, in 1977 Kenny remarked, 'in many ways *Rigmarole* likes to indulge itself by clothing what it publishes in an "artefact" guise … [T]his design should be, that it's operating in "rapport" with the work itself and that should be its criteria' (206). In broader terms, he reflected, 'I saw a magazine as the more public manifestation of what might otherwise go in private correspondence, living room confrontations, readings, workshops, and the private act of writing' (204).

As with the assumptions behind the limited-edition book, Kenny clearly saw *Rigmarole of the Hours* as hopefully having an intense, rather than a broad, relationship with readers. In one sense, his methodology was indicative of the reality that the writers he was publishing were not well-known outside literary circles, and his press had limited financial resources; but in another way, the question hovered as to whether any other ambition was simply irrelevant. The magazine incorporated the question: was it a beautiful aristocratic gesture or another democratic transgression? With hindsight, that became a central paradox of the 1970s.

As I have suggested earlier, the rise of many of the small magazines was implicated in generational opposition to the Vietnam War and the concurrent rise of alternative media. There was a revolution on some levels at least, but it was not to last, and according to John McLaren's argument in *Writing in Hope and Fear* such rhetoric dissipated: 'What began as direct engagement with life ... finished as a pure aesthetics of language' (183). Perhaps support for such an argument is discernible in the small-magazine aesthetics of Kris Hemensley and Ken Bolton, for example, but McLaren was widely generalising. It was a pre-post-modern moment, if you can forgive the tautology. But it needs to be noted that McLaren's line was a materialist defence of *Overland*'s long tradition that Australian culture needs to be read in concert with the changes to the means of production, distribution and exchange.

Speaking of the counterculture over the period, he added, '[T]he rebellion thus remained middle-class, concerned with the distribution and acquisition of emotional well-being rather than its production' (197). But *Overland* was always working within an evangelical Left tradition that desired to reach beyond middle-class readers, whereas segments of the libertarian New Left (Frank Moorhouse, in particular, in Sydney), were intent on marginalising the notion of class by the end of the 1970s. Something else became clear: large media organisations, national and international, were in the process of commodifying upsurges such as women's liberation (for example, the production of *Cleo* by the Packer family) and, more significantly, the popular, once the desired territory of the Left, was being stylised by conservative forces and made marketable.

While *New Poetry* wanted to look good, there was always a tendency during the 1970s to account for the occasional, and a sense of not wanting to be taken too seriously — of parody — which was subeconomic. *9-2-5* (edited by Pi O, Thalia, Jas H Duke and Jeltje, under the banner of Collective Effort Press) was a publication ostensibly about work which was cheaply produced, and largely given away free. Pi O claimed in conversation that *9-2-5* had the widest distribution of any poetry publication in the country ('Respectable or risqué' n.p.), but such claims could never be verified given the non-commodified nature of the magazine, and they remained as another contribution to the developing 1970s mythology of neo-romantic gesturing.

In late 2010, in response to a series of questions from *Meanjin*, Pi O described the contents as 'GREAT', and that it started because 'no one wanted to publish us ... so we pooled our resources and our efforts' (35). The magazine did not take advertising or accept grants:

> No! We were/are Anarchists and don't want to rely on government grants or any other kind of patronage ... [W]e saw too many poets being eaten up by whom or who didn't get a grant, and who was or wasn't fashionable at the time ...

He went on to say that it had succeeded beyond their wildest dreams:

> We inaugurated the advent of performance poetry in Australia ... [W]e printed and published the first visual poetry anthology in Australia ... [W]e gave voice to workers, who didn't have a voice. (35)

Similar to *Fitzrot* and *9-2-5*, *Dodo*, from Sydney, edited by Tom Thompson, Keith Shadwick and Michael Witts, was printed in pages and assembled and stapled by the editors, with a distribution that was confined to inner-suburbs bookshops and free copies. It was pretty typical of much of the small-press activity in the way in which it was almost a reaction to the agenda of the other magazines. Denholm said of it: 'The editors regard the magazine as being different from the usual university-type literary product, and also avoiding as much as possible "the in-group mentality" of a lot of little presses' (1: 83). Its production standards would ensure that it would not sell many copies and it would be confined to speaking largely to other authors, but that was what it

Figure 6: Cover of 9-2-5, no 2

Figure 7: Cover of Dodo (1976)

set out to do, not unlike many of the other little magazines. The agenda was craft-like, unpretentious, yet caught within a ghetto of relatively like-minded people.

A similar venture was *Meuse*, which originated from students at the University of Sydney in 1977. Its first editors were Bill Farrow and Les Wicks, and according to Denholm its first issue 'was a mixture of roneo and silk-screen mediums; the second fifty pages quarto offset' (2:183). It was deliberately discursive in terms of its scattergun design standards, and employed different sizes for different issues; contributors included Ania Walwicz, Brian Cole, Tom Thompson, Anna Couani and Gig Ryan. It published six times, the last edition, the *Last Meuse*, being in 1980, published by Grant Caldwell and Geoff Aldridge. They also published *Throat*, an anthology.

On the whole, the magazines in the 1970s tended to survive longer than their precursors in the late 1960s, but, as the decade swirled with pent-up activity after the 'revolutions' of 1968, it was almost inevitable that some would not stay the course. Still, in their own way they encouraged writers. There was an understated bohemian belief that regularity might even be 'middle-class' and that sometimes magazines should appear only when there was enough good stuff around to justify it. At the start of the new decade (1980), *Polar Bear*, edited by Nicholas Pounder, made a brief, attractive appearance in blue wraparound covers. *Khasmick Quarterly*, a poetry magazine, began in 1974 in Sydney, published a series of chapbooks, and registered as an all-women publishing company in 1975, and from 1976 published women's writing on a bi-annual basis. *Leatherjacket*, another poetry magazine, organised by Robert Adamson, Ken Quinnell, John Forbes and John Tranter, came out in 1972 and lasted for two issues with a print run of around 100 copies. *Meuse* was published from Sydney with a liberal use of photographs, graphics and cartoons. Meanwhile, in the early years of the decade, roneoing still persisted in A4 and A5 sizes through the agency of *Foundation* (edited by Robert Hughes and others) in 1975, and *Parachute Poems* (edited by Mal Morgan).

It was a time for grand pronouncements and some posturing; Kris Hemensley and Pi O have demonstrated that in their desire to create ideological agendas and engage in myth-making. So much so that *Foundation*'s editor, Robert Hughes (not the art critic), made one of the most sweeping statements of the decade:

> During the final years of this century and the early years of the next, the most powerful poets in the English language will be Australian ... [O]ur culture has matured, the first truly Australian poets are writing now. (Qtd. in Denholm 1: 90)

He claimed that *Foundation* would be 'the most important set of literary documents extant in Australian literature'. Contributors included Shelton Lea, Pi O, Robert Harris, Michael Dugan and Kris Hemensley. History is in the process of deciding the truth of the assertion, but his statement reflected much of the outrageous, super-confident nature of the time.

Another experiment in de-commodification, and an example of the ongoing anxiety of poets as to their marginalised art form, was *Street Poems*, a single sheet of poems handed out free around Melbourne between 1974 and 1977 by Lucky Tom (or Poor Tom) and Ken Smeaton. They claimed the magazine was 'living poetry ... poetry of the streets'. It was, according to Jenni Brown, trying 'to reverse the crimes against poetry (which) come from attitudes of apathy, indifference and inertia' (qtd. in Denholm 2: 225).

The subculture of poetry, as expressed in the frenetic activity of the little magazines, as we have seen, always had its rivalries, perceptions of dominance and cliques, not unlike any largely bohemian activity. The *Saturday Club Book of Poetry*, for example, had been established in 1972 by Pat Laird, and published quarterly about then, and by all accounts it provided an outlet for poets who would not be accepted by established literary magazines; but during the late 1970s it changed its title to *Scopp* through Pat Laird's The Saturday Centre in Sydney, involving writers such as Philip Hammial, Rae Desmond Jones and Joanne Burns. Laird said she was 'sick to death of the small-mindedness of the so called "poetry scene" with its cliques, its snobbishness' (qtd. in Denholm 2: 215). But she was not happy over the life of the publication:

'Costs are huge, our grant is a joke — $200 an issue — and prejudices from the Literati, the bureaucracy and the intelligentsia of the underground are immense' (215). The venture in both its manifestations ran at a loss.

The Saturday Centre also published a series of books, but due to the withdrawal of funding from the Literature Board, *Scopp* stopped in 1978. Poetry it seemed would never become widespread or commercial and the tension brought out division in the ranks of the poets. Even so, the mere existence of the myriad small magazines during the 1970s provided them with inspiration. Pam Brown has cited recently, in retrospect, the influence *Magic Sam* in Sydney exerted over her early writing, along with, to a lesser extent, the *Ear in the Wheatfield* in Melbourne (qtd. in Wakeling).

An extremely short-lived venture was *Manic Magazine* in Melbourne, surviving in colour offset form for one issue only, edited by Russell Deeble (then a high profile poet), with its advertising representative being Sweeney Reed, the son of John and Sunday Reed. It became, like some of the other publications of the time, retrospectively reified as a scarce commodity for antiquarian booksellers forty years later, due to its lack of longevity. The Reed name also invoked potential connections to the bohemian Melbourne artistic establishment of Sidney Nolan, Albert Tucker and others. The first issue in Volume 1 in March 1970 published the local poet Shelton Lea alongside a story by the then unknown Peter Carey, and overseas names such as Basil Bunting, Gary Snyder, Brian Patten and Tom Pickard. Graphically sophisticated for the time in an A4 offset format with some colour reproductions, *Manic* disappeared almost without trace when its publisher, Still Earth Publications, went out of business.

In contrast, *Tabloid Story* was never a straight commodity, in that it was a free giveaway in host journals without a specific exchange value, so it managed a limited independence reliant on state support through the Literature Board. It was in one way free of the grotty problems of paying bills, other than to its writers, but in another sense it did not exist, as it, too, was dependent on the patronage of its hosts. *Tabloid Story* had evaded the tyranny of the glass ceiling of limited distribution, albeit it briefly, but as with a number of other publications of the decade, it could not have existed without government subsidies. In a sense then, its 'democracy' was paid for and could not last unless it established itself as a 'monumental' site, as had *Meanjin* and *Southerly*. By its very nature, *Tabloid Story*, in its desire to popularise the short story, was a move away from monumentalism.

7. Academic developments and other problems

All this activity and jockeying for visibility was a welcome development for a culture too often made timid by what AA Phillips had identified in the 1950s as the 'cultural cringe'. In its own way it was a grassroots upsurge, not necessarily led by the universities, but it played a part in opening up the possibilities of an Australian literature. If as Nile suggests, quoting Roland Barthes, 'literature is what is studied inside of universities, in that universities legitimate and give value to canonical texts' (202), it was not until the 1970s that some progress was made in introducing some Australian books to curricula. There had been proponents for many years in and outside the system — such as Colin Roderick, Nettie Palmer, PR Stephensen, Rex Ingamells and Miles Franklin — and in 1940 Brian Elliott became the first specialist appointment at the University of Adelaide. Even so, scholars such as Leonie Kramer and JM Stewart still actively questioned whether there was 'enough of it' to study:

> [T]he rise to prominence of the university critic in the generation following the 1960s coincided with a perceptible increase not only in new titles appearing each year but also the number of Australian books being reprinted — and this factor alone was forcing a critical rethink. (Nile 206)

Founded in 1963, *Australian Literary Studies* pre-empted, and later articulated, the changes. *Australian Literary Studies* was solely dedicated to critical work on Australian literature, and was the first journal of its type. Further formalisation followed in 1977 with the foundation of the Australian Association for the study of Australian Literature (ASAL). According to Denholm, *Australian Literary Studies* was founded on the suggestion of James McAuley at the University of Tasmania (2: 68) and Laurie Hergenhan became its first editor and over much of its life its mainstay. According to Michael Wilding, McAuley, because of his conservative leanings, wanted to counter the promotion of Australian literature along the radical nationalist lines promoted by *Meanjin* and *Overland* at the time (*Australian Literary Studies* 76). Furthermore, the aim was that '*Australian Literary Studies* would be professional — not amateur, enthusiastic and radical' ('Letter to the author').

Hergenhan moved to the University of Queensland in 1971, and after 1976 *Australian Literary Studies* was published by the University of Queensland Press. He had an eye on the past and the future, so much so that in October 1977, when publishing the special issue, 'New Writing in Australia', he in some senses formalised such activities to a naturally conservative constituency, and made them visible as possible inclusions in courses. Hergenhan, being a proponent of Australian literature, saw it as an evolving tradition and was not averse to associating and working with the editors of the new magazines. Indeed, in February 1976, he participated in 'an invasion of the Literature Board' at Writers Week in Adelaide, as a member of the newly formed Australian Small Magazines Association, in the Association's quest for better distribution and reduced postage for small presses. No other academic journal in Australia at that time would have joined in such activism.

Although *Australian Literary Studies* was different from the general criteria for this study in that it was largely a journal of criticism, its importance cannot be understated. It was a journal with an influence in excess of its limited circulation, a characteristic common to little magazines, which traditionally have been in and out of the marketplace. Looking back over the fifty years since the magazine's inception, Michael Wilding noted Hergenhan's 'openness and eclecticism ... [H]is vision was to expand the boundaries of Australian literature, rather than reduce them ... [He] was open to moves to extend the traditional concerns of literary criticism'. Of the 'New Writing' issue, Wilding stated that it provided 'a serious representation of the emerging novelists and poets well in advance of their general recognition elsewhere' ('History of scholarly journals' 33). *Australian Literary Studies* continued to be published in association with the English Department at the University of Queensland and would spearhead critical work on the writings of David Malouf, Peter Carey, Murray Bail, Frank Moorhouse and others of the generation of the 1960s and 1970s. On Hergenhan's retirement from the University of Queensland, the new editor became Leigh Dale, who was later to move to the University of Wollongong. From 1993, *Australian Literary Studies* went online.

As already suggested, a consistent problem for all literary (or small) magazines whose editors wished to sell copies was distribution in a book and magazine marketplace dominated by several large multinational publishers. In terms of newsagents, there were one or two large distributors (such as Gordon and Gotch) who dealt in volume-based turnover. This issue was to dominate the thinking of most magazine editors throughout the period of my study. Underlying the issue with distribution was the extent to which any small magazine could achieve a level of commodification or acceptance into the marketplace. By and large, the magazines (including the established journals, *Southerly*, *Meanjin*, *Overland* and *Quadrant*) were marginal to the book trade and, apart from *Quadrant*, invisible in newsagents. Booksellers usually found that literary magazines only sold slowly and in smallish numbers. Often the stocking of magazines was at the whim of friendly bookshops in the inner cities and universities — a difficult situation for consumers in that if they did not see the product they would not buy it, therefore conforming expectations that that type of magazine would not sell. During the 1980s, *Australian Short Stories*, edited by Bruce Pascoe, managed to achieve newsagent distribution due to its small, populist format, but that case has been the exception. Also, *Australian Short Stories* was a portable product — it looked and felt like a magazine — in contrast to the other literary magazines, which were becoming both chunkier and less frequently published. By the new millennium, some literary magazines (such as *Southerly* and *Heat*) were published only twice a year, bringing into question whether they were in fact magazines or books.

After the relatively static social and cultural landscape of the 1950s, dominated by a desire for security after World War II and the Cold War, the number of literary magazines remained static, and entrenched in their positions. The 1970s, in contrast, as I have suggested, highlighted a plethora of new publications that threw down the gauntlet to the established magazines and funding bodies, even though the established magazines were feeling the strain. For example, in 1975, the Literature Board of the Australia Council met with magazine editors of subsidised magazines on 20 February in Melbourne. In a statement to the Board, the editors asked it to consider a commitment to, in some cases, support for three years, as well as to consider more promotional activities, in recognition of the fact that 'the magazines cannot exist on the open market, any more than individual writers, drama companies and the like' (qtd. in Shapcott, *The Literature Board* 241), to which the Board agreed. A year later, at the Adelaide Festival in March 1976, a UNESCO seminar of literary editors was held, and on 5 March the minutes of an adjoining meeting of the Literature Board recorded that the business of their meeting was interrupted without prior arrangement by a delegation from the UNESCO seminar. This delegation represented mostly a range of the new magazines — *Etymspheres*, *Magic Sam*, *Meanjin*, *Contempa*, *Hecate*, *Tabloid Story*, the *Ear in the Wheatfield*, *Poetry Australia*, *Aspect*, *Fitzrot*, *Australasian Small Press Review* and *Australian Literary Studies*. Member of the Literature Board Elizabeth Riddell was overheard asking the Director, 'Who are these people?' The magazine delegation was concerned with increasing subsidies, typesetting facilities and the cost of postage.

There were to be several more meetings, and a series of recommendations regarding magazines over the next two years, canvassing ideas such as diversifying funding towards the newer publications and addressing printing costs and problems of distribution. For example, a Literary Magazine Editors' seminar was held at Aquinas College, University of Adelaide, organised by Elaine Lindsay under the auspices of the Literature Board, between 22 and 24 February 1978, at which the Australian Small Magazine Association (ASMA) was formed, an idea that would resurface in the 2000s under the name SPUNC [Small Press Underground Networking Community]. Most of the magazines were represented and the themes of the earlier meeting in 1976 were rehashed, including the problem of distribution (as a result of which, a pilot distribution scheme and production of a catalogue of small presses was proposed dependent on Government funding). There was the inevitable disagreement about who got Literature Board funding and why, and the high cost of postage. The Australian Small Magazine Association agreed to a plan to push for more money for magazines that had a circulation of fewer than 750 copies. Participants appeared divided as to the success of the meeting. Stephen Measday from *Real Poetry* said, 'We're from the third world of magazines, i.e. those who never get any worthwhile subsidies … unlike those grossly over-subsidised mags who also attended the seminar' (qtd. in Lindsay 7). Laurie Hergenhan of *Australian Literary Studies* remarked that in 1978 there was more cohesion, as in '1976 discussion was often handicapped by an apparent lack of common interests' (qtd. in Lindsay 5).

The report from the 1976 meeting had represented the dichotomy between the establishment publications, such as *Meanjin* and *Overland*, and new publications, such as *Magic Sam*, the *Ear in the Wheatfield*, the *Saturday Club Book of Poetry* and *Etymspheres*. Jim Davidson of *Meanjin*, though, stressed collaboration with the new, whereas Stephen Murray-Smith of *Overland* was downright stroppy. Even so, his comments were perceptive as to the practical hurdles the magazines would meet both then and over the next forty years. Of the problem of subscriptions, he noted, 'I find that people who are prepared to pay a market price for a car or a coat are horrified to be asked to pay a market price for ideas and the words they come in' (*Australian literary magazines* 2). He was cynical as to whether any magazine could attract advertisers, and as to link-ups with institutions such as universities, his comments were crudely perceptive:

> You can become allied to an institution. *Quadrant* has the CIA, *Meanjin* has the University of Melbourne, *Westerly* had the student union of the UWA, and so on. It sounds a good idea but [it] is a hell of a lot of sack for a very little bit of bread. (3)

Comparing the situation to the US, where he claimed magazines could be adornments to universities, he added, 'in Australia they are seen as a damned nuisance'. Murray-Smith, although employed by the University of Melbourne for much of his working life, nevertheless ran *Overland* as a fiercely independent organisation. In turn, he was dubious as to whether any of the magazines could break out of the circulation- and distribution-ceiling, and believed that co-operation was difficult because 'resentments and jealousies abound', and 'there are magazines which pride themselves on their limited readership' (3). He seemed to think that some of the new magazines of the 1970s were ego trips and examples of petit-bourgeois radicalism.

During the 1978 meeting of editors, Richard Jones, of the distribution firm Book People of Australia, centred in Melbourne, spoke about the recurring theme of the problems of distribution for magazines. 'Marketing magazines is a different and more difficult proposition than books', he said in a talk that confirmed what the editors already knew: that only about 10 per cent of bookshops would stock them, and that editors should disregard the chain booksellers and newsagents as being too difficult to crack (13). He noted basic marketing problems, such as unattractive production standards with the magazines — 'the covers did not seem to grab enough attention,' he was told by booksellers — and he advocated the idea of 'concept selling' with posters and stands, along the lines of the theme 'contemporary Australian literature' (16). He effectively told the gathering that, on the whole, their magazines were not attractive-looking enough to sell on an open market. There was some resistance to this idea and a feeling in the meeting, which contained an assortment of very single-minded (and to an extent esoteric) publishers, that his proposals would lead to standardisation.

The Literature Board did eventually decide in September 1986 that small magazines with a distribution of less than 500 copies with a national readership were eligible to apply for one-off projects, with no guarantee of continuing funding. However, in broad terms, the activities of the Board could not paper over the cracks of the relative rigidity of a small marketplace. Such were the contradictions that, by the conclusion of the 1970s, most of the newer magazines listed above would have ceased publication and probably not for funding reasons alone. For example, *Fitzrot* never had a circulation outside Melbourne, and did not aspire to one, it seemed, as it was privately published and presented so as to deliberately resist co-option or commodification.

Etymspheres, the *Ear in the Wheatfield*, *Rigmarole of the Hours* and *Magic Sam* were up-front about their avant-garde aspirations and non-commercial intentions, and were, in many respects, journals for other writers and not the general reader. Michael Wilding suggested in 1977, speaking of his own involvement in the movement, that 'you produce books you want to produce, and mail them to people you want to see them' ('A survey' 125). This was very much the way Hemensley and Billeter (*Etymspheres*) saw their roles as magazine editors. Wilding quoted Hemensley:

> [H]e thought he had a readership of no more than 200 people for his work,
> he didn't want to print more, that was all he wanted to communicate with,
> I rejected what I thought was the negative elitism of his attitude. (126)

Wilding inadvertently exposed that there was always an aristocratic element to much of the counterculture and its opposition to mass society. I see this as an interesting junction in the 1970s as Wilding was being utopian, but some of his contemporaries were not even being idealistic. The political defeat of the 1960s was working itself through in contrary ways.

The work of Hemensley, Billeter and others in their magazine grouping was intensely self-referential, and almost 'pre-post-modern'. In micro-terms, a good number of the new magazines exhibited such tendencies. The popular could then often be constructed as uncreative, a totalising notion in itself. To be fair to these editors, who largely published poetry, circulation would always be limited unless individual poets had the visibility of Les Murray or

Bruce Dawe at that time. They were publishing largely with their own limited financial resources (albeit it slightly mediated by subsidies from the Literature Board) and had no distribution arrangements to speak of. But they were not alone in the 'limited-edition' community — there were other magazines like this, such as *Magic Sam* in Sydney, edited by Ken Bolton.

In 1977, *Magic Sam*'s editorial policy read: 'The magazine's policy (as an ideal) is to publish work that is intelligent and aware and intellectually "on" and formally self-aware' (Bolton 216). Ken Bolton and Anna Couani's editorial statement in the 'New Writing' issue of *Australian Literary Studies* is militantly anti-realist, and suspicious of naturalism in both art and literature. Bolton, after leaving Sydney in the early 1980s, would go on to involvement in the Experimental Art Foundation in Adelaide and then to publish an occasional magazine in the 1990s called *Otis Rush*, which revisited his writerly predilections:

> Much of Australian writing is craft: craft objects built around one or other standard fond idea or attitude: a humble reflection (never a thesis) occasioned by a real (i.e. false but well described) event, often situated in the landscape that evoked it ... We'd like the magazine to be comparable to the overseas magazines we like — for example *Big Sky* and *ZZZZ* (both US). (216)

In broad terms, a group of magazines revolved around the aesthetics of Hemensley's the *Ear in the Wheatfield*, *Magic Sam*, *Etymspheres* and *Rigmarole of the Hours*, established after Robert Kenny left *Contempa* in 1974. *Etymspheres* (1974-75) was founded by Walter Billeter and John Jenkins in 1973, the first issue appearing in 1974. Billeter saw it as a space where he could explore and publish works in translation and 'texts that were too long to find their way into existing magazines ... I live and work here — a foreigner to the land, to the language. It is a position I share with about a third of this country's population' (219). He was very conscious that writing in Australia could open itself up to international perspectives, and he saw Hemensley, Kenny, Jenkins and others as acting in, rather than withdrawing from, the public sphere. He was conscious, too, of the creative 'reflection upon the individual's place in society and it's major product: consciousness' (221).

As Michael Wilding has suggested, internationalism was a hope and although he was concerned at the political naïvety of some of the small-press movement he was then idealistic as to the outcomes. Thus *Aspect (Art & Literature)*, edited by Rudi Krausmann in Sydney, was a part of that potential frame, and there were crossovers between writers and magazines across Australia. Of *Aspect*, Michael Denholm commented, 'The intention of the journal is to create an open forum within the limited area of art and literature' (2: 61). The first issue appeared in the winter of 1975. It was glossy by the standards of the day, in an A5 format, and perfect-bound to appeal to art galleries and bookshops. *Aspect* was internationalist in all respects, at a time when it was fashionable to distrust the 'old' Australia. But the problem was that Australia was still colonial without even being a republic, and had not come to terms with its own 'cultural cringe', let alone been able to confidently develop a multifarious national literature. *Aspect* demonstrated a desire for sophistication when Australia, like an adolescent, was all over the place, and in and out of love with itself.

For what it is worth, even a glance at the editors of the new journals reveals that they were mainly males, although whether this was because second-wave feminism was still attempting to march through society and the results were not yet visible might be a question worth considering. Even taking this into account, the journals were on the whole led by men. An exception was Carole Ferrier, who with Carmel Shute launched *Hecate* in Brisbane in January 1975 with a wide-ranging issue containing stories, poetry, reviews and articles on women and film, in a magazine that became assertively Radical Feminist with a socialist-theoretical bias. As with a number of other magazines, its genesis was university-based — the Postgraduates Association and the Women's Rights Committee of the University of Queensland were involved. According to Denholm, *Hecate* 'partly emerged out of the fourth issue of *Refractory Girl* which was produced in Brisbane and the enthusiasm to start a local magazine which it engendered' (1: 92). Its aim was to publish serious feminist criticism and to consider the question of the integration of feminism and socialism, so the magazine was named after Hecate, 'the goddess invoked by women who desired freedom from male tyranny' (92). *Hecate* would continue in that vein: its second issue included articles on prostitution and sexual politics published in a paperback-style, stapled format.

Compared to *Luna*, published from Melbourne, *Hecate* was perceptibly abrasive and didactic. In terms of my overall criteria of a magazine that gives a considerable proportion of its space to original creative writing, there were not many other magazines that were ostensibly feminist during the decade. Yet *Fin*, edited by Anitra Nelson, which first appeared in 1975, published four issues in a stapled and roneoed quarto broadsheet, in response to an increasing amount of unpublished material surrounding feminism. The quarterly women's studies journal *Refractory Girl* (started in 1972) did also have some literary content, and received assistance from the Literature Board between 1976 and 1978.

In saying that, individual female poets were avowedly feminist in most of their publications. Kate Jennings published the groundbreaking feminist anthology *Mother I'm Rooted* (Outback Press) in 1975, which set agendas, and to a degree, announced a potential new poetic establishment which could not be ignored, even by the established magazines.

As the decade was characterised by passionate argument, polarised position-making became a part of the aesthetics of publishing. *Contempa* (after Robert Kenny withdrew his involvement in 1974) rejected the 'avant-garde'/self-referential direction of Kris Hemensley and Ken Bolton, and defined itself as a 'broad' church showcasing the wide range of new writing. I enjoyed publishing Les Murray and Pi O in the same issue to illustrate my point after Kenny had earlier expressed his belief that *Contempa* should have closed down after his departure.

Magazines like *Contempa* were very much products of the 1970s and had not demonstrated that they could survive for at least a decade like the established, yet still financially precarious, journals such as *Overland*, *Meanjin* and *Quadrant*. In saying that, it was clear that the new publications had thrown down the gauntlet. For example, with the resignation of long-time editor Clem Christesen in 1975, the new editor of *Meanjin*, Jim Davidson, was intent on making the magazine more sensitive to the social and political changes of the 1970s. As Lee, Mead and Murnane noted, 'his principal work, and hardest of all, was to establish a new constituency without losing the old' (228) by publishing a wide range of 'avant-garde' material and opening the magazine to a newer generation such as Moorhouse and Carey to name a few. He also appointed Kris Hemensley as the new poetry editor in 1975, a radical move to engage with Hemensley's circle of writers and poets. Davidson wanted *Meanjin* discussed in poetry circles, as the new poetry of the time was a good part of the general cultural upsurge, yet he noted that 'poets are basically Balkan chieftains, constantly fighting one another ... [T]he poets have this delusion that they are the Union Jack in the corner of the flag' (232). In any case, he commissioned timely essays from poets with a growing profile, such as John Tranter's 'Growing Old Gracefully: The Generation of '68', which gave credence to the reputations of Alan Wearne, Robert Adamson, Vicki Viidikas, Rae Desmond Jones and Laurie Duggan due to its publication in the pages of *Meanjin*, and contained timely remarks such as this by John Tranter (in considering the aftermath of the sacking of the Labor Government in November 1975): 'It was as though ... the poets voted informal, came in off the streets and locked the door' (277).

Davidson noted how Moorhouse had articulated a view that *Meanjin* was stuck in the past. For example, when speaking in 1974 at a student literary festival at Melbourne University, he described *Meanjin* 'as aboriginal for "rejected by the *New Yorker*"' (J Davidson, 'A cork' 134). In an interview with Jenny Lee published in 1990, he felt that his priority 'was to get the writers back on side — people like Frank Moorhouse, who was crucial and quite open-minded' (J Davidson, 'Making *Meanjin* survive' 229). Davidson instituted a new format, a part of which was to engage, in his view, with the perception in Sydney that *Meanjin* was too Melbourne-centric. Thus he organised the 'St Petersburg or Tinsel Town' conference which became one of a number of themed issues. In 1981, in a sense reviewing *Meanjin*'s re-evaluation during the decade, Davidson spoke of looking for short stories that had

> quickness, freshness, or whatever ... [W]hile *Meanjin* at one level seeks to place new writing in the context of Australian culture and society generally, we are more concerned that the stories published are among the best offering and directly engage the audience ... Despite rumour to the contrary, *Meanjin* is open to the 'new'. ('Editor's statements' 249)

This was evidence of Davidson's awareness that the magazine had had to resurrect itself in the 1970s if it was to continue in relevant ways: 'In fact a new wave, a new spirit in writing is long overdue' (250). He asserted that the project was still evolving, while identifying that the magazine's audience 'probably consists largely of graduates, and those who see themselves as taking an interest in the arts'.

Furthermore, he stated that 'new support has been found for *Meanjin*'s understanding of Australian culture as a continuous spectrum and a continuing process'. *Meanjin*, he stated, was a clear delineation from 'so-called "coterie" magazines, those of which a high proportion of their readers are themselves creative writers'. This was a comment aimed at the fistful of new publications catering for ascendant poets and prose writers, who had not been prepared to wait for the establishment to recognise them. He also identified that 'our readership has changed with the decade. Less than one half of the current subscribers took the journal in 1974'. In any case, he recognised that *Meanjin* should be wary about cultural waves: 'This basic fact of cultural life should not, however, lead an editor into a position of weak-kneed trendiness, into publishing material which is thought to be modish' (251). Looking back in 1990 he was suspicious of the magazine's relationship with the University of Melbourne, noting how it had supporters in Ray Marginson and Geoffrey Serle, but that, 'accaland is the intellectual Safeways. It doesn't like culture too much in the raw' (233). In a portent of what was to accelerate over the 1980s and 1990s, after the conservative onslaught of the Fraser Liberal Government in 1975, he said:

> [A]lot of academics were very depressed. The kind of freewheeling intellectual inquiry which had been going on in the Whitlam years to some degree ceased. Partly it had been replaced by greater professionalism, but I think part of that was also people were abandoning public issues for their own careers. (233)

In terms of short stories, *Meanjin* only published on average eight or nine a year, compared to *Inprint* and *Tabloid Story*, whose mission was militantly in favour of the genre; but the mere fact of longevity and acquired prestige meant that the magazine was one of *the* places to publish for established and up-and-coming authors in the 1970s. *Meanjin*, in other words, could afford to be generous, even with the many changes it knew it had to relate to.

Australian Literary Studies had legitimised the new writing in academic circles when it published its 'New Writing' issue in 1977, much of which was devoted to position statements from writers rather than academics. *Hecate* had a defined constituency, that of writing and criticism in the area of feminist literature, and would continue beyond the 1970s. *Australian Literary Studies* was already well-established, and the only academic journal of Australian Literary Studies in the country, so it continued, along with *Overland, Meanjin, Westerly* and *Quadrant*, to be well-supported by the Board.

While the magazines of the Left — *Overland, Meanjin* and the ever-changing number of small magazines — were idealistically pitching themselves through the years of the Whitlam Labor Government (1972-75) and inheriting the social and political changes recurrent through the remainder of the decade, the only magazine of the Right, *Quadrant*, was intent on forging its conservative literary and political agendas despite any perceived passions. It had always played the ideological card to ensure state funding, despite its avowed espousal of free market economics and small government. Writing in 1988, the then director of the Literature Board of the Australia Council, Thomas Shapcott, suggested that 'more than any magazine subsidised by the Board, *Quadrant* has received detailed attention and consideration and has been subject to major scrutiny and investigation' (*The Literature Board* 250). After the controversial sacking of the Whitlam Labor Government in November 1975 by the then Governor General Sir John Kerr, *Quadrant* made renewed representations to the Australia Council for increased funding. Earlier in 1975, the magazine had pressed the Board, as it wished to change publication frequency, but the Board was concerned as to the level of literary content in the magazine (251).

Over subsequent years, and into the early 1980s, *Quadrant* made enquiries regarding funding through higher levels of the Australia Council and through the then Minister for Home Affairs and the Prime Minister in March 1980. Again in May 1986, the editor of *Quadrant*, Peter Coleman, complained to the Federal Ombudsman over funding and cited 'political bias', but the Ombudsman was not all that impressed with the argument (255). Even so, *Quadrant*'s grant had increased substantially over the period of complaint, even though the Board's concern over its percentage of literary content was still apparent in 1986, as the year's issues were devoted to 50 per cent current affairs and political debate, and only 14 per cent original creative writing. This was in strict variance to stated policy in terms of support for other literary publications.

The intellectual Right had always coalesced around the pages of *Quadrant* whereas in my view the promotion of original Australian literature had been largely a nationalistic project propagated by the Left, in the hands of *Overland* and *Meanjin*, and then through and after the 1970s in the more libertarian agendas of the newer magazines who were attempting to acknowledge the changing nature of Australia. In saying that, *Quadrant* regularly published original creative writing.

In the period between 1968-2012, issues over survival for the magazines always reappeared in different ways. In the discussions between magazine editors and the Literature Board during 1975-76 and through into the 1980s, a recurrent theme would always be the problem of distribution. At one stage in 1976, Pat Woolley, the Board's promotional agent, produced special catalogues for booksellers extolling the virtues of subsidised books and magazines, and an Australasian Small Press Association was formed, amongst other initiatives, but the reality of a small market in a large land-mass remained to haunt those concerned.

The 1970s saw, as in the new millennium, an upsurge of committed individuals prepared to take on the task of publishing the 'new', and attempts to bring together these people into common cause, something quite difficult in an industry marked by individuality and ultimately, in a capitalist economy, private interest. If the 1960s had indicated anything, it was that a strong thread of anarchic individualism prevailed in the protest movement and the subsequent political formations. The 1970s inherited much of that suspicion of collective thought and action, even if the latter was sometimes romanticised. An anarchist collective is of course an oxymoron, and those who started many of the new magazines were militantly individualistic — which, on reflection, worked against the longevity of publications as much as the lack of resources may have done. By way of contrast, the persistence of *Overland*, in particular, was fueled by not only Stephen Murray-Smith, but also the collective spirit of the organising group.

In 2006, SPUNC (the Small Press Underground Networking Community) was formed in Melbourne to represent the interests of a growing band of small presses in a similar way to the formation of the ASMA established in February 1978 at a meeting in Adelaide of literary magazine editors, sponsored by the Literature Board. ASMA consisted of twenty-two magazines, with the brief of lobbying on postage, a book bounty for magazines, distribution and a typesetting service, with its executive officer being Tom Thompson. It lasted for only a year and it appears that, like many trade organisations made of members of limited resources, the effort of running their own businesses was all-consuming. There is evidence to suggest that such initiatives could well have been ahead of their time in that there was (and is) little or nothing the state can do if Australians as a whole are not interested in their own literature.

In 1973, a National Book Council was formed with the express purpose of bringing together booksellers, librarians, publishers and authors in the common purpose of promoting Australian writing. Its first initiative was the creation of the Banjo Awards for Australian Literature, which would go on to become a major promotional tool for publishers, and which was later won by Geoffrey Serle's *From the Deserts Prophets Come* — an apt description for what many had considered the cultural environment of Australia up until the social and political changes of the 1970s.

The task would be to convert more Australians to what was produced locally. In 1975, the inaugural meeting of the Australian Independent Publishers Association took place in Melbourne with membership open to all Australian-owned publishers whose head offices were located in Australia. According to Michael Denholm, 'thus the organisation provides a marked contrast to the Australian Book Publisher's Association, although it is possible to hold membership of both' (1: 4). In contrast to many of the members of the fledgling National Book Council, most of the new members were medium to small publishers, with no representation from the literary/small magazines. In 1976 they ranged from publishers of local history such as Lowden Publishing from Kilmore in Victoria (run by a local dairy farmer, Jim Lowden) to A&R in Sydney, to Rigby Ltd from Adelaide (a major educational publisher of Australiana and children's literature), to the avant-garde Outback Press and Wild & Woolley and the new travel publisher Lonely Planet, which clearly had commercial ambitions. The Chairman of the association was self-confessed Maoist Geoff Gold from Widescope, who held to the line then espoused by the Communist/Marxist Leninist Party of radical support for the Australian bourgeoisie in its battles with 'multinational imperialism'. Overt nationalism was in the air, particularly after 1975.

Also, in response to a changing publishing climate, a group of newly independent local publishers of fiction and non-fiction, such as the aforementioned Lonely Planet, Widescope, Outback Press and Wild & Woolley, along with McPhee Gribble and a rollcall of the small magazines, supported a distribution company called Book People of Australia to represent them to the book trade, set up in Melbourne in 1975. Established by Richard Jones, Book People of Australia originally operated out of a small shop front in suburban Burwood, and then later in a far more expensive warehouse in the centre of the city. By September 1977, it represented 110 publishers (most of whom were very small), including magazines, but their two major concerns were cash flow problems and convincing retailers of the value of the local product. Also, Pat Woolley of Wild & Woolley distributed some presses and a range of small presses such as Black Sparrow, City Lights and New Directions from Sydney as Allbooks. Book People of Australia went into receivership in 1979 and the warehouse and offices were taken over by Book Collective. Book Collective consisted of the larger publishers who had been on the list, including Outback Press, Widescope and the expanding Lonely Planet, which had been established in 1978 as a protective device against any future collapse of Book People of Australia.

Modelled along the lines of Book People in California, the plan for Book People of Australia was to sell alternative publications from a wide range of clients, but unlike in the United States, the Australian market was much smaller and freight costs were prohibitive to many locations. Even so, Book People of Australia pioneered the distribution of the early titles of McPhee Gribble (such as Helen Garner's first book, *Monkey Grip*) into the marketplace, along with other publishers. Eventually, McPhee Gribble would enter into an agreement with Penguin Books, and the remainder of the list — with the exception of the larger publishers who already had their own marketing arrangements, or who were developing them, like Lonely Planet, as products of the 1970s — either ceased publication, or amalgamated. There were to be a number of other largely fitful initiatives at distribution in the 1980s. Other Book Services in 1981, a mail-order distribution service and, in 1984, a Victorian collective of five small publishers, received a Victorian Government grant of $100 000 to promote selected small presses under the working name of Collected Works. By 1985 it represented twenty-seven publishers, but as a distribution arm it would not last for long. Eventually, the initiative morphed into the creation of The Collected Works Bookshop in Melbourne, which became an important centre for small-press and specialist literary publications under the guidance of Kris Hemensley. It was still operating in 2010.

The decade, then, responded to a crowd of new voices looking for validation and exposure, and with that came a sense of desperation at problems that sometimes seemed insurmountable, such as distribution. The formation of several associations to represent the interests of small publishers was a mark of this, but also a tendency towards bureaucracy in the arts, a symptom that shows that periods of upheaval are also crises of direction. It goes without saying that the decade was one where a belief in state intervention in the economy predominated, but by the 1980s economic rationalism would become the ruling idea, and with it, little magazines would see themselves as having to adopt more realistic approaches to issues of publication, distribution and exchange. Peter Pierce neatly summed it up in 1981:

> [C]heaper production costs and a more buoyant economy were the practical foundations of the hopes with which many 'little magazines' were begun early in the 1970s. As those conditions no longer obtain, fewer 'little mags' are likely to flourish in the next decade. (226)

For all that, the support of the Literature Board had been vital to the magazines, and its role cautionary and proactive when necessary. Thomas Shapcott (the then Director of the renamed Literary Arts Board of the Australia Council), surveying the scene after the events, as it were, in 1988, noted that seven magazines continued to be funded — *Meanjin*, *Southerly*, *Quadrant*, *Overland*, *Westerly*, *ALS* and *Poetry Australia*. He added: '*New Poetry*, *Makar*, *Dharma*, *Contempa* and *Tabloid Story* have all ceased publication, for various reasons' (*The Literature Board* 236). He noted of *New Poetry* that in his opinion 'there was perceptible falling off in the quality of the later work published'. He also noted some financial difficulties. With *Makar*, 'its editor,

Martin Duwell, found it impossible to maintain the considerable financial commitment from his own resources to continue the journal'; and of *Tabloid Story*, '*TS* was one of the great innovative journals of the 1970s' but by the early 1980s 'it had served its purpose' because many more individual collections of short fiction were being published and in 1983 'the new magazine *Australian Short Stories* made its first appearance, with excellent distribution through newsagents'. And of the others who had folded, '*Dharma* and *Contempa* were very much magazines of the early 70s and their life was tied closely to the commitment of the particular editors who ran them' (237).

But they had achieved something at least. As I have stated elsewhere, 'many small presses and literary publications of the 1970s and early 80s, were the feeding ground, and home, for the new writers of the time; many of whom became established names by the conclusion of the 1980s' ('Respectable or risqué' n.p.). I explained further: '[T]hese small presses and magazines were the equivalent of our contemporary Creative Writing classes in finding and encouraging potential writers'. But the difference then was that the activity was voluntary, ungraded and non-institutional compared to the early years of the millennium. Rjurik Davidson, in an article that discussed the pros and cons of creative writing courses in 2010, and their possible commodification in the contemporary educational market, quotes a publisher called 'Errol', in a survey of students, academics and publishers and their responses to the value of courses. 'Errol' ruminates on the 1970s:

> [T]here was a much smaller pool of authors ... fewer publishers [and] no literary agents. We were more inclined to take on things that were perhaps a bit rough around the edges in the hope that we could work with the author and polish them up ... [W]e used to do more work in those days. All sorts of things have happened since then. Literary agents have come along ... [C]reative writing courses have given people much more technique and sense of the marketplace and what's required and so on. (Qtd. in R Davidson 107)

There is some evidence, then, that publication was easier in the 1970s. It was certainly the case, ironically, that better author visibility could be gained through the little magazines, even though there were fewer publishers. The decade had seen the consolidation of the more academic journals such as *Meanjin* and *Southerly*, and break-outs of avant-garde spirit with the *Ear in the Wheatfield* and *Etymspheres*. Thus 'the space between university-based journals and commercial magazines published by large media companies would remain the site of editorial dreams, intellectual stake-outs and brief moments of brilliant success as new magazines were born and old magazines re-born' (Carter & Osborne 256).

Tabloid Story had been a brave, subsidised dream; many of the very small publications were carryovers from the utopianism of the late 1960s and there were glimpses at new models, but conceptual and practical restrictions inhibited the landscape. There were fitful attempts at market penetration and commodification, and conversely, wilful attempts at recreating preindustrial forms. All in all, the decade was innovative, but there was no hard evidence to suggest that the market for the literary magazine had grown, as many of the initiatives were overly dependent on government subsidies. In terms of literary book-publishing during the decade, the explosion in the number of new titles was almost totally due to the publishing subsidy scheme of the Australia Council; in fact, almost the whole of the new fiction lists of Penguin Australia, Outback Press, Wild & Woolley and the University of Queensland Press were subsidised. The 1980s and 1990s would throw up more specialised challenges, in an environment where the level of government assistance in the arts remained relatively static.

8. A more 'realistic' decade

The 1980s were also a period of intense political and social upheaval. The 1970s had seen the onset of a New Left, opposition to the Vietnam War, women's liberation and so forth, but the extent to which such changes were and became mainstream has been open to debate ever since. Prior to the dismissal of the Whitlam Labor Government, though, notions that the state could play a proactive role in social engineering were relatively common. With the advent of the conservative Fraser Liberal Government there was a growing belief that welfare and income maintenance by governments was an intrusion into the body politic. If generalisations can be made about the decade, one would be that a social climate developed which was becoming intolerant of ideological alternatives to the marketplace. Globalisation started to become the buzz word in popular discourse; in the economic substructure, it meant the onset of free trade across the world, which became shorthand for the triumph of the transnational corporations. Locally, the workplace was beginning to be restructured, and casualisation became commonplace across sectors other than retail and agricultural production.

The 1970s had seen an expansion of state promotion of the arts through the creation of The Australia Council by the then Government, modelled on the structure of the Canada Council. Whether support for the arts would achieve bipartisanship into the 1980s would be fascinating to watch. Needless to say, the arts became an industry of sorts during this decade after the experiments of the 1970s. Of the 1980s, Paul Kelly has suggested:

> [T]he upshot is that the 1980s was Australia's decade of creative destruction. It witnessed business shake out, financial excess, economic restructuring, individual greed ... [But] the decade saw the collapse of the Australian settlement, the old protected fortress Australia. (130)

Kelly was of course acknowledging capitalism's ability to revolutionise the means of production and the extent to which such changes infiltrate the prevailing culture. Even so, state intervention often has modernised shifts in the means of production. In this case the social engineering encouraged by Whitlam in the 1970s became bolder and more respectable in the 1980s in Australia as markets grew larger and more heterogeneous. Some writers such as David Malouf and Peter Carey were on their way to establishing international reputations.

The 1970s could be seen as the necessary nationalist phase, with an eye on the international. It could also be argued that after the pioneering work of the contradictory 1970s, the Australian middle class became far more heterogeneous, more 'multicultural'. Consequently, during the 1980s many book publishers published a wide range of authors, and the decade was a boom-time for local authors; but by its conclusion, large multinational firms subsumed smaller independents — such as McPhee Gribble to Penguin in 1989, and the venerable Angus and Robertson to Harper Collins in 1989. Yet as Gelder and Salzman have demonstrated in *The New Diversity*, published Australian literature became more open-ended, experimental and multicultural during the 1980s, inheriting the innovations of the 1970s. The contents of the literary magazines reflected these changes, and led to in some cases specialist magazines such as *Outrider: The Journal of Multicultural Literature*. Specialisation became widespread during the 1980s. Indigenous authors were also published in the journals, a tendency that began in the 1970s, yet there was not an Indigenous/black literary journal as such, although Magdabala Books, an exclusively Indigenous publisher, was established in Broome.

The 1970s period was a relatively brief flowering of nationalism or self-awareness, which was soon to be renegotiated with the deregulation and internationalisation of the economy, but also with pervasive trends in the universities. The interregnum (for better or for worse) that the 1970s provided was too brief a time for consolidation of a diverse national self-awareness. Forces were waiting in the wings, however. For example, Robert Dixon makes the case that there was a strong link between the rise of literary theory (largely French post-structuralism) and that of economic rationalism under the Hawke-Keating governments in the 1980s. Discussing one of the main protagonists of the theories, Meaghan Morris, Dixon notes that in Morris's book — *Ecstasy and Economics*, published in 1992 — she expresses the view that forms of protectionism belong in the past:

> [F]or Morris, there is no question of protectionism, for in a post-colonial culture there is no imminent national identity to protect. Rather, the question is how to work in such a context. (200)

Michael Wilding, writing in 1978, prefigured what would be a general shift away from the modernising yet national moment that was the 1970s by suggesting that

> the problem for Australian writers today is that the 'Australian' proclamations have seemed to be the preserve of the conservative — conservative both politically and aesthetically. Until now the celebration of rural Australia has seemed to be the preserve of the nationalist conservative — not of the radical or alternative consciousness. ('Tabloid story' 308)

After the disillusionment of the late 1970s, the Left in Australia had largely discarded its precursors such as Henry Lawson, and its early trade union history, in a moment that both marginalised utopian notions into the convenient past and made discussions of local ownership difficult to sustain during a period when the brief nationalist surge of the 1970s had waned. AA Phillips's 'cultural cringe' had been a rather gentlemanly expression of cultural frustration in the late 1950s, but by the 1970s, after the final fall of the European empires in the Third World, nationalism became more strident and even fashionable for a time. Culturally, however, Australia had always had a comprador bourgeoisie, a class of mainly buyers rather than innovators and creators. By the 1980s most Australian cultural consumers and producers remained psychic and commercial compradors. Their interests lay in promoting imports rather than culturally unreliable local products. The cultural elites, in the universities at least, had always been susceptible to this, something AA Phillips had stressed in terms of their deference to Oxford and Cambridge back in 1950. Therefore their support (apart from the remnants of the true believers in a national literature) for local literary and small magazines would remain on shaky ground through the 1980s, 1990s and into the new millennium.

Concurrently, Robert Dixon claimed another complication: '[I]n the 1980s, then, the cult of theoretical expertise continued to fracture the public sphere for Australian literature' (198). He stated that the Dawkins reforms in the educational system 'helped to produce a new humanities reshaped in the image of corporate culture and technocratic expertise' (201). Or, as Brian Castro has more recently put it, perhaps the entire literary project is problematic: 'The tacit assumption that literature has something to do with the amelioration and tempering of society was always an idea waiting to fail'. Castro went on to say that 'ethical' critics such as Matthew Arnold, Raymond Williams and FR Leavis were inevitably going against the thrust of mass representation, and then came

> on the one hand, French theory, the semioticians and the 'boa deconstrictors', who disengaged language from real presences, prophesying the end of the human subject. On the other, cultural analysts were busy turning the pleasure of the text into unreadable jargon. (20)

Put another way, such changes in teaching and promotion in the universities influenced a generation of students to possibly disregard much of 'the local' and the popularity of any discussion pertaining to it. The effects of this would filter into publishing programs, and the ability of local literary magazines to survive or even prosper.

Despite such complexities, by the early 1990s, some Australian independents were beginning to rise, such as Text Publishing, Scribe, Allen & Unwin and the much smaller Giramondo Publishing. Despite this visibility for Australian authors in their own market, and a decided increase in the overall percentage of Australian books being sold to readers, the number of small publishers was being pruned, and trade terms in the retail book trade had changed compared to the 1970s when many booksellers would stock a few copies of pretty well everything that was published, whether it was a small magazine or a book from one of the small book publishers, as a co-operative gesture. But by at least the mid-1980s, the trade was competing with a variety of new media for the educational and entertainment dollar. Another feature of the Australian book trade in the 1980s was the onset of the marketing potential of genre fiction, in that booksellers and publishers united in promoting categories such as 'chick lit', speculative fiction, romance and so forth onto a developing market. This resulted in a move away from author-based general fiction into another subcategory of literary fiction, which brought with it notions of marginality, which had not been previously considered. It would spell promotional difficulties for literary magazines. Several authors, though, particularly in the 1990s, escaped the genre-specific prescriptions of the trade. Helen Garner and Tim Winton both became respected literary and bestselling authors.

The 1980s also witnessed the opening up of the Australian economy under the Hawke/Keating Labor Governments, the floating of the dollar and the reduction of tariff barriers for Australian manufacturing. In terms of publishing, this meant the disappearance of the book bounty for local printers, even if the Australia Council's publishing subsidy scheme remained in place. In real terms, some of the 1970s magazines printed issues with the minimum page-counts of a book, thus qualifying as a subsidised book; such a concession was not available in the 1980s.

In contrast to the 1970s, book and magazine distribution became more centralised, and dealing on sale or return exclusively to retailers made it more difficult for small presses to promote new authors and innovative titles.

This was unlike in the 1970s, when new authors such as Carey, Moorhouse, Bail and Wilding could count on having at least a few copies of their books in bookshops, as the trade terms were largely firm sale, making booksellers aware that they had to clear existing stock. Increased government educational spending during the 1970s meant that large library suppliers such as James Bennett in Sydney ordered sizeable orders of pretty well anything published, which was of great assistance to small publishers. Although sale or return terms had existed in the trade since the depression of the 1930s (Carter & Galligan 77), firm sale predominated after the Second World War until the late 1970s, to disappear when newsagents and chain retailers were offered sale or return on paperbacks, as with the popular magazines they stocked. The decline of first publication in hardback, during the 1970s, also worked against firm sale terms of trade.

Trade discount terms had also changed. Retailers (bookshops and newsagents) were demanding 40 per cent of the recommended retail price in contrast to the 1970s, when the standard discount had been 33.3 per cent firm sale. Bookshops, in broad terms, were becoming stock warehouses where bestsellers would predominate even more strongly and the shelf-life of new titles was becoming shorter and shorter. The relationship to the little magazine was to force it increasingly into smaller bookshops, so that there was never a sales presence in many areas of the country including regional towns and city suburbs. The demographics of bookselling was also changing in that, after Collins Booksellers, under the direction of Michael Zifcak, pioneered branches in the new shopping centres in the suburbs of the major cities, Angus and Robertson and the United States-based group, Borders, followed in the late 1990s. Newsagents and department stores had also been selling mass-market paperbacks and bestselling sport and cooking titles for some time. By the conclusion of the 1980s bookselling was a two-tiered story: independent bookshops on the one hand and the book chains on the other, often selling radically different types of titles.

The 1970s had established that state support for the arts was acceptable, and in the 1980s, this became a bipartisan position as the arts were being accepted as an industry at last in Australia. Even so, after the defeat of the Whitlam Labor government in 1975, the Australia Council suffered a 40 per cent staff reduction and a decline in finance of more than 39 per cent between 1975 and 1982 (Denholm 2: 8). By 1980-81 total payments to individual writers dropped by 52 per cent. The election of the Hawke Labor government came with a pledge to restore funding, but this pledge was effectively put in place only marginally, along with cutbacks to the administrative budget (9). In 1984 the Literature Board's assistance to magazines represented 10.2 per cent of the total budget, and it then offered assistance to 21 of the 46 magazines applying in 1985. In broad terms, despite the high profile of the activities of the Literature Board, in 1986 it only received 6 per cent of Australia Council funds.

Grants for writers continued through the Australia Council, and in each state capital, writers' centres, in response to an upsurge in community arts, were set up to cater for beginner writers — ports of call for previously isolated people at considerable expense to the taxpayer. Unfortunately, over time they came to largely spend their budgets on salaries to staff and city rents so as to organise workshops and seminars. This could be viewed as, perhaps, a form of tokenism and paternalism favoured by state arts departments who could be seen to be throwing money at the problems of writers struggling in a small market. They were a formalisation of the grassroots activities of the earlier decade without the desire to add value to initiatives. Basically, they provided places to meet when writers wanted publication, money and time to write. However, there was no overt criticism from writers, by that time accustomed to economic dependency.

On the much more localised level (and indeed the almost subeconomic level) of small-press publishing, the story of the literary/small magazines of the decade was of consolidation for the highly subsidised *Overland*, *Meanjin*, *Quadrant* and *Southerly* and largely a struggle for the remainder of the newer magazines. But even for the established magazines there was no such thing as surpluses fuelled by bestselling titles and extensive backlists. There were also little of the anarchic, freewheeling, irresponsible initiatives of the 1970s, yet there were some new births, among them *Scripsi, Voiceworks, Brave New Word, Tirra Lirra, Mattoid, Australian Short Stories, Going Down Swinging* and *Island* (formerly the *Tasmanian Review*).

Broadly, despite difficult economic conditions throughout Australia, the decade supported a range of publications, some of which reflected the changing socio-political environment. An example of this occurred in March 1986, when the Literature Board convened a major meeting of literary magazine editors in Canberra prior to the National Word Festival (*The Literature Board* 246). Twenty-eight magazines were represented, the largest magazine seminar conducted by the Board to that date, which demonstrated that the 1970s may well have seen an upsurge in publishing possibilities (much of which were short-lived) but that in the 1980s, a strong tradition was continuing, albeit in less flamboyant terms.

And the same problems and issues were repeating themselves. Geoffrey Dutton, writing in the *Bulletin* during 1983, had noted that

> the unsung heroes of Australian literature are the editors of literary magazines and their assistants. Nearly every writer of note in Australia has contributed to these magazines and many had their first work published in them. Some, such as *Angry Penguins*, also brought the work of young artists Sidney Nolan and Arthur Boyd to public notice then. (Qtd. in *The Literature Board* 248)

He went on to speak of the almost daily reality: '[L]iterary magazines are always in financial difficulties and, in our commercial society, this means that they will always be little magazines'. But he went on to warn against problems that came with being small:

> At a seminar on literary magazines a few years ago at the Adelaide festival, I listened, at first with amusement and then with disgust, to several snarling editors, whose magazines circulated to a couple of hundred of their mates at the most, abusing the Literature Board for supporting *Meanjin, Quadrant, Overland* and so on. (Qtd. in *The Literature Board* 248-9)

Apart from the sometimes competitive and uncharitable behaviour in literary circles, the sector was still dependent on its main benefactor, the Australia Council, and whether that would diminish only history would tell.

The *Australian Book Review* underwent a rebirth during the 1980s. Then a journal largely of book reviews, the *Australian Book Review* had had a number of manifestations. Founded originally in 1961 in Adelaide by Max Harris, Rosemary Wighton and Geoffrey Dutton, it was published in a letterpress format, largely four times a year, until it ceased with Volume 12 in November 1973. Harris was the controversial publisher of *Angry Penguins* during the 1940s and ran his Mary Martin discount bookshop in the centre of Adelaide for many years. After discussions initiated by Barrett Reid and the National Book Council in Melbourne, it was decided to reactivate the magazine as the official journal of the National Book Council in June 1978, to be published by Peter Issacson Publications in Prahran. In a sense the *Australian Book Review* was a natural partner for the National Book Council, which brought together librarians, publishers, booksellers and authors; and its reincarnation came with bookseller contacts through Michael Zifcak of Collins Book Depot. The first issue of the *Australian Book Review* for 1982 was published with a print run of 8000 copies, including a scheme whereby large booksellers purchased 'bulk copies at run on costs to give, with their compliments, to appropriate customers' (Denholm 2: 115).

A notable feature of the *Australian Book Review* in the late 1970s was that it set out to review or notice as many new books as it could, in all fields including gardening and farming, as opposed to its current policy which is very selective. If a book did not receive a full review it was at least given a short descriptive listing, evidence of a more open policy in that period towards book reviewing. The *Australian Book Review* became a monthly, was printed in a cheap newsprint, saddle-stitch format, with advertisements from publishers and booksellers, very much like a commercial magazine compared to the literary magazines, which persisted with perfect-bound, more expensive formats. It has been, over its life, the only regular review journal for Australian books.

John McLaren was the new editor until Kerryn Goldsworthy in 1986. She continued till 1987, after which the editors were Louise Adler in 1988, and Rosemary Sorensen between 1989 and 1995. Helen Daniel was the editor between 1995-2000, and she brought to the *Australian Book Review* a modernising influence due to her interest in transgressive fiction and the stable of new fabulist writers (such as Peter Carey and Murray Bail). She was already discussing these authors in her book reviews in publications such as the *Age*, the *Australian* and the *Sydney Morning Herald*, in published criticism such as *Liars: Australian New Novelists* (Penguin 1988), and in the volumes she edited, like *Expressway* (Penguin 1988).

Australian literature had moved away, for better or worse, from what Patrick White had once called 'dung-coloured realism', and Daniel wanted the reading public to become aware of it. A new literary establishment had been created during the 1980s, which reflected the deregulation of the economy and the heightened visibility of Australian books after the messy innovations of the 1970s. Helen Daniel played a significant agenda-setting role. After the National Book Council closed down in 1997 the *Australian Book Review* became an entity in its own right and it gradually broadened its scope to include more essays and some original creative writing, under the editorship of Peter Rose during the 2000s. Even so, during the same period, the *Australian Book Review* has substantially reduced coverage of Australian publications, and currently reviews are far more selective.

Because it is Australia's only monthly journal primarily devoted to reviewing new books, the *Australian Book Review* has been able to attract high levels of sponsorship, making it currently Australia's most highly subsidised literary publication, even if it departs from my general criteria for a little magazine. Currently, it is supported by the Literature Board of the Australia

Council, Arts Victoria, Arts SA, Flinders University, the Sydney Myer Foundation and the Copyright Agency Limited, and it has a budget that far exceeds that of any of the other established magazines. Its basic format of looking like a magazine rather than a book remains the same, and it can, unlike the others, attract some advertisements from publishers, due to its having a widespread circulation in libraries. Even so, its circulation is limited compared to the book review pages in the *Age*, the *Sydney Morning Herald* and the *Weekend Australian*. In the current climate, it is pursuing initiatives such as publishing essays and short fiction, along with offering special online supplements and poetry competitions to appeal to a demographic outside what Mark Davis has referred to as 'the true believers'. Thus it hopes to increase its somewhat limited circulation.

Going Down Swinging was founded in Melbourne in 1980 by two new writers, Kevin Brophy and Myron Lysenko, and they aimed to provide a forum for new writers, especially prose writers. Reflecting on the birth in 'The Formative Years', Myron Lysenko explains it in 1970s terms — bohemian to an extent, and spontaneous:

> We spoke to a few editors of litmags and asked them how to do it ... [A]ll we had to do was let writers know we were going to publish a magazine, select the appropriate work and then take it to the printers. We weren't told how to sell the magazines because that didn't seem to be important ... The first issue came back from the printers on May 29th 1980 and it had taken us eighteen months to produce it. (n.p.)

The first edition had a print run of 600 copies and the second 300 copies. Kevin Brophy typed the first few issues on his IBM golf-ball electric typewriter, and for the first ten years it was funded out of the editors' pockets until it received Arts Victoria funding until 1994. The early issues, which were published irregularly, contained prose that was experimental at heart and partially reflected the editors' tastes, such as Samuel Beckett, Richard Brautigan and Charles Bukowski. Ania Walwicz's deconstructive work was an early favourite, and interviews with Peter Carey and Michael Wilding were also another feature. After the late 1980s, *Going Down Swinging* started to appear less regularly, and by 2010, it was published as an annual collection, making it effectively an anthology rather than a magazine by most definitions. Over that time, *Going Down Swinging* started out saddle-stitch (stapled) with cheap card covers but by the time it had become an annual it was glossy, and more expensively produced. *Going Down Swinging* also took the form of a CD.

By contrast, in 1981 *Scripsi* started out differently, more 'professionally', as was the tenor of the 1980s — with over 200 pages, perfect-bound, with gloss covers and all the marks of literary prestige, a clear attempt at creating a splash in Melbourne literary circles as a high cultural product. Edited by Peter Craven, (who would become one of Australia's best-known literary critics) and Michael Heyward (later of Text Publishing), *Scripsi*'s agenda was internationalist, in the sense that they published what they considered to be the best local work alongside some big names from overseas. The editors were also not afraid to publish special issues such as the James Joyce centenary issue in November 1982. Peter Craven has said that *Scripsi* 'was an attempt to do a magazine that took stock of the great world, and which also published the best Australian work ... [W]e started Scripsi because Michael Heyward was ... panting for glory' (41). Initially published at the University of Melbourne by the Scripsi Society, after five years it established itself at Ormond College. There were interviews with major critical figures such as Northrop Frye and Basil Bunting, alongside Gary Snyder, Peter Porter, John Forbes, Murray Bail, Helen Garner and Gerald Murnane. This was an impressive rollcall of authors (local and international) who were generally unavailable to other small magazines of the time, one that incorporated an undoubted sense of 'cringe' in that the local really had to be validated internationally.

In terms of its production values, 'the old wraparound dust-jacket covers came about when someone left the info off the spine' (41). Craven believes that *Scripsi* helped create an environment where books were evaluated. According to Stuart Sayers ('A home' 15), circulation in 1986 was 2000 copies and its budget $50 000. The magazine lasted until 1994, through the at times unconventional assistance of the then Sub Dean of Arts at the university Dinny O'Hearn. Despite bitter disputes with the Literature Board, it received generous subsidies — for example, between 1983-86 it received $34 500, which was roughly similar to amounts received by *Meanjin*, *Overland* and *Southerly* over the same period (Shapcott, *The Literature Board* 258). It was a very effective moment that helped to establish the reputations of several authors and the nascent literary credentials of its editors. Often the story of small magazines is also the story of pushing forward editors' names and agenda-setting into a broader public sphere, even if the publications do not last. This was the case with many of the small poetry magazines of the 1970s through the work of John Tranter, Robert Adamson and Kris Hemensley, to name a few.

As we have often seen, the birth of new literary magazines is often a moment of hopeless idealism. In 1982, despite significant changes to the efficacy of the trade union movement with the onset of economic rationalism, a magazine (*Carringbush Writing*) was formed in Melbourne that was quoted in the *Age* as 'wanting to create a new readership for Australian fiction … by holding readings in schools, universities and places of work and by establishing a strong connection with trade unions' (qtd. in Denholm 2: 129). Its editors were Maree Teychenne, Sally Webb and Karin Altmann, and by all accounts it only had two issues. Taking its name from 'Carringbush', the fictitious name given to the Melbourne suburb of Collingwood by the communist writer Frank Hardy in his novel *Power without Glory* in the early 1950s, it was a quarto-sized journal of limited copies that published two other well-known left-wing authors in its first edition, John Morrison and Dorothy Hewett. Frank Hardy was then still alive and associated with the magazine. Of interest was that the advent of *Carringbush Writing* was an attempt, it seemed, at revitalising *Overland*'s old agenda during the 1950s of seeking distribution among trade union members, in its original manifestation as the *Realist Writer*. By the 1980s, though, white Australian fiction was almost a century away from its egalitarian roots in the 1890s, and becoming increasingly marginalised both within university English departments and by over-specialisation in publishing and bookselling. Popular culture had captured the common reader, by all accounts. *Carringbush Writing* could go down as one of the most utopian and brief moments in the story of the little magazine.

There were, though, other such moments in the 1980s. Although not strictly along the lines of my criteria as a magazine that published primarily original creative writing, *Access* first appeared in early 1982, distributed to newsagents. It was modelled loosely along the lines of the newly defunct *Nation Review*, which had published political comment, cartoons (by Michael Leunig) and columns by writers such as Mungo MacCallum, in a generally left-wing framework of opposition to uranium mining and wood-chipping. It was produced and published by Rolf Heimann from Melbourne and published some short fiction and artwork, which made it an interesting experiment as to how broad magazines might survive in newsagents dominated by niche publications. Originally published monthly, it became a bi-monthly. By 1983, the monthly print run was 4000, down from 8000, as there were problems with distribution and plenty of returns (Linnell 9). By the winter of 1985 it had published twenty-one issues.

Although the *Nation Review* and the *National Times* had published short fiction during the 1970s and early 1980s, it appeared then that the worlds of creative writing and journalism were becoming even more compartmentalised in public perception. The *Adelaide Review* published fiction during the 1980s, at times with government support, but its commitment was peripatetic: payment to writers only occasionally, and in wine, according to Frank Moorhouse; and although it was a magazine of the arts, it developed over time as a lifestyle publication, where original fiction was not central to the kinds of representations it wished to pursue. It was only distributed in Adelaide and could not garner a national profile.

The tension between the local, the parochial and the national would always persist. As we have seen, a strong sense of regionalism was promoted in Western Australia and in Queensland, but it was extremely difficult to set a new publication anywhere, let alone one that stressed a desire to only speak locally. *Carringbush Writing* had been an example of this even though it seemed to desire to promote a writing that was in the social realist tradition. Yet, as with the strange manifestations of the literary magazine, its genesis has a lot to do with writers, rather than the expressed desires of readers at any one time. So, in 1983, *Peninsula Writing* was created by Liam Davison and Warrick Wynne, both of whom lived on the Mornington Peninsula south of Melbourne, which they hoped would provide 'a forum for writers from the Mornington Peninsula and create a new interest in their work' (Denholm 2: 198). It appeared four times a year, in a stapled quarto-size booklet, for a couple of years, and contributors included Fiona Capp, David Kerr and Peter Murphy. Its guiding mission, similar to many of the other publications of the time, was to promote what was in front of the editors, which could not be sustained beyond the 'local'.

Last but not least, the 1980s bore evidence of a more confident gay and lesbian community after the political break-outs in the 1970s. Alongside writing by women, gay authors were making statements as to the 'difference' displayed in particular texts and in what it meant to be gay. Debates as to definitions characterised some of the published anthologies such as in Dennis Altman's introduction to *Edge City on Two Different Plans* (1983).

Michael Hurley claimed of the 1980s:

> [W]hen one looks at the major literary journals and magazines of the 1980s, there is little evidence that they provided a proving ground for writing from gay and lesbian perspectives ... [G]iven this environment, many lesbian and gay writers preferred independent publishing ventures and worked in experimental and/or non-commercial formats. (208)

Sybylla Press in Melbourne, for example, published the work of Finola Moorhead and Mary Fallon. In any case, the decade saw the publication of a an increasingly wide range of books and anthologies featuring openly gay and lesbian writers. Even so, there was no gay literary magazine as such until the publication of *Cargo* in 1987, which continued for fourteen issues until 1993. Produced by Black Wattle Press in Leichardt, NSW, it featured (among others) authors who later gained visibility: Gary Dunne, Margaret Bradstock, Pam Brown, Susan Hampton, Susan Hawthorne, Roberta Snow, Michael Farrell, Dorothy Porter and Sasha Soldatow. Generally it contained forty to fifty pages of A5-size and was stapled. Editors included Jill Taylor (nee Jones) and Lauren McKinnon. Black Wattle also published thirteen books by gay authors over the period. The little magazine was then acting out its traditional role of foregrounding the work of the marginal, the unknown and the non-commercial.

9. NEW EDITORS

In 1982 Jim Davidson resigned as editor of *Meanjin*, and he wrote to Clem Christesen on 31 March expressing his gratitude for the opportunity of taking over during the 1970s, but spoke of rising cost pressures and cost cutting. 'There is now half the office staff we had in 1974', he wrote, but there had been in his estimation 'the cultivation of the concept of a cluster of constituencies' (qtd. in Lee, Mead & Murnane 295). The new editor became Judith Brett, previously a Lecturer in Politics at the University of Melbourne. According to Lee, Mead and Murnane, she 'was committed to maintaining the magazine as a broad review of ideas with a strong contemporary focus — as a journal of Australian writing rather than a literary magazine in the narrowest sense' (298). A feature of Brett's editorship was the publication of an emerging group of women and migrant writers. In 1983, there was a special issue on immigration and culture reflecting the kind of diversification during the 1980s; and, 'there was a strong sense that the centre of gravity was shifting as new, heterogeneous creative movements rose to challenge the earlier nationalist project, with its promotion of a unitary, "mainstream" Australian culture' (298).

The academic Sneja Gunew was one such promoter of difference and multiculturalism in her essay published in 1983, 'Migrant Women Writers — Who's on Whose Margins'. This offered an argument about alternative canons and a reformation of critical language from a Deleuzian perspective (invoking Said, Foucault et al.), privileging authors such as Zeny Giles,

Antigone Kefala, Ania Walwicz and Anna Couani. Brett articulated as much: '*Meanjin* is now concerned with cultural politics and with what can be called the politics of representation, and both these challenge the possibility of keeping political and literary questions apart just as surely as did the earlier conjunction' (Brett 320). In a joist at the past, she added: 'until recently in Australia, the domain of the "literary" has been predominately the domain of middle-class white Anglo-Celtic men'. The challenge then for 'the other' had been sent out.

Implicit in such changes was the reassessment of the legacy of Australian radical nationalism. Such a deconstructive fermentation would inadvertently ally itself with the forces of economic rationalism and globalisation and would be played out over the 1990s and the early years of the new millennium. In any case, there were seminal pieces published in *Meanjin* which would attempt a reassessment, such as Graeme Smith's 'Making Folk Music' in 1985, following on from Humphrey McQueen's *A New Britania* in 1972.

Judith Brett left in 1987 and was followed by Jenny Lee, who would open it up to further possibilities that would reflect the changes in intellectual priorities in the universities. For example, there was Simon During's assertion for a broad cultural studies approach in 'Professing the Popular' in 1990, where he reflected on the continuing adherence to established literary canons at places such as Cambridge compared to a more 'egalitarian' Australia experience. Jim Davidson, commenting in 1990 — in effect on the perceived urgencies of the 1980s and on issues for what was to follow in the 1990s — was astute, and demonstrated his historian's eye:

> [T]he combination of popular culture and multiculturalism, while in the end it may be fruitful, in the short run is culturally confusing. The present mood, to some degree from necessity, is so deconstructionist that it's very hard to see exactly what the next step will be. There have to be some givens for a creative cultural climate. ('Making *Meanjin* survive' 230)

Jenny Lee would have her work cut out for her to take *Meanjin* through a time of social fragmentation, historic amnesia and accelerating commodification of cultural difference. One response was to continue Brett's tradition of themed issues in response to what she saw as the increased plurality of Australian intellectual life. In respect to poetry, 'while poetry now is still fuelled by the energies released in the 1970s with the emergence of the New Poetry, the divisiveness of that time is gradually yielding to a new plurality ...' She further claimed, optimistically, that due to live performances, 'poetry has shed much of its esoteric image and reasserted its central place in cultural life' (qtd. in Lee, Mead & Murnane 353). Philip Mead, was poetry editor between 1987 and 1994.

While *Scripsi* and *Meanjin* could count on (up to a point) an established network in and around the University of Melbourne, traditionally the centre of educational prestige in that city, other births were more tenuous and less respectable, and indeed, less resourced and less ambitious. *Brave New Word* had first appeared out of idealistic discussions among students at the Chisholm Institute of Technology (later to become part of Monash University) in January 1981. The first editors were Peter Haddow, Ric Burtan, Karen McLean, Frank Ryder and Theresa Wattis. A general forum-type publication which aimed to provide a space for struggling new, and not so new, writers, it came into existence with none of the literary pedigree of *Scripsi*, yet it scored quite a coup in its first issue with an interview with one of the then rising stars of Australian letters, Frank Moorhouse, then writer in residence at the University of Melbourne. It would last for four years and publish a wide range of authors including Brian Castro, Kevin Brophy and Eric Beach. Interestingly, *Brave New Word* sported glossy covers but the contents were much thinner than *Scripsi*. Like many of the other little magazines in this study, *Brave New Word* was always under-resourced and it had distribution problems; for instance, after 1984 Theresa Wattis contributed financially to the magazine (Denholm 2: 124). But as with the others, it published the first work of writers, and the venture was an expression of a group of people asking the inevitable question, 'Why can't new writers get published?' As in the 1970s, most of the small magazines were products of their time and the obsessions largely of editors who were not business people.

Mattoid was another one that began as an expression of student frustrations in the first creative writing courses, the students wondering where on earth their work might appear. Denholm has claimed that its birth in November 1976 was a result of 'student frustration and student funding' (2: 179) at the Gordon Institute of Technology (now Deakin University). They received $500 from the Student's Representative Council to fund the initial idea. The name means 'of an erratic mind, half fool, half genius', and it would sum up the positives and negatives of starting any new magazine. The early editors were Vicki Jones and Brian Fraser and over time it published a range of relatively well-known and unknown authors. Early in the 1980s, Wendy Morgan introduced supplements and a more serious literary focus, with the involvement of staff such as Sneja Gunew, so that finally by 1986, when Senior Lecturer Brian Edwards took over, it became a very serious review of current criticism along with original creative writing. Edwards (later with Robyn Gardiner) would publish it from the School of Humanities at Deakin throughout the rest of the 1980s, the 1990s and into the early years of the 2000s, but it appeared less frequently, and by 2010 it had not appeared for several years. It began its life cheaply in a stapled format and over the years became chunkier and more expensive-looking, but it never achieved any significant market penetration. Its critical articles were on occasion from high-profile overseas academics, but by that time, academic discourse was becoming over-specialised, and academics were withdrawing from any ambition to speak in a public sphere.

Mattoid was hardly alone in what was to become its designated space. Structuralism and post-structuralism had fundamentally affected the type of language employed by many academics, and it is not irresponsible to say that such discourse was what gave some of the magazines cultural credibility — almost as if, in the 1980s, many thought that that was what they had to do. David Carter traces such moves — in academic criticism, at least — to the *Foreign Bodies Conference of 1981*, and the *ASAL Conference of 1982* as precursors to the broader influence of post-structuralist and deconstructive theories of textuality which would be absorbed into the mainstream of Australian literary criticism during the 1980s ('Critics, writers, intellectuals', 281-2). Many of the magazines reflected that influence.

The quasi-Marxist publications *Thesis Eleven* and *Arena* started publishing 'important'-looking themed issues twice a year, leaving behind, it seemed, a desire to find an audience outside university departments. Creative writers, on the other hand, would always desire as many readers as possible, so, despite the pruning of ambition in the 1980s, they would continue to be ambitious and relatively utopian. Denholm in his introduction to his second volume on small magazines duly noted the ongoing value of the small magazine in nurturing and creating a critical environment for writers. In specific terms, he noted that writers such as Helen Garner, Beverley Farmer and Elizabeth Jolley were first published by small presses:

> With the takeover of most large Australian publishing firms by multinational corporations the small press helps to ensure that many books of quality are still published in Australia even if they may not be very profitable. (2: 27)

However, Denholm was not as forthcoming in regards to what he saw as a retreat towards obscurantism in the 1980s. He made a large generalisation about a wide range of fledgling publications, commenting on a decade that retreated from 'large' statements: '[T]he eighties have seen the rise to prominence of magazines interested in modernism and in concerns such as structuralism, semiotics and deconstruction'.

Referring specifically to a newer brand of art theory publication — in particular, *Art & Text* edited by Paul Taylor and to a lesser extent *On the Beach* and *Tension* — he accused them of 'a disturbing unwillingness to express their views in a simple clear manner'. Acknowledging that some of the new magazines were a welcome trend away from 'the Puritanism of the old left and the conservatism of the right', he went further: '[I]ronically the interest in the text and in literature and in art as modes of play and pleasure in a time of consensus and conservatism can be seen as a retreat from the world of these writers and artists ... ' (27). Or, as Stephens has put it,

> the desire for a rebellious, transformative politics can still be read in the peculiarly unreflective romanticism of the postmodern aesthetic. All kinds of political longings are displaced onto an aesthetic sphere which fancifully is viewed as an autonomous and, by definition, an ethical domain. (126)

Notwithstanding that, the politics of little magazines is usually the enunciation of various forms of alienation from the perceived mainstream. An example could have been *Otis Rush* (new writing, new art and reviews), published by the Experimental Arts Foundation in Adelaide, and edited by Ken Bolton who had published *Magic Sam* in the late 1970s and early 1980s. Originally a quarterly, *Otis Rush* appeared thirteen times over eleven years (1987-96), making it more of an anthology, in a perfect-bound book format, than a regular magazine. For the little/literary magazine, the pressures have always been acute, given the disparate nature of intentions. Was it better not to 'dumb down' and concentrate on publishing in technical terms a 'limited edition' that was specialised, or to invest (in all ways) in a desire to find new readers when the available evidence (to the 1980s at least) was that Australia was still resistant to such entreaties?

There had presumably been break-outs from this frame, such as *Australian Short Stories*, but it remained extremely difficult to sell more than 2000 copies of any one publication. Kris Hemensley had, in effect, resigned himself to this in the 1970s with the *Ear in the Wheatfield* and *Three Blind Mice*, but the question also remained as to whether such magazines wanted more readers other than like-minded writers. Poetry was a mini-issue within a larger problem of publishing from a niche to a niche market. Also, the evidence from the 1970s suggested that possibly twenty of the publications were largely attempts at being noticed rather than ideas about communication.

As mentioned previously, *Australian Short Stories* inherited, in a sense, the unfinished project that *Tabloid Story* set for itself in the 1970s: that of trying to popularise the short story out of its ghetto in the academy. Even there, Australian literature was having to work its way through the structures and contend with the international bias of cultural studies, structuralism and post-structuralism, and the distribution problems in the marketplace still cast a pall over optimism. Even so, *Billy Blue*, an innovative publication produced in Sydney with the assistance of John Clemenger Advertising, was pioneering innovative artwork, publishing articles and stories alongside advertising. This suggested a model for the future, but since it was distributed free in Sydney throughout the 1980s, it was not a model that arts administrators could relate to. The magazine also was not prepared to ask for support.

Established in Melbourne in 1982 by Bruce Pascoe and Nancy Phelan, publishing under the name of Pascoe Phelan, *Australian Short Stories* would publish two series; the first series ran from 1982 to 1995 (with fifty-one issues), and the second series ran from 1995 to 1998 four times a year. It was an optimistic venture because the two borrowed heavily to produce the first issue. With the first issue 20 000 copies of the magazine went on sale in newsagents and bookshops around the country. Stuart Sayers of the *Age* reported that 'Bruce Pascoe is convinced Australians still have an appetite for short stories — provided our writers write readable and believable fiction, stories that reflect the nature of life in this country' ('Stories in search' 14).

Thomas Shapcott commented on the effective handover of Literature Board support from *Tabloid Story* to *Australian Short Stories*, of which the great majority of the grant was designated towards payments to writers. Speaking of *Tabloid Story*, he said:

> It began as a magazine designed to draw attention to 'the new wave' of Australian short story writers: by the 1980s there had been a significant increase in the number of book collections of recent stories — both by individual writers through to anthologies. In 1983 the new magazine *Australian Short Stories* made its first appearance, with excellent distribution through newsagents. *Tabloid Story* had served its purpose. (*The Literature Board* 236)

Could the short story once again be as popular as it was when Henry Lawson and Steele Rudd were writing? But compared to back then, Australia in the 1980s was becoming multicultural and more diverse in all ways, and the

Figure 8: Cover of Australian Short Stories, *vol 1, no 2 (1983)*

rise of new media such as radio and television created a radically different landscape from when the printed word was pre-eminent in a smaller country. Bruce Pascoe was then a radical nationalist in many respects, who favoured a different type of story from the fabulism promoted by Frank Moorhouse and Murray Bail. Thus on the whole the stories he published were broadly realist in mode and naturalistic in orientation, which could have attracted 'average' readers (if there is ever such a thing) — but this made the magazine unrepresentative of the new writing. Perhaps, though, the reason for the magazine's initial sales success was its representation of a more nostalgic, smaller and manageable Australia. Pascoe was reported in the *Age* as saying that 'academic esoteric or banal stories of discreetly thwarted passion' are eschewed (qtd. in Denholm 2: 120). In broad terms also, Pascoe and Phelan's orientation was toward bush settings, an irony given that the history of the short story in Australia was largely one of a flight from tales of the countryside into tales of the city, and particularly narratives of the inner city. Notwithstanding, Gordon and Gotch, the largest newspaper and magazine distribution of that time, agreed to distribute it to its outlets.

The magazine itself was published in a small paperback-size format of approximately sixty to eighty pages with colour covers and perfect binding (not unlike the later issues of *Inprint*, which went to perfect binding for its last few years). Its format endeared it to the relative product standardisation at work in newsagents, and by all accounts it achieved steady sales for the majority of its publication life. Denholm reported that, published bi-monthly, it sold 7500 copies each issue, but towards the end of the 1990s it started to encounter financial difficulties and ceased publication. Over its life, however, it had popularised the work of a host of writers — including Marion Halligan, Beverley Farmer, Barry Dickins, Robert Drewe, James McQueen, Nigel Krauth, Jennifer Dabbs, Moya Costello and Tim Winton, to name only a few — and this facilitated a resurgence in the publication of individual short story collections and anthologies during the 1980s.

Australian Short Stories would not be the only example of state-sponsored intervention to try to popularise the short story. Between 1985 and 1986, the

Figure 9: Cover of Island, no 129 (2012)

Adelaide Review, a free arts and lifestyle giveaway, received support from the Literature Board to pay writers, which was seen by the Board as another chance at exposure (Shapcott, *The Literature Board* 239), even though the publication lacked a national profile. The problem, though, was that popular newspapers and magazines (such as the *Adelaide Review*) were not prepared to pay creative writers on a regular basis without subsidies, so the short story remained for much of the fifty years of this study, a cute artistic 'other' to the daily urgencies of journalism.

One magazine that largely shrugged off the perceived post-structuralist ascendancy and was published outside the Melbourne/Sydney nexus was the *Tasmanian Review*, first published in 1979 from Hobart. After 1980 it changed its name to *Island*, and in the 1980s it became a lively combination of original creative writing and accessible articles. Granted there is no such thing as a 'general reader', but *Island* was not content to limit its range of reading possibilities. The first editors were Michael Denholm and Andrew Sant, and contributors were a catholic blend of people such as Les Murray, Frank Moorhouse, Donald Horne, Gwen Harwood, Humphrey McQueen and Hugh Stretton. *Island* established itself as an ongoing publication during the 1980s. It was Tasmania's only literary/small magazine and as a result it received support from stakeholders such as the University of Tasmania, Arts Tasmania and the Australia Council. In the merry-go-round of becoming known and asking for support from grant bodies, *Island* was, like *Westerly* in Perth, in a better position than some new aspirants in Victoria and New South Wales, in that they could appeal to representing their regions in a national context and local context.

Another magazine that could be seen to be appealing to special interests and thus creating a niche for itself was *Voiceworks*. In 1983, Express Media, the publisher of what became Voiceworks, was established in Melbourne as Express Media Power Workshops. *Voiceworks* (the newsletter) was launched by Prime Minister Bob Hawke and rock guru Molly Meldrum in 1985 (the International Year of Youth) to publicise the organisation's workshops.

At the time of writing, Express Media currently has three full-time staff, a General Manager, an Artistic Director and the editor of the magazine, within a structure that includes an editorial committee made up of young people who assist the editor in producing the magazine. Contributors have to be less than twenty-five years old. From around the twelfth issue, *Voiceworks* began to publish a quarterly eighty-page magazine. Currently it has published 84 issues, usually in a largish size format with colour, gloss covers and some of the early work of a number of writers who would go on to publish more widely.

Voiceworks has survived for over two and a half decades through not only the voluntary labour of participants, but through extensive subsidy support from state and federal arts bodies (Arts Vic, The Australia Council, the City of Melbourne, the Copyright Agency Ltd) and a number of private sponsors, including the popular author of Young Adult fiction John Marsden. Express Media has always been able to appeal to grant bodies from a politically sensitive niche position in that it represents young people. Whether this is a form of tokenism, or something that should be judged over time as public money spent in necessary 'seeding', is a double-barrelled question. In broad terms, *Voiceworks* has been one of the most highly subsidised publications in Australian small press history and it has published the early work of many aspiring authors. Given its 'youth' brief, it has the advantage of a discernible constituency, but the disadvantage of not being able to operate outside that grouping.

Gaining a niche, then, has been rather important in starting up a publication and sustaining it over time. *Voiceworks* has proven that, but *Outrider: Journal of Multicultural Literature in Australia*, which Denholm has described as 'a journal of ethnic literature in Australia' (2: 194), managed to make its mark by appealing to cultural administrators who were nervous by the 1980s as to the ongoing debate over multiculturalism and the attendant issues of inclusiveness and difference. This debate, on an academic level, was pursued vigorously by Sneja Gunew and Wenche Ommundsen in the late

1980s and early 1990s. The publication of *Outrider* was also a realisation that Australia had a changed demographic.

Outrider published literary prose, poetry and contributions that dealt with ethnic literature in Australia, and poems were printed in their original language as well as in translation. Contributors included Maria Lewitt, Walter Adamson, Lolo Houbein, Judah Waten, Manfred Jurgensen and Cornelius Vleeskens. Although the guidelines for assistance from the Literature Board stipulated at the time that 'any magazine applying for a grant should have produced at least three issues' (Shapcott, *The Literature Board* 237), the Board made an exception in *Outrider*'s case, following the *Multicultural Writing Conference* in Manly, New South Wales, in July 1983, where a motion was passed requesting assistance from the Australia Council. The Board approved an 'in principal' establishment grant of $12 000 for two issues in 1984 (238). Following the decision, *Outrider* put out a statement: '[I]ts aim is to extend the concept of Australian literature by presenting works of ethnic writers … [E]ach volume will feature one ethnic writer … [T]he aim of *Outrider* shall remain, above all, literary and ecumenical' (qtd. in *The Literature Board* 238). The original editorial committee consisted of Manfred Jurgensen, Serge Liberman and correspondents Sneja Gunew, Lola Houbein and Margot Luke. The Board was impressed by the well-developed editorial policy it received with the application.

The magazine published from 1984 until 1994, semi-annually until 1989 and annually from 1990 — from Queensland by Phoenix Publications and from an address in Melbourne until 1996. According to Sonia Mycak, the first issue was 'unambiguously designated as a multicultural or ethnic journal', but 'by 1988, when the bicentennial issue of the journal was published, the subtitle had lost its overly multicultural focus' (272) as it changed to *Outrider: Australian Writing Now*, and became an anthology of contemporary Australian literature which does not accept the distinctions of 'mainstream', 'ethnic', or 'marginal' (273). Mycak claims that the editor, Manfred Jurgensen, was striving to reach out to a wider social network than a purely multicultural niche publication. *Outrider* was handsomely produced to look like a book, with an implication of permanence. It would go on to publish a series of writers who were 'ethnic' or who identified with the notion. There was evidence that the magazine was tapping into an established community of interest, as it performed pioneering work in redefining what an Australian literature could be.

Another magazine that has survived for over two decades was first published in 1986. *Verandah* is a literary journal first published by students at the Toorak Campus of Victoria College in Melbourne. It has traditionally provided an outlet for student writing at Deakin University (which subsumed Victoria College), and over time it began to publish once a year, making it an annual anthology and not a magazine given the criteria I am using here. Apart from student writers, it has published a number of more well-known writers such as Garry Disher. The creative writing course at Victoria College was one of the first such courses in Australia and boasted teachers such as Judith Rodriguez and Gerald Murnane, and it was ample evidence of what was to follow throughout Australia in the way that student demand in the creative industries would grow and inform the content of the little magazines, particularly in the early 2000s. In micro-terms, universities and colleges responded by publishing some form of publication by students such as annual anthologies. The business of ongoing support for the publication of any nationally published literary magazines remained outside their orbit. Whereas in the 1970s grungy, newsprint little magazines were acceptable, and influenced, on occasions, by the revolutionary nature of the student press of that time, educational institutions wanted by the 1980s to make a statement about their position in a growing educational market. *Verandah* is still publishing annually.

Tirra Lirra, calling itself the quarterly magazine for the Yarra Valley in Victoria but not associated with any institution, was created in 1990. Edited by Eva Windisch and Julian Spencer, it published in spurts, in a relatively glossy format, until around 2003 when it went online and, like some others which had done the same, was then difficult to track. From northeastern New South Wales, *Ulitarra* appeared, published by Kardoorier Press in Armidale and with links to Taree on the mid-north coast. It was launched in Sydney in 1992 by Les Murray and Michael Wilding and published twice-yearly until 2001. Gaining respect in literary circles over its life, it attracted Robert Adamson as poetry editor for a time and Michael Sharkey between 1992 and 2001.

Visibility, particularly in the eastern states, had, as we have seen, been *Westerly*'s frustration in its quest to showcase what Western Australia had to offer: it seemed hard for readers elsewhere to imagine that it was also a national magazine. The Northern Territory was even further away in many eyes, but its literary traditions have been locally known. *Northern Perspective*, published from Darwin, has had two lives in effect: from 1977 to 1997 (twenty issues) and from 1998 to 1999 (two issues). Initially it was published by Darwin Community College at Casuarina, but then by the Darwin Institute of Technology and from 1988 by Northern Territory University (now Charles Darwin University) as a magazine that concentrates on Territorian themes and issues through articles and creative writing. Denholm described a typical issue as consisting of 'a section featuring general articles ... and a section devoted to creative writing and short reviews' (2: 190). According to Thomas Shapcott, it 'has done much to encourage Creative Writing in the Northern Territory' (*The Literature Board* 239) and it was clearly a journal which took to heart its local constituency, a vital part of the traditional role of a certain type of literary magazine. This was something which would mitigate against mass sales (and indeed commodification), yet be important to its local community. With that type of publication, its use value made it distinctive.

Also in the 1980s, presumably out of sight and mind prior to the internet, there were a number of publications from Queensland, even though the Bjelke-Petersen National Party government reigned supreme. As we have seen, *Makar* and *Australian Literary Studies* were continuous and respectable projects, yet there were a number of very idiosyncratic magazines such as *Phoenix Australia*, which was associated with the Sunshine Coast Literary

Society and was a purely private venture, duplicated and hand-bound and published by Les Alcorn. It published between 1975 and 1978 and struggled under parochial pressures.

The magazines discussed here differ from the established journals in that very few of them achieved visibility in newspapers or on radio, where literary matters were highlighted. Economically Australia, it seemed, was unable to sustain more than a handful of magazines. Broadly speaking, Australia could not promote and sustain more than a small group of high-profile writers, let alone promote unknown writers. The 1980s had then seen, essentially, a return to the status quo. As in the 1970s, most of the activity was centred on the population centres of Sydney and Melbourne, and attempts to set up in the smaller capitals were always difficult. Yet *Westerly* was still soldiering on, and in Brisbane, *Imago* was published for the first time in 1989 by the School of Communication at the Queensland University of Technology, one of the newer universities which had previously been a College of Advanced Education or Teachers' College. Its full title was *Imago: New Writing* and it was published until 2001, edited by Philip Neilsen, in a forum-format with short fiction, some poetry, articles and reviews. Like much from that state prior to the advent of the *Griffith Review* in the early 2000s, *Imago* was rarely seen outside Queensland, and therefore could not gain the cultural traction of an established magazine. In a format sense, it was the A5-size equivalent of a smallish paperback book, and it was the case of a magazine that relied on the passion of one key individual. Like other initiatives over the years, *Imago* was paid for by the Queensland University of Technology and Arts Queensland, and for whatever reason, had little other regular income, making it institution- and grant-bound.

The history of the magazines has surely shown that institutions are welcome supports, but they can make the future unsustainable if overly relied upon. After 2001, *Imago* was effectively replaced by *Dotlit*, an online creative writing journal edited by Neilsen and Donna Lee Brien, which ceased publishing and then was reborn in 2005 with new editors Nike Bourke, Stuart Glover, Craig Bolland and Glen Thomas. It then unfortunately ceased publication by 2008, similar to a number of other online journals. Was it because writers and readers thought online publication too easy an option? Irrespective of the standard of the contents, many online journals would disappear even though they were a cheap option for backers such as universities who wished to raise their creative writing profile.

In general terms, a notable feature of the newer magazines of the 1980s was that they attempted professionalisation in a decade that demonstrated all the marks of necessary commodification. Although there had been some fitful models of formats that were portable and potentially populist, such as *Tabloid Story* in the 1970s, consolidation was the key word for the more conservative 1980s. As I have suggested elsewhere in regard to the general history of the genre,

> another striking feature is the monumentalism inscribed in the artefact that is the literary magazine: as the years rolled on, the magazines looked even chunkier, more expensively produced, more like books because that is the way they are taken seriously, or so the story goes. ('Respectable or risqué' n.p.)

In other words, it appears that such formats were the only way for magazines to be stocked in an increasingly professionalised book trade. However, there had been significant changes in the electronic media during the 1970s, as Enzensberger noted in 1976:

> [T]hese new forms of media are constantly forming new connections both with each other and with older media like printing, radio, film, television, telephone, teletype, radar, and so on. They are clearly coming together to form a universal system. (20)

He went on: '[M]onopoly capitalism develops the consciousness-shaping industry more quickly and more extensively than other sectors of production' (21).

An interesting playing-out of the contradiction in the 1970s was the tolerance for 'grungy' publications such as the first bestseller for the nascent travel publisher Lonely Planet, *Across Asia on the Cheap*, which, in its first edition, was stapled and cheaply produced, but which had identified a big gap in the market for travel guides. Lonely Planet identified a hippy-inspired, cheap-travel youth market, in similar ways to the way in which a new crop of rock magazines had tapped into the relative deconstruction of high/popular culture. In the literary area, the irony was that the experimentation of the 1970s magazines had partly prepared the path for authors in the 1980s by publishing their very early work. It is true that many of the small 1970s magazines were products of that decade and the tone of the era — ephemeral, irresponsible and performative. Yet eras of consolidation are often prefigured by periods of 'anarchy', and so it was with the 1970s. Another 1970s characteristic — spontaneity and small-scale 'craft' production, manifested in many of the little magazines — would of course run dry over time in an exchange economy.

Volunteerism, bourgeois or otherwise, is built on the ability of individuals and groups to give freely of their time, and often some people are more equal than others, given their personal income. Many of the magazine editors in the 1970s were in their twenties and without family responsibilities, but by the end of the decade they had set about making careers, and their idealistic magazines dropped by the wayside. More to the point, many of the magazines of the 1970s were examples of youthful impetuosity and were intended as such.

Another comparison with the 1970s is also intriguing. The small magazines of the 1970s not only catered for the 'poetry wars' and the new Australian poetry, to put it briefly, but they attempted to reactivate the short story from its post-war marketing malaise — examples of which were *Tabloid Story*, *Inprint*, *Overland* and *Westerly*. Short fiction had famously been the training ground for Frank Moorhouse, Tim Winton and Robert Drewe. While there was still short fiction in the journals during the 1980s, publishers inherited the innovations and published more individual collections in the decade. After the 1980s, though, the form would go back to a its undernourished publishing niche in the 1990s — even despite the efforts of Bruce Pascoe with his *Australian Short Stories* — to then undergo a renaissance in the 2000s through the initial work of *Sleepers Publishing* and *Wet Ink*.

Typical of the 1970s, magazines such as *Tabloid Story* put together by Frank Moorhouse and Michael Wilding were personal creations which lasted as long as individual passions. By the end of the 1970s, Moorhouse and Wilding decided to hand the magazine over to a collective in Melbourne, comprising Laurie Clancy, Lucy Frost and John Timlin, who continued the work of trying to find host journals. However, the idea had run its course and most of the mass-market host journals had been exhausted, such as the *National Times*, the *Bulletin* and *Nation Review*. *Australian Short Stories*, as we have seen, was a brave venture that lasted the subsequent decade. An A3-size publication, it had by all accounts a print run of 20 000 copies when it first appeared in 1982 (Denholm 2: 119), a rare event for a literary/small magazine in Australia. If Denholm's suggestion as to its circulation is correct, *Australian Short Stories* had cracked the glass ceiling of distribution for a small magazine in Australia for a short time at least. *Quadrant* had achieved newsagent distribution for some years prior to 1981, but it was a conservative journal.

10. Changes among the established magazines

As we have seen, *Overland* had been Stephen Murray-Smith's 'baby' since its formation in 1954 when it incorporated with the *Realist Writer*. He rejected the notion that culture was exclusively produced to cater for elites, and drew inspiration from a notion of an egalitarian Australia. *Overland* in a sense was Murray-Smith's way of promoting an intellectual culture that could show the way to a democratic Left alternative with Australian roots. The masthead incorporated Joseph Furphy's famous dictum ('Temper democratic, bias offensively Australian') minus the word 'offensively'. During the 1970s, *Overland* was attacked by the new wave as one of the 'Golden Oldies' (with the implication that it was an establishment journal, which must have been amusing to Murray-Smith, who had battled through the height of the Cold War and the frosty intellectual environment of the 1950s.

Stylistically, though, it had not adapted to the cultural changes of the 1960s and 1970s, and its fiction was largely realist in orientation. It must be acknowledged, however, that the magazine was one of the first to publish the fabulist Peter Carey, who saw himself as a writer of relatively experimental fictions. *Overland* nonetheless broadly represented an exhausted tradition in the eyes of some. Aligning himself at the time with a broadly avant-garde, small-press tradition, Michael Wilding, writing in the 'New Writing in Australia' edition of *Australian Literary Studies* in 1977, said:

> [T]hough *Overland* has included pieces of the new writing, its overall tone has always been the old realist aesthetic — the reduced social realist mode — reduced from socialist realism, which in itself was reduced from 19th century bourgeois critical realism. ('A survey' 124)

In broad terms, none of the established magazines, such as *Overland*, *Meanjin* or *Southerly*, were represented in that issue of *Australian Literary Studies*. The new writing was presumably the preserve of the newer little magazines. Jim Davidson, when he took over at *Meanjin*, made considerable overtures towards what he saw as the new wave. His magazine needed modernisation and ways in which it could strive for new constituencies of readers. In saying that, it was obvious that established cultural visibility still had the power to promote previously semi-underground writers such as Hemensley and Tranter, whereas *Overland* was wary of such influences. This was possibly because — if the evidence of John McLaren's comments on the time are any indication — the old Left were still suspicious of the anarchic New Left in the way it wished it could avoid the boring business of political economy.

In 1981 Murray-Smith made it clear that the *Overland* project was still in place. He was suspicious of the new wave, and he wanted to keep a social realist tradition in place:

> If I favour anything, it would be stories with a humorous component ... but the best story I ever published, John Morrison's 'Pioneers', was anything but humorous; and very firmly set in a traditional story-telling manner. ('Editor's statements' 266)

Yet he was also wary of 'stories with a message': 'We soon learnt that fine thoughts butter no parsnips' (266).

He was rather grumpy, it appears, after years of battling for the magazine's survival against the odds during the Cold War, but in that way he articulated his ideas of the magazine's audience and intentions:

> On the whole we are not particularly impressed by the quality of the stories we receive ... The only audience I have in mind is a kind of generalized and rather vague view of who comprises the *Overland* readership. This is probably far broader than the readership of any other Australian literary magazine, and influences our choice to the extent that we favour readable, interesting, non-mannerist stories ... (266)

All in all, it appears that he was not impressed by the new writing of the 1970s, in particular the short story, which everyone else was claiming a renaissance. 'I fancy that interest in the short story, both in *Overland* and elsewhere, has declined', he added (266).

Gradually *Overland* modernised its layout and content during the 1980s. In terms of the poetry, Barrett Reid had been the poetry editor from the early 1970s and had published a range of relatively avant-garde poets with links into the new poetry including Shelton Lea, Robert Harris, Jennifer Maiden and Robert Adamson. Reid brought with him a tradition tracing back to the 1940s in Brisbane and a briefly published magazine called *Barjai*. He had had links to Max Harris and the distinctly modernist painters such as Sidney Nolan and Albert Tucker. Michael Dugan, networker par excellence, was also friendly with 'Barrie' (as Reid was known), and introduced him to new poets and provided a link into the small-press scene. In a sense then, Reid was always open to the new, whereas Murray-Smith and Turner wondered whether the baby would be thrown out with the bath-water in the days of the fashionable New Left. The magazine had been for years printed in letterpress by Bob Cugley at the National Press in Latrobe Street, Melbourne, for concessional rates, but offset printing offered different challenges. With Murray-Smith's death in 1988, Barrett Reid took over the editorship from 1988 to 1993. Later, a stalwart of *Overland* over many years, John McLaren, became editor until mid-1997 when Ian Syson took over.

Syson, a former electrician at Mount Isa mines in Queensland, took out his PhD in working-class literature from the University of Queensland under the supervision of the socialist feminist Carole Ferrier. He was in many respects an ideal new editor for *Overland*, as he was intent on synchronising its realist tradition with new developments in Australian writing, particularly in and around Melbourne. Syson says that he 'wanted to make it into an aggressively and proudly left/antagonistic magazine. I also wanted to include more working class themes and writers' ('Letter to the author' 2). Coincidentally, mainstream publishers (such as Picador and HarperCollins) were promoting a 'grunge' realism of sorts, written by authors such as John Birmingham, Christos Tsiolkas, Andrew McGahan and Luke Davies. It had been years since the first flushes of such developments in the hands of Hunter S Thompson, Tom Wolfe and Gay Talese; even so, in Australia, the experimental writers, in this respect, were always slower finding market appeal due to a much smaller population. Publishing decisions, then, were always riskier.

Syson promoted Tsiolkas as in a sense a new realist, who was in touch with new social formations where class was a determinant but had slippery manifestations with the advent of post-industrial layers of the workforce. McLaren explains: 'Ian Syson, however, argues that the best of grunge writing follows the tradition of social realist writing, and that its outrage is itself the solution, the rejection of an unjust society as the necessary first step to building a new one' (208). Perhaps the realisation was that as time went on people identified with lifestyle rather than with locality and class. Syson, although sensitive to what appeared to be the new social formations, held relatively rigid ideas as to the nature of fictional realism, and it would be several years before the short fiction in *Overland* became more eclectic and less determinist in its orientations. Syson, whether he liked it or not, had to contend with a social landscape that had changed from being based on a discernible class base, the concept of which had sustained *Overland* through the Cold War. The true believers were ageing, and in the West there was the development (since the 1960s) of a new service subclass, members of which were the consumers of cultural products such as *Overland*. Bourdieu has suggested that this new subclass bases its aestheticism

> on a rejection of everything in themselves which is finite, definite, final ... that is, a refusal to be pinned down in a particular site ... [T]hey see

themselves as unclassifiable, 'excluded', 'dropped out', 'marginal', anything rather than categorised, assigned to a class, a determinate place in social space. (Distinction 370)

Under Syson, non-fiction became more combative in the hands of New Left Marxists. Throughout Syson's editorship, he also expressed concerns that cultural hegemony had not shifted all that far, even after the advent of a New Left. His argument was that there was a soft Left literary establishment, particularly in Melbourne — represented by high-profile figures such as the academic Robert Manne — who were given carte blanche by publications such as the *Age* to offer up soft Left views on issues. Syson often promoted the views of Mark Davis, author of *Gangland*, who argued that the cultural elites were basically baby boomers unable to let go of perceived cultural power. This dilemma was nothing new for *Overland*, as it had always constructed itself as on the outer, particularly through the Cold War, when it was politically marginalised. Paradoxically, by the 1990s it could be said that the magazine was established because it had been around for a long time and was therefore a good place to publish.

In recollection, though, Syson saw his changes as having twin aims:
In fact there was something quite conservative and retrograde in what I was doing. I was trying to recapture a lost readership first and foremost because I believed that a lot of old (flush) lefties should be contributing to the culture and finances of the magazine. There was also a young humanist left cohort that had never felt attached to the magazine when it should have been their natural home. Though I guess the idea of a new demographic was in our sights as a secondary aim. ('Letter to the author' 2)

Syson made the magazine more appealing to a newer generations of writers and readers, and, while remaining aware of its radical nationalist tradition, he wanted it to be relevant in rapidly changing times, and not an image (for better or worse) of the past. A part of that drive was awareness that the poetry *Overland* published needed to be reflective of new experiments; thus he appointed Pam Brown, a well-known experimental poet, as poetry editor.

Overland became more noticed by a new and perhaps younger audience. I pissed off a few people as well. Some older readers thought I was rude and

> disrespectful — they had Stephen Murray-Smith whizzing in his grave every other issue. Other older readers liked the fight we brought back to the mag. We increased circulation and impact quite markedly while I was editor. The *Overland* lecture series was an unqualified success. We also opened the door to the brave new electronic world via a web presence and *Overland* Express. (3)

Syson had made moves towards a new demographic and had also reasserted his perception that class-based politics had not disappeared.

Although *Overland* came with ideological baggage (in some eyes), it was always able to mobilise and appeal to its left-wing community for support and encouragement. Regularly through its history it had always had a sinking fund of supporters' donations, which, if it looked like special pleading, was also evidence of an active, committed base — something which many newer magazines of the 1970s never had the time to establish, or the inclination to pursue. Syson believes that the changes that he made, and that Nathan Hollier was to make, 'were ones that enabled the present editor Jeff Sparrow to make the successful wrench into the new media' (3). Typically feisty, Syson saw the *Overland* project as 'conducted in a space defined by its alterity. But it's a slightly daggy space as well, a place where a yobbo Marxist like myself can have a bit of fun blowing raspberries at the right' (3). Because of such strong characters, *Overland*'s ideological base, which was criticised in the libertarian 1960s for a lack of spontaneity, provided the organisational base by which it survived through the 1980s and 1990s, decades in which the Left (or what was left of the Left) was largely under attack.

Nathan Hollier (after being the associate editor between 1998 and 2002) became the co-editor with Katherine Wilson in 2003 when Ian Syson resigned to concentrate on his full-time position lecturing at Victoria University. *Overland* had been published since 1990 by the OL Society (a company limited by guarantee), formed after the death of its founder, Stephen Murray-Smith. Hollier wrote to the Board of the OL Society in December 2002 of his intents as editor, with Katherine Wilson; he articulated the need to promote discussion of the magazine's motto, 'Temper democratic, bias Australian'

('What can we hope to achieve' 1) and wrote that he believed in the way *Overland* addressed issues in language that was jargon-free and accessible. He noted that he thought that 'non-regular readers have a range of perceptions of the magazine, most of which appear to be shaped by its position within Australian culture a decade ago or more' (1), something which Syson had been acutely aware of. *Overland* should lead debate and come up with new ideas, he went on, and in typical ideological style he suggested that *Overland* 'should hope to be a popular forum for trade union, activist, academic, Green and left-ALP debate' (1). It was an unequivocal reaffirmation of the traditional *Overland* mission of being the literary magazine of the Left (with Green tinges) — something which marked it out from the other magazines.

Hollier also noted how Ian Syson had lifted the magazine's profile within the mainstream media as well as within alternative media such as the radical community radio station 3CR, and stated that if *Overland* was to continue to be relevant it must keep working at broad promotion across different social platforms. Inevitably, the question of increased retail sales and subscriptions raised its head, as *Overland*, like all the other magazines, had to work very hard to lift circulation, even though it had been going for over fifty years: 'The one concern with this is our aging subscriber base and an apparent lack of a subscribing culture among younger people' (2). Sponsorship, he felt, was a recurring problem, which in fact he was not confident about due to the political nature of the magazine, and due to the fact that *Overland* faced problems such as 'snobbery':

> History suggests that it is not possible in Australia to be widely regarded as 'first class', in terms of intellectual and aesthetic quality, if one is also inclusive in one's approach and democratic of bias. (2)

This was a fascinating observation that articulated what made *Overland* different, and, to an extent, what attracted some readers to magazines such as *Meanjin* and *Southerly*, who desired a hierarchy.

The look of *Overland* was also different — more of an accessible magazine, less like a 'book' — with some idea of the general reader outside academic circles and the latest intellectual obsession. Hollier's implication was that ordinary Australians might not have intellectual interests, and that the 'cultural cringe' was deep in the national psyche, as AA Phillips had suggested.

> This is a problem the magazine continues to come up against in the public sphere, not only in the mainstream media and within the perceptions of such people who are connected with *Quadrant*, but also ... many connected to *Meanjin*, *Arena*, and others. (3)

He wanted to break down the perception, but as was the way with a number of literary magazines in a small cultural space like Australia, he noted that 'we are consistently attacked by radicals, poets and younger writers as being part of the "establishment"'(3). It was the case that *Overland* had been around for a long time, and longevity had made it an institution.

Sales and subscriptions continued to grow over the period of the new editors, but not rapidly, because retail sales continued to be a problem, something *Overland* shared with most of the other magazines. In 2003, *Overland* had problems with its then distributor, Dennis Jones and Associates, in that concerns were expressed over prompt servicing of friendly retail outlets. The print run was just over 2000 copies each issue for 2003, made up of roughly 1000 subscribers per edition, it reported to the Australia Council.

Ian Syson also gave Hollier and Wilson his advice and reflected on his role, in his typical feisty style, after a number of years jostling with what he considered the Melbourne literary establishment, or those who thought of themselves in such a way. He praised the invaluable work of the co-ordinator, Alex Skutenko, in the day-to-day operations of *Overland* ('Editing *Overland*' 1). He noted that advertising was a hard nut to crack, and he did not really know of any solution, and of sponsorship he said: 'I don't think we're the kind of magazine that will attract corporate sponsorship and if we ever do I'll possibly wonder where you've gone wrong'. He also reflected on what he thought he had achieved:

> I always saw my role as being [that] of reinterpreting *Overland*'s original function in terms of today's changed culture and society. The extent to which this was successful is measured by the number of old lefties

who said we'd returned *Overland* to its proper role combined with those younger readers who felt that it was becoming more relevant. (2)

He made a no-holds-barred rundown of promotional possibilities around Melbourne — who to target and who to ignore — which raised the question that, for all its overall relatively evangelical brief, *Overland* was, as with *Meanjin*, very much a creature of Melbourne, traditionally the home of ideas and radical tendencies in Australia. It was centred in Victoria, and the pressures of keeping a magazine visible in such a town took considerable energy, let alone the demands from around the rest of the country.

Meanjin also went through many changes in the 1980s. After Davidson left in 1982 it has had a series of editors, including Judith Brett (1982-87), Jenny Lee (1987-94) and Christina Thompson (1994-98), all of whom had different tastes; but there was little doubt that the magazine was coming to terms with the changing intellectual climate of cultural theory, particularly during Jenny Lee's time as editor. The fourth editor, Lee arrived in 1987, and said, 'The most advanced piece of equipment in the office was an IBM golf ball typewriter. The magazine was costing almost as much to typeset as to print' (qtd. in Edgar & Geddes 19). She saw that she had to respond to diversifying trends in Australian literature, and in response appointed Gerald Murnane as fiction consultant in 1988:

> [O]ne of my longer term ambitions was to open the magazine up, which meant taking unsolicited material seriously ... [W]hat we could offer ... was editorial support for people to write things they really wanted to write. It's a risky strategy, because you don't end up publishing a lot of name authors. (19)

Meanjin had begun a long period of readjustment, after the stalwart Clem Christesen retired, and its fortunes were to fluctuate with politics within the University of Melbourne and changing demographics in the wider community.

11. A MAGAZINE APART

By contrast, *Quadrant* only prided itself on not needing to change with the times. In fact the basic cover design of its April 2011 issue used the same typeface, and was printed on similar paper stock (a type of newsprint), as that it used in the 1970s. Yet it has maintained widespread newsagent distribution in an effort to reach a non-coterie audience — 'so it does make literature and literary discussion available to a casual, browsing public' in contrast to the other magazines, according to Michael Wilding ('Letter to the author').

Quadrant had always prided itself on being Australia's only conservative literary magazine, so in a sense it has seen no reason to update itself, unlike *Meanjin* and *Overland*, on the so-called Left. Its raison d'être has been to resist trends and fashions. Largely, it has been a magazine of politics and opinion with relatively marginal adherence to original literary work, something which the Literature Board of the Australia Council had questioned in the past. To a lesser degree, the same could be said for *Meanjin* and *Overland*; even so, they have consistently dedicated a greater proportion of their pages to original creative writing. As discussed previously in Chapter Six, *Quadrant* has, on occasions, made political representations whenever it has felt that its interests have been under attack — confident, it seems, in the belief that it is on sure ground in an Australia that has largely resisted radical ideas, and ideas in general. But it must be said that the great majority of little magazines in this country are (and have not been) political in the strict sense. A rollcall, particularly of the 1970s, reveals a list of publications that were broadly libertarian, individualistic in the extreme, and concerned only in publishing new writers, irrespective of any ideological framing. A similar pattern of magazines largely eschewing overt political positions would develop during the 1980s, 1990s and into the new millennium.

Quadrant still describes itself as 'Australia's leading journal of ideas, essays, literature, poetry, and political and historical debate' (*Quadrant Magazine* n.p.). In 2011 it was published ten times a year, with double editions in January-February and July-August, so it has never been backward in coming forward, charting out a territory for itself that is adversarial and, in earlier times, anti-communist. The magazine was founded in 1956 by Richard Krygier, a Polish/Jewish refugee from war-torn Europe, and poet James McAuley (famous for the anti-modernist Ern Malley hoax in the 1940s). It was published under the auspices of the Australian Committee for Cultural Freedom, the Australian arm of the Congress for Cultural Freedom, a group allegedly funded by the US Central Intelligence Agency (the CIA) — the influence of which *Quadrant* still disputes on its website. In broad terms, *Quadrant* has seen its mission as exposing academic shoddiness; it deplores the polarisation of the arts; it has been critical of universities which, its editors think, have come under the spell of political correctness; and it has turned a sceptical eye on what it sees as fads such as post-modernism, cultural relativism, multiculturalism and radical environmentalism.

Quadrant has always been able to call on a conservative community of business allies and sponsors who have donated money and in-kind resources. The annual *Quadrant* lecture, for example, is an example of how a small magazine can assemble together like-minded people and engage in agenda-setting. The former Liberal Prime Minister John Howard has been a speaker. Editors of the magazine have tended to last for long periods: James McAuley (1956-67), Peter Coleman (1967-90), Robert Manne (1990-97), Paddy McGuinness (1997-2007) and currently Keith Windschuttle (a Marxist during the 1970s). All of these editors are, and have been, relatively high-profile public figures. Robert Manne became known in the 1980s and 1990s as an anti-communist intellectual, but by 1997, with his resignation from *Quadrant*, his politics were becoming increasingly small 'l' liberal. Peter Coleman was a state Liberal and later federal Member of Parliament. Windschuttle has vigorously engaged in the so-called culture wars, and his scepticism as to the veracity of much of the writing of Indigenous history has made him a divisive figure. The current editorial advisory board consists of conservative newspaper columnists and former Governor-General and Labor politician Bill Hayden. The literary editor for quite some time has been the poet Les Murray, also a critic of 'trendy' positions and anti-establishment fads.

Whatever can be said about *Quadrant*, and plenty has been, the fact that it does not in any way aspire to being on the cutting edge has assured it of a secure, relatively easy, reactionary space. It has defined itself as 'other' to the rest of the magazines, so much so that, as late as December 2009, it was still complaining about where it stood in relation to 'the others'. Mary-Anne Toy reported in the *Sydney Morning Herald* that *Quadrant* had accused the Australia Council of political bias after its annual grant for 2010 was cut by 30 per cent, from $50 000 to $35 000. Windschuttle was reported as saying, 'Throughout the 11 years of the Howard government, its appointees never reduced the funding of overly left-wing publications like *Meanjin*, *Overland* and the *Australian Book Review*' (qtd. in Toy 4).

Two magazines became eligible for funding that year, the *Griffith Review* and *Wet Ink* — the obvious culprits in *Quadrant*'s eyes for its loss of funding. Whether they were left-wing is another question. The Australia Council's director of literature, Susan Hayes, was reported as suggesting 'that the board was also concerned that *Quadrant* and some other magazines were using too narrow a field of contributors, and it was not the only magazine to lose funding' (Toy 4). John Tranter has made the point that *Quadrant* is essentially a journal of political commentary compared to other literary magazines such as the *Australian Book Review*, yet 'poems, and reviews and stories make up only a part of its contents. But by my rough calculation *Quadrant* has asked for and received more than $1 million in literary subsidy since it began' ('Poems' 27).

Quadrant's influential backers will ensure its survival in one form or another, and, more importantly, it has not had the stress of adapting with the times, such as is the case with small magazines on the Left, which seem to have been manoeuvring in circles. For example, *Meanjin* appears to be unsure whether it is of the Left or of an asymmetrical, apolitical, new social class. The *Griffith Review* is clearly a Left/liberal manifestation, allied to a publishing triumvirate in Melbourne around Text Publishing, Scribe and Black Inc., which has established cultural visibility. Apart from *Overland*, the remainder are creative writing magazines, largely unconcerned with political agenda-setting.

12. WHITHER THE UNIVERSITIES

Broadly speaking, there had been a move away from university involvement in supporting literary magazines in the 1980s and 1990s. In terms of support for book publishing, university presses were declining in number as the text-book market (particularly in the humanities) was undercut by course readers for students, and the corporatisation of the universities meant that idealism was not cost-effective. There had been upsurges in activity, such as the University of Queensland Press's program of local-fiction publishing in the 1970s under the management of Frank Thompson, but university presses largely abandoned local fiction until *Heat* magazine, through Ivor Indyk and Giramondo Publishing, was conceived in 1996 in the Writing and Society Research Group at the University of Western Sydney. In 2005, UWA Publishing announced a plan to publish a new series of literary fiction from post-graduate students in Australian creative writing courses, and also in the mid-2000s, Central Queensland University Press published a range of fiction and non-fiction titles (largely regional histories) under the idiosyncratic guidance of David Myers.

Sam Martin has claimed that this is evidence of active involvement by universities ('Publish or perish' n.p.). In my view, however, the reality is one of declining responsibility for community involvement despite the examples Martin cites, as they are stories of wilful individuals such as Thompson and Indyk pushing particular agendas. In terms of the literary magazines, the

University of Melbourne was still involved with *Meanjin*, but by the early 2000s its publishing arrangement had changed. At the same time, *Westerly* was publishing less and less at the University of Western Australia; *Southerly* was still at the University of Sydney; *Island* was loosely associated with the University of Tasmania; Victoria University was involved with *Overland* with in-kind support; and Griffith University made a bold move with the *Griffith Review*. Other than that, the trade conditions in book publishing had changed and idealism was confined to groups outside universities. The rise of marketing departments resulted in the general view of 'what was in it for us?' and number-crunching over enrolment levels. Looking closely, none of the newer universities apart from Griffith University (which was started in the late 1960s) were involved with any of the new magazines, even though they were enrolling thousands of creative writing students. In consequence, co-operation would be left to individuals and small groups, which had always been the sustaining narrative of the literary magazine in Australia.

13.   A BRAVE NEW WORLD

The 1980s had seen the consolidation of established magazines, and the dropping off of several newcomers, because publishing a literary magazine involves decisions that are radically different from other types of publishing. People do not set out to make money, so in a sense the literary magazine is both an amateur and professional space, with one foot in commerce and the other in aesthetics. The variety of shapes and sizes, formats, types of typography and unrealistic ambitions was testament to that. The literary magazine is a strange, wilful beast indeed and its manifestations over the next two decades were testament to that, too.

Of vital importance to the way magazines looked in the 1990s was the introduction, and eventual universality, of desktop publishing around the middle of the decade. Desktop publishing was a further refinement on the offset revolution, providing better design flexibility and further consolidating the professional appearance of all magazines, particularly the literary magazine. People could publish idiosyncratic zines in limited editions, but for any magazine that aspired to an audience, slick design was a given.

Aside from the secure adversarial role that *Quadrant* had defined for itself, any new magazine would also have to work with a changing social landscape that had been developing since the late 1960s. By the 1990s, there was evidence that many of the magazines were still republishing the culturally and politically correct 1970s social myths. They were also beginning to chronicle changes that could have been the self-fulfilling prophecies of an expanding yet culturally insecure new class influenced by a suspicion of inefficient meta-narratives. John Frow has claimed that members of this new class were excellent consumers of post-modernist cultural products. His claims support other theorists such as Pierre Bourdieu, Fred Pfeil and Barbara and John Ehrenreich, in a frame that postulates the slippery nature of class formation in the latter years of the twentieth century (Frow 89-105). How the magazines would respond would be a central question to watch. Another one could be: Would the literary magazine continue as a site of discussion, given the fundamental technological changes, and the decentred social landscape?

Another journal appeared in 1994, entitled *Republica* and edited by George Papaellinas, an up-and-coming author of Greek-Cypriot background. Published initially under the Angus and Robertson imprint (which had been taken over by the large multinational HarperCollins in 1989), *Republica* lasted for four issues, containing long essays on aspects of cultural change, with an emphasis on multicultural discourse in the new Australia, and publishing quite a long list of esteemed authors in editions of at least 280 pages. Meanwhile, *Meanjin* and *Southerly* were looking more like books as the 1980s wore on, but *Republica*, as a biannual publication, was not one thing or the other. Despite its impressive contents, it was an expensive proposition for any publisher, and would require considerable investment in the short-term before subscriptions could be obtained — a hard ask for a biannual journal in a small market, where subscribers look for regularity and where the economic viability of those that are already established is an open question.

14. Everything that is solid melts

> *The new value placed on the transitory, the elusive and the ephemeral, the very celebration of dynamism, discloses a longing for an undefiled, immaculate and stable present.* (Jurgen Habermas qtd. in Harvey 325)

Habermas was of course speaking of his idea that post-modernism (I use the term here in reference to the contemporary social mood of late capitalism) is, if anything, an unresolved modernism that has not as yet worked through its contradictions. In a similar way, the changes in the informational means of production were flying every which way by the year 2000.

Capitalism, as a social and economic system, works through creative destruction in search of new profit-taking, and social value is expressed through commodification; that is, monetary value determines social value. It largely pays no respect to relatively unprofitable enterprise such as book publishing, which has always been a low-profit business, even in boom times. There have been periods of reasonable profitability, mainly in North America and Europe during periods where the form was the dominant media, but in Australia a survey of 228 businesses in 2000-01 by the Australian Bureau of Statistics revealed that although publishers generated an income of $1.36 billion (of which literary publishing is a small percentage of turnover), expenses were $1.32 billion, a profit of only around 6 per cent (qtd. in Webster 84). The least profitable publishing enterprise of all is the literary magazine, as it has always been in permanent crisis, and runs at a loss if subsidies are calculated. Thus the question developing in the 2000s was how the literary magazine would survive in any format alongside the advent of the worldwide web around 2000.

In 2007 the author Richard Flanagan attempted to sum up his despair as to the state of contemporary literary publishing. Most of the small magazines under discussion either call themselves literary or are perceived as such by a society obsessed with labels and niches, so his comments are relevant and would prefigure what would happen to the magazines after the year 2000. He noted that

> the fervent Australian nationalism that fused radicalism with cultural exploration and created both a market for Australian books and an extraordinary gallery of writers and publishers to produce them is dying. People feel betrayed by the idea of Australia, for Australia is no longer an idea with which all Australians wish to identify. (133)

Also in 2007, David Carter put it another way:

> The 'national' no longer provides a compelling frame for either consumers or producers (although as historians of the book we need to be wary of assuming that this was ever the case for those outside a small intellectual minority). ('Boom, bust or business' 245)

It was an effective summary of the legacy the 1980s had left for those publishing literature in the 1990s and the early 2000s. The point made by Carter in parenthesis is also timely, in that literary publishing and the little magazine that published writing have always been marginal to popular culture in Australia, and increasingly during the 1990s, the growth of new media and competition for the entertainment dollar became acute. A further interesting observation would be Carter's warning against generalising (outside of a small intellectual minority), because nationalism was still a major narrative in popular culture (with sport and romantic Australiana). More to the point, the Left, constructed in this instance as dominating the intellectual class, had abandoned its role in further developing an Australian national identity after the fall of the Whitlam government in 1975, leaving a massive space for conservatives such as John Howard to exploit.

Peter Kirkpatrick summed up the changes to suggest that the boom in literary publishing during the 1980s and 1990s was a blip fuelled by factors 'including the impact on national culture of the bicentenary, the growing significance of the Literature Board funding and the rise of Creative Writing courses in the universities'. He added that 'the corresponding rise of cultural studies as well as global changes to the publishing industry … [are] now having their effects' (qtd. in Neill, 'Lost for words' 2). This, he has further explained elsewhere, was the result of a diversifying educational environment in terms of the teaching of Australian literature: '[T]he interdisciplinary drive of the new humanities has actually increased the range of Australian literature being taught' (Kirkpatrick 21). In other words, the incorporation of Australian literature into Cultural Studies and creative writing units has meant that 'it's become less a specialisation and more mainstream' (21). The extent to which students of Australian literature and creative writing would support the local publishing industry, including the magazines, was a factor that would impact on the magazines in the 1990s and continue into the 2000s in curious ways.

Meanwhile, Mark Davis, the author of *Gangland* (1997) — an attack on what Davis then saw as the baby boomer, Left-liberal elites, who were clogging up literary and journalistic opinion — had pretty well announced the death of literary publishing in Australia in 2006 in an article entitled 'The Decline of the Literary Paradigm in Australian Publishing' in *Heat*, which later folded as a magazine in early 2011. Discussing developments in publishing and in general culture over two decades, Davis noted key factors such as the introduction of the Nielsen BookScan, which provided publishers with more up-to-date and detailed sales information, thus leading to the recognition of the high sales of genre fiction and the predominance of non-fiction titles in bestseller lists. Davis concluded that literary fiction, as it has been promoted in Australia, was on the way out against a backdrop of structural changes to publishing:

> Since the mid-1990s the industry has globalised and consolidated to become an information-based business, beholden, in the case of nine out of ten of Australia's top companies, to global media giants. (119)

He noted how the industry has adapted to modern marketing techniques, and further noted that a radically different reality is at work from the 1960s, 1970s and 1980s, when there was heavy government support, along with the wave of nationalism that Flanagan alluded to, and when books were free of sales tax, and so forth. Davis added that 'the decline of the literary paradigm isn't simply to do with literature but with a broader reconceptualisation of the public sphere itself' (121). Of the economic ground beneath all of this, 'the abandonment of fixed exchange rates in the early 1980s ... and the axing by the Howard Government in 1996 of the Book Bounty had a disproportionate effect on literary titles since most illustrated titles were already printed offshore'.

Other factors have been the rise of 'celebrity' authors and subsequent profiling on the mass media, resulting in a short shelf-life of four to six weeks in shops. Although consumers may identify the magazines on the whole as literary, their shelf-life is usually two to three months in independent bookshops at most, and most of their sales are via subscription. Yet Davis noted factors that appear to be having effects, such as a decline in reading among the young, and the growth of interactive multimedia, niche markets and a trend to 'narrow casting' (127). He stated that 'analysis of the undergraduate offerings of leading Australian universities shows an overall decline in the teaching of contemporary Australian literature' (128). Therefore there may be, in the 2000s, a generation unreceptive to an overall discourse about contemporary writing and ideas in the journals. Whether this generation would demand that journals become more niche-orientated and serve their community of interest is interesting when one looks at the new journals that appeared after 2000.

Davis had other acute observations that feed into this discussion:
> Literary journals such as the *Australian Book Review* and *Meanjin* and the book pages of broadsheet newspapers have set themselves up as

nostalgic guardians of a (Mid-list) literary culture at odds with both the 'postmodern' academy and the new commercial imperatives. (129)

He claimed that the magazines were, to an extent, living off their reputations, in highly subsidised ways, and that after 2005 specifically, an under-resourced batch of new magazines posed a threat to this establishment, through new formats and by publishing many unknown authors. Evidence of this has been available 'in the rise of alternative literary festivals, a live reading circuit' (130), and more experimental publishers such as Sleepers in Melbourne. There was a triumphalist tone to his piece in that Davis seemed to be talking about the declining influence of the kind of elites he had little time for when he wrote *Gangland*.

The article was not without its critics, such as the then editor of *Overland*, Nathan Hollier, who argued about Davis's understanding of economics and power, and who was clearly defending the idea of a national project in the face of scepticism. Hollier suggested that

> Davis' diagnosis of the 'death' of literature seems informed by a desire, very common among cultural studies intellectuals influenced by postmodernism, to assert that they have a unique insight into contemporary social change and the future shape of society, and that, alone among the fusty halls of academe, they are 'down with the kids' (hence the emphasis on new technology and the attraction to the idea of historical spirit). ('Diagnosing the death' 14)

All well and good, as there is always the ghost of a 'cultural cringe' in Australia, and much of it has come from the cool indifference of much of cultural studies in the universities. However, Hollier's attack had an element of trying to shoot the messenger, as much of what Davis was suggesting could very well be still working its way through current social formations — which is not going to be good news for the literary magazines in this discussion. Most of them, in the first instance, are about the 'local', due to the mere fact of where they publish, irrespective of their ultimate ambitions. The extent to which the new grassroots movements Davis speaks of will be co-opted by the remnants of his old establishment, such as the literary pages of the

Age, would be fascinating to watch. Token gestures would probably result. In broad terms, Davis's prescription that 'the cultural nationalist, protectionist moment is over' (131) is astute, if uncomfortable, and would be a situation that the magazines had to face whether they like it or not. In other words, what we see as Australian literature has been promoted and sustained by an ageing generation of 'true believers'.

If Davis is right (and he could well be), cultural nationalism was a brief phase compared to the 'cultural cringe' of most of the twentieth century in Australia, first identified, as I have previously discussed, by AA Phillips in his article of the same name. Phillips 'identified a species he called "the denaturalised intellectual" as the Cringe's unhappiest victim — and cursed him down to "his indifferent eyebrows"' (McPhee 58). Although we might not see ourselves as second-rate English scholars, readers and writers any more, we may well have new masters, as Hilary McPhee suggested in 2010 when she wrote that

> nearly twelve years of the Howard government, followed by three years of Rudd and Gillard, have ensured that the old Cringe, which Phillips saw as a form of estrangement of the intellectual, has morphed into a kind of stylish but timid conformity. (60)

There is some evidence that these symptoms can be discerned in a number of the newer magazines.

Davis's discussion of the declining viability behind literary fiction was a description of a commerce that was relatively flush compared to the commercial realities of the magazines. The magazines have always (with rare exceptions such as *Australian Short Stories*) been even more marginal to marketers and thus bookshops than literary fiction, for they are not in the business of selling these types of magazines. When stocked by booksellers, the reason has often been that they are doing something 'worthy'. Thus, in effect, the boom of the 1970s was a crack in time, and those magazines which continued through the 1980s and 1990s had to, in varying degrees, adjust to the new climate described above, accept their ongoing marginalisation or plan different strategies.

Also, there would not be much joy coming out of the much vaunted creative industries in and around the universities, despite rhetoric about student publication. Richard Florida had published *The Rise of the Creative Class* in 2003, in which he argued that there was in a shift in some Western economies, where creativity had presumably morphed into the creation of class fractions that were inspiring new ways of conceptualising problems and solutions and creating new kinds of jobs in a lateral environment. Much of that argument is naïve, as it precludes land, labour and capital in wealth creation, shown graphically by the global financial crisis in 2008. Malcolm King offered up one of the consequences, stating that '[i]t's clear when university teachers and marketers talk about creativity or creative writing what they are really talking about is another C-word: commodification' (27).

In between time, in Australia at least, considerable amounts of federal research money was thrown in the direction of the creative industries by institutions such as the Queensland University of Technology in Brisbane, which had been creating interdisciplinary creative arts faculties — unlike the older universities, which were holding onto their traditional hierarchical structures. During the 2000s, though, somewhere in all this discourse, little practical assistance was on offer to the literary magazine, which had to negotiate its way through significant changes in its own corner of the creative industry. In broad terms, the 2000s witnessed a growth in arts bureaucracies and of research into the industry, but with marginal adherence to the effectiveness of grassroots business models. Rhetoric, rather than action, was on the rise. Concurrently, creative writing as a discipline in the humanities was trying to find its feet surrounded by a battle over its own theory and practice with little time to consider its role in an open-ended national project, or even to consider whether that was relevant.

Whether creative writing students and teachers supported the magazines of the 1990s and the early millennium would turn out to be a moot point.

15. New magazines

In any case, the early years of the new millennium, unpredictably, witnessed the birth of a number of new magazines — partly, it appears, as a response to a publishing crisis for new writers. It was also apparent that non-fiction (as a broad definition) was outselling fiction in the marketplace. Most of the new magazines would then heavily promote essays and creative non-fiction in such an environment.

In 2003, Griffith University decided to upgrade its intellectual profile (at a time when most universities were leaving the difficult business of supporting such unpredictable ventures) by creating the *Griffith Review* under the editorship of Julianne Schultz, a professor at Griffith University. The *Griffith Review* was offered financial and in-kind support from the university, in an interesting move from an institution that was not a part of the Group of Eight.[2] The charter for Schultz was to make the *Griffith Review* largely a non-fiction journal that would participate and prefigure national debate. This was during a time when the conventional wisdom in publishing continually stressed that literary fiction did not sell but that non-fiction in its various guises did well. Unknown authors, though, were rarely published in its pages.

---

[2] The Group of Eight (Go8) is a coalition of what are considered to be leading Australian universities, distinguished from other Australian universities in a number of ways. For more details, see https://go8.edu.au.

Phillip Edmonds

Figure 10: Cover of the Griffith Review, no 35

Thus the *Griffith Review* has successfully anticipated republican debates, for example, and initiated themed issues such as 'Re-imagining Australia'. Schultz was a public intellectual during a time when university-employed academics were withdrawing from public space into specialised enclaves. In a sense, she shrewdly anticipated developments in the zeitgeist, publishing articles, for instance, by Marcia Langton, Noel Pearson and Peter Sutton, whose views were contrary to the established wisdom on Indigenous policy after the 1970s. In its early years, the *Griffith Review* was designed like a book, consisted of over 200 pages, and consolidated the general move, over three decades, away from magazine formats to chunkier, more 'serious' constructions.

The creation of the *Griffith Review* was the most serious incursion undertaken by a university into publishing a literary magazine in decades. The University of Melbourne had supported *Meanjin* for many years after Clem Christesen moved it to Melbourne from Brisbane; the University of Sydney had consistently helped out *Southerly*; and more recently, Victoria University has been giving *Overland* in-kind and facility support. But overall, the universities had retreated from involvement. Griffith gave the new magazine offices to use and the facility of some paid full- and part-time staff, amongst other in-kind support, to start the magazine. By the late 2000s, the *Griffith Review* was seen as a place to publish, having achieved promotional visibility; and because of its regularity and design, it made the leap from a little magazine into that of a hegemonic site of perceived significance.

The facilities mentioned above meant that the *Griffith Review* could promote itself vigorously at literary festivals and set up its own lectures and functions to market its themed issues. Concurrently, it often sold some of its essays and non-fiction to newspapers such as the *Age* and the *Australian* as well as to the Australian Broadcasting Corporation. Initially, it was distributed by ABC books, through the high-profile publisher Allen & Unwin. These developments were taking place at a time when *Meanjin* was moving away from its former political, non-fiction constituency as an agenda-setter and endeavouring to hook up with a younger, less seemingly didactic demographic. More to the point, there had not been a journal of such ambition in Australia for decades. Whether it was a literary magazine was another question, in that — although it published original short fiction (usually the winners of Griffith University's annual Josephine Ulrick Prizes for Literature and Poetry) and the odd poem — original creative writing was a small part of the magazine. By 2010, it was publishing fiction largely in one edition a year as an annual fiction issue to seemingly satisfy the grant requirements of the Literature Board. Other changes included a co-publishing arrangement with Text Publishing in Melbourne, giving the magazine more of a promotional profile. The 2010 annual fiction edition contained nineteen fiction authors, plus memoir writing, an essay and some poetry. A good number of the fiction authors were also Text authors.

It is rare in Australia for a little magazine to have a large distributor, thereby offering up the possibility that a magazine could achieve higher sales because it is seen to be available. Having a base in both Brisbane and Melbourne has also meant that the *Griffith Review* is visible outside the enclaves of the respective inner cities, which have been the ghetto of most magazines. The rise of the *Griffith Review* also went some way to highlighting the fact that Brisbane (and Queensland) was not the cultural backwater it had once been seen to be (by those in the south) under the Bjelke-Petersen National Party government in the 1970s and into the early 1980s. I would argue that it has a level of organisational support not seen in Australia so far: it is a professional journal, light years away from the more occasional, craft-based, small-scale publications which have characterised much of the story so far.

So, then, the *Griffith Review* was making waves during a time when *Meanjin* was forced into a corner, without the unequivocal support that *Griffith Review* attracted from its host. As evidence of the instability, *Meanjin* had six editors between 1982 and 2011: Judith Brett (1982-87), Jenny Lee (1987-94), Christina Thompson (1994-98), Stephanie Holt (1998-2001), Ian Britain (2001-08) and Sophie Cunningham (2008-11). Lee, Thompson, Holt and Cunningham could be seen as innovators influenced by cultural studies, feminism and changing demographics, whereas Britain was a historian (not unlike Jim Davidson) — he was very much out of the Clem Christesen tradition, when the magazine had built up a stable constituency and, it seemed, an identifiable readership. As with all cultural icons, perception is everything — which is not to say that *Meanjin* was not a pre-eminent place for new writers to publish, but that challenges were appearing from *Heat* and the *Griffith Review*, both of which magazines had managed to create enough prestige to signal that they were significant.

In the early 2000s, *Meanjin* seemed wedged between the *Griffith Review* and *Overland* in terms of its Left/liberal constituency in a small marketplace. *Meanjin* was also not largely a magazine of original creative writing, which might give it another form of difference. Cunningham's predecessor, Ian Britain, had during his time as editor become notable for his themed issues, including one on rock and roll which sold out; but in 2008 Cunningham jettisoned that format — unlike the *Griffith Review*, which was persisting with what it saw as a useful publishing frame and marketing device. Allied to that, Ivor Indyk's press, Giramondo, had initiated a literary publishing program that featured writers such as Brian Castro, and most importantly, the Miles Franklin winner, Alexis Wright. This gave Giramondo, and by reflection *Heat*, established literary credentials necessary in any battle over hierarchy.

In 2007, the University of Melbourne decided to 'spill' the existing board of the magazine over a proposal to give the administration and distribution over to Melbourne University Publishing. Ian Britain resisted the changes, along the lines that he felt that they could compromise the magazine's independence and the print-based nature of the publication. In February 2008 he was replaced by Sophie Cunningham, and *Meanjin* moved to Melbourne University Press, and a new editorial board was appointed. Despite the magazine's perceived prominence, it, too, suffered from too few paid staff. In 2008, Cunningham said that her office manager had not had a holiday over the past two years (Ommundsen & Jacklin 64). Nevertheless, *Meanjin*, although over the years having disputes as to its assistance levels from the Australia Council, assumed, like any cultural institution of over fifty years' duration, that it was significant and should be supported in a general debate about support. As Ommundsen and Jacklin suggested, the debate was about

> issues such as their perennially low circulation on the one hand, and their critical importance in providing a platform for new writing on the other. In the intervening ten or twelve years, the issues remain the same, the one significant addition being the possibilities of digital delivery and the potential, thereby, to increase readership. (65)

Irrespective of debates about hard-copy or online format, magazine editors are unanimous about the fact that the long-term role of their publications is to provide a platform for new literary talent. Examples have been Alice Pung, who was first published in *Meanjin* in 2002, and who later went on to publish *Unpolished Gem* in 2007 through Black Inc. Other journals can cite similar examples from their own experience. *Wet Ink*, which was established in 2005, published many, not to mention *Overland* and some of the others. Although statistics surrounding the number of copies sold and subscription levels are often difficult to trace, any magazine that sells more than 2000 copies is doing well in the current climate. The reach of a magazine is also important, and in *Meanjin*'s case (in 2008) it 'indicates that roughly two thirds of its subscription-base is Victorian, just over one sixth is from interstate, and just less than one-sixth is international' (67). This suggests that the magazine, even after over fifty years of being Australia's pre-eminent literary publication, was then in some respects not a national publication.

The *Meanjin* name did not even make distribution to the retail trade any easier, it seemed. Ian Britain, during his time as editor, was 'shocked at the ABC bookshops that refused to stock *Meanjin* because their commitment was to a similar periodical (the *Griffith Review*) which they partly sponsor' (qtd. in Ommundsen & Jacklin 67). He noted how *Meanjin* had good media representation on different ABC shows 'and yet the ABC shops for whatever reasons would not stock us' (67). This was one example of the problems that literary magazines had at the retail end, probably because bookshops were not really much good at selling magazines (and would demand 40 per cent discounts, whereas magazines usually attracted 25 per cent). It was also because the retail book trade, excluding the large chains, is tribal and disconnected, while in the chains themselves, the book trade is at the whims of central buyers, who are often out of touch with local developments. In other words, some shops would stock copies of one magazine and hope to sell them, while the newer magazines could be intermittent and hard to track — further emphasising that the literary magazine, during most of its incarnations in Australia, has been a stubbornly difficult and problematic commodity.

Nevertheless, in 2008, Cunningham expressed her frustrations with Pan Macmillan, *Meanjin*'s national trade distributor: 'There is a tension between the needs of a large distribution warehouse that works with thousands of titles and the needs of a small quarterly journal' (qtd. in Ommundsen & Jacklin 68). In other words, *Meanjin*, like many of the others, was continually having frustrations with distributors whose priorities were bestselling titles. Meanwhile for bookshops, the issue was that you could really only sell magazines face-out, given you had the space. Some magazines such as the *Lifted Brow*, *Voiceworks*, *Wet Ink* and *Overland*, were satisfied using smaller companies who specialised in niche magazines. As I have detailed, the situation was not radically different from the 1970s, even if booksellers then were more nationalistic.

Cunningham was hopeful of attracting a younger readership through her radical revamp of the design — colour and illustrations plus photographic essays — while retaining the journal's longstanding subscribers. She hoped the new design would also improve retail sales, attributing the American journal *McSweeney's*, founded by Dave Eggers, as an influence on her design changes. *Meanjin* was being renovated and whether enough people would like it would be another question. As Gruber put it at the time:

> [A] fresh lick of paint will hopefully dispel conceptions that *Meanjin* is a fuddy-duddy. Cunningham's is a tricky inheritance, however, will the groovy new look alienate the loyal readership, which tends to be over 50? (13)

Meanwhile in 2005, a new publishing house, Sleepers, published an annual short fiction anthology, the *Sleepers Almanac* — evidence of new challenges to the established magazines (and publishers), who were the only real survivors of the 1990s. *Wet Ink* was also established in 2005, with the express intention of promoting what its editors saw as a new wave of writing. Later that decade, in Melbourne — traditionally the home of the little magazine — *Harvest*, the *Lifted Brow*, *Etchings* and *Kill Your Darlings* were created, suggesting a desire on the part of those involved to be proactive rather than reactive in general terms. Each of these magazines were born (apart from *Kill Your Darlings*) for better or worse, in an optimistic, credit-filled economic climate prior to the first global financial crisis in 2009.

Also, all of the above inherited the massive changes in computerised technology, so that their publications aspired to market visibility and to an extent the advantages of digital printing during the mid-2000s. Digital printing had the potential to change the face of book publishing through print-on-demand options for short runs of non-commercial books, as a way around previously expensive short offset runs, where economies of scale could not be achieved. For magazines, though, which printed over 500 copies, digital printing had limited appeal, as they were tied into printing a designated number of copies to satisfy subscribers and retail sales. In this way, the magazines were a cumbersome product without the potential flexibility of the book. In any case, of the magazines listed above, none, it seemed, would look ephemeral, temporary, or cheap like many of the little magazines of the 1970s.

The birth of *Wet Ink* in Adelaide in late 2005 prefigured much of the upsurge in small-press publishing over the next five years. *Wet Ink* was formed by a group largely associated with the creative writing program at the University of Adelaide, plus two people from a design company (SlincCreative) who had been thinking of a similar idea — which was to create a magazine for new writers. Planning took place over most of 2005, and the first edition appeared in December 2005, launched in Adelaide by JM Coetzee. The group made the decision to involve relatively unknown people in editorial

Figure 11: Cover of Wet Ink, no 25 (2011)

decisions; and in producing the magazine, they elected two managing editors, Dominique Wilson and myself. Emmett Stinson, a postgraduate student, came up with the name after some meetings brainstorming ideas. The first two poetry editors also — Stephen Lawrence and Heather Taylor Johnson — brought infectious energy to the group.

There was a strong sense of organisation, and a desire to create something sustainable. Several years before I had theorised my frustrations with existing literary publications and suggested a new model that could be different from highly subsidised and expensively produced magazines that remained in permanent crisis ('Respectable or risqué'). *Wet Ink* was designed as a new model that could appeal to general readers (a third way in fact): a magazine that looked good while being portable at the same time. It would be a creative writing magazine, containing short fiction, some poetry and creative non-fiction without any academic pretensions — a forum, if you like, for different writers and styles, and for the type of pluralism that was evident at grassroots levels of the writing community. It was to be a magazine that did not pretend to be a book, and did not have a stapled 'mass' look. The original group wanted to create a structure that was as independent as possible — they did not want to be too tied to a university, or too dependent on grants and subsidies. This was a very idealistic idea, for a product that was then not in existence. So as to create the necessary capital for the first issues, an advertising representative was hired on commission — an idea which small magazines in Australia had rarely been able to contemplate.

Wet Ink would be a magazine of new writing, devoting most of its pages to original creative writing from around Australia. We wanted to provide more space for writers without feeling the need to publish scholarly articles. Its first editorial was another way of saying that original creative writing is research in its own terms and should be judged as such. *Wet Ink* would go on to become a magazine devoted largely to original creative writing and some non-fiction, a utopian gesture which was intensely ideological in that new writers usually are not bankable commodities in an era where idealism generally, since the 1970s at least, has a pragmatic, promotional edge.

There was no direct sponsorship or subsidy from any one educational institution, and it would take time to establish a subscription list. There was also evidence that creative writing courses in universities and colleges were setting up a great deal of unmet desire among budding writers around Australia. *Wet Ink* was to be a magazine based in the community, yet somewhere along the line it would cater to this new constituency. Its model was ideology-free compared to *Meanjin*, *Overland* and *Quadrant*, which might prove to a bonus or a promotional headache as time went on. In the first editorial Dominique Wilson and I wrote that there was talent 'crying out for exposure' and added:

> There is also a sense that our cultural administrators and policy makers are blasé about the current situation. Thirty years after the innovations of the Australia Council, the limited level of international success some Australian authors have achieved has become a self-satisfied mantra in publishing and arts administration. We believe the production of creative writing requires positive outlets of dissemination, rather than being continually marginalised, for better or worse, in universities. (Edmonds & Wilson 1)

This was a similar articulation to the sentiments expressed by AA Phillips in his essay, 'The Cultural Cringe', in 1950. The magazine was the first attempt at creating an ongoing publication in Adelaide since the 1970s. The length of time between attempts was partly due to problems such as a smallish population base.

Wet Ink's advent was positively received and actively encouraged by people like the then Chair of Creative Writing at Adelaide University, Nicholas Jose, who realised that it could have a positive spin-off effect locally and nationally. Even so, *Wet Ink* made three applications for support from Arts SA in the first three years of the magazine, and all of them were rejected; and there was some indifference within the university. One application, in 2006, was rejected because the magazine refused to quantify the number of South Australians it would publish in the following financial year, another under the pretext of it being a student publication. Yet it clearly was not, and did not intend to be, a student publication — especially because the student anthology model was outworn by then and very difficult to sell.

In any case, the Literature Board granted *Wet Ink* some support in 2006. A distributor, Bookwise, was found, enabling the magazine to find exposure in interstate bookshops and newsagents, and the group worked assiduously on promoting the name around the country, knowing that the magazine could not rely on any one city for support. Coming from Adelaide was a weakness in that the place was relatively small and unconfident as to its representations — but it was also a strength, in that the magazine had to work to find exposure. The magazine also had to overcome recurring cash flow problems in its first three years, but by 2009 a reasonably healthy subscriber-base was established, which helped it weather such periods.

The format of *Wet Ink* was designed with A5 colour covers, perfect-bound, of roughly 60-70 pages, and with no gloss stock or colour photos (either inside or out), so as to look good yet be a magazine and not a book. In broad terms, the early models for size (if not contents) were *Overland* and the *Australian Book Review*. Despite its conservative use of paper stock, the magazine was unashamedly attractive, and in that way, it threw down the gauntlet to the design values of the established magazines. This was celebrated by Jane Sullivan in March 2007 in the *Age*, when noting how the magazine was responding to an upsurge in new writing and small-press activity:

> I'm particularly impressed with *Wet Ink* ... a lively and beautifully produced literary magazine from an Adelaide based team ... In true democratic style, the work of established and emerging writers sits alongside the work of complete newcomers. ('Bright spots' 30)

In the five years from 2005-2010, *Wet Ink* had published more original creative writing (mostly short fiction), but also creative non-fiction and poetry, than any other small magazine in the country, and had been instrumental in giving writers the confidence to continue. The magazine played a role in reactivating the small-press scene around Australia by offering a model of what was possible, and — in Adelaide at least — contributing to an upsurge in grassroots activity in and around a conservative city. One example was

Staples. Instead of waiting for official blessing, a postgraduate at Adelaide University, Shannon Burns, started *Staples* in 2007, a zine-sized, stapled publication similar to some of the cheaper models of the early 1970s. Apart from the need to produce it cheaply, Burns saw it 'as a place where the work would be privileged rather than any pretentious format' ('Letter to the author' 1). It appeared seven times and published an impressive range of known and unknown writers.

In broad terms, *Wet Ink* was the first serious attempt to create an ongoing publication in Adelaide for thirty years, and there was some understated resentment. There was a view held that I was an 'outsider', coming to Adelaide from Victoria, via Queensland, and that Dominique Wilson was an unknown postgraduate student at the time. As I mentioned above, at one meeting with Arts South Australia in 2006, the editorial team of *Wet Ink* was asked to give a percentage of how many South Australian authors it would publish in the following year. The team declined to answer, along the lines that the editors, did not, and would not, choose material on such a parochial basis. In any case, *Wet Ink* qualified for federal Literature Board support that year.

Among the writers supported by *Wet Ink* were Chris Womersley, Favel Parrett, Wayne Macauley, Sally Breen, Patrick Holland, AS Patric, Catherine Harris, Siall Waterbright, Krissy Kneen, David Jagger, Ronnie Scott, James May, Felicity Castagna, Josephine Rowe, Amy Espeseth and Gretchen Shirm — up-and-coming authors, some of whom would go on to publish individual collections of short fiction. Alongside them were established names such as Mike Ladd, Nigel Krauth, Judith Rodriguez, Thomas Shapcott, John Kinsella and Michael Wilding, among others. In other words, there was a blend of known and new, alongside an interview in each issue.

In the editorial for the twenty-second issue, marking the fifth birthday of the magazine, Wilson and I wrote:

> [W]e have been acutely conscious of the fact that there are many writers and readers outside the literary networks of the major cities who want to

be connected, and we want to hear from you. Overseas, we sell copies in Singapore, NZ, the US, Canada, the UK ... And even Dubai. (1)

This had been achieved, partly, because the internet had offered up cheap ways of promotion. Unfortunately, apart from the *Australian*, the Melbourne *Age* had never reviewed *Wet Ink* in its five years of publication. In 2010, despite some of the more established magazines being caught up in a merry-go-round of status listing of peer-reviewed journals, *Wet Ink* resisted the urge, believing that it was a gun to the head of the possibility to further create a broader audience for new Australian writing. And the editors of *Wet Ink*, although it had a limited online presence, were confident in the belief that readers would continue to support hard-copy publications.

Because of its regional base, *Wet Ink* had to be outward-looking, and the model was idealistically populist. In fact, after the launch in Adelaide in 2005, Dominique Wilson stated that *Wet Ink* was not going to be a literary magazine with a capital 'L', articulating the fear that in Australia, all too often, the literary was unfairly marginalised, and also giving voice to a recognition that, for whatever reason, the cultural landscape was too diversified to only respond to hierarchy. Even so, *Wet Ink* also wanted to get away from the specialised and inward-looking language which had characterised the pages of many of the other publications.

After five years, the magazine had survived without institutional support, apart from some advertising, through intense voluntary labour in the first two year. However, it moved to partial remuneration for key staff after 2007 — a realistic move, as the experience of Australian small magazines is that it is impossible to create sustainable models on the back of the unpaid surplus value of voluntary labour over long periods. If the original group had any aspirations for longevity, it did not dare to state them openly in 2005. Yet the magazine had survived through having a relatively diversified cash flow, even though it could not then appeal for donations from an established community, in contrast to magazines such as *Overland*, which had been branded in an ideological fashion. *Wet Ink* would have to also meet the challenge of the e-revolution and an ongoing crisis in retail book and magazine selling after 2010.

In 2007, two years after *Wet Ink* appeared, *Harvest* was formed in Melbourne, and was, unashamedly, intent on publishing new writers. The founding editors were Davina Bell, Julia Carlomagno and Rachael Howlett, and its first issue in June 2008 was an aesthetic triumph, in that it was printed on recycled paper with a heavy reliance on colour reproductions throughout, printed on very expensive paper stock. Whether that kind of production was sustainable over the longer term would be an interesting question. The editors described it as 'Melbourne-born, Melbourne-bred, and Melbourne-based' (*Harvest* n.p.) — a description which is an advantage in Australia if starting a new magazine, but which might be a hindrance if wanting to continue and attract readers from around the rest of the country. The original *Harvest* group was brought together by RMIT's Professional Writing and Editing course (and some initial funding from RMIT), and the initial publicity stressed idealism and a desire to 'produce a tactile and engaging publication for a well-read audience. An audience that believes that good writing can be both attractive and intelligent' (n.p.).

The editors stated a belief that their magazine offered 'a visceral experience, a pleasure to sit down and read' as opposed to cyber-reading. They saw online sites mainly as a gateway to print. Fiona Gruber reported that

> they call themselves a magazine because they say journal sounds too stuffy, and cite as inspirations the irrepressively hip and quirky American journal *McSweeny's Quarterly Concern* ... and the Australian quarterly *Dumbo Feather*, which specialises in autobiographical pieces. (13)

This was very laudable as, on the whole, the literary magazine in Australia was rarely a site for adventurous design. The problem for *Harvest* was that it was publishing into a much smaller market than *McSweeny's*. Short and relatively expensive print runs had, and still are, a problem in Australia.

The first poetry editor was Geoff Lemon, who was replaced by Josephine Rowe in mid-2009. By the start of 2011, *Harvest* had published five issues over a three-and-a-half year period, suggesting either that it was not the plan to publish quarterly, or that a more periodical plan was acceptable. Even so, it is hard for any small magazine to establish a subscription when it appears occasionally. To appear regularly, a magazine needs a growing number of subscribers to generate cash flow. *Harvest* in those five issues published a range of new authors including Jessica Au, Patrick Cullen, Nathan Curnow and Ryan O'Neill, among others who would go on to publish individual books, along with members of a group of writers who had previously been in a strata that was unpublicised.

Both *Wet Ink* and *Harvest* threw down a challenge to *Overland* and *Meanjin*, who were looking at ways to modernise and revamp their production values. In particular, *Meanjin* went through a thorough redesign under Sophie Cunningham, introducing coloured sections and funky typefaces, and at a later stage it put 'the best of new writing in Australia' on the masthead. Coincidentally, *Wet Ink* had on its masthead 'the magazine of new writing', and it would not be long before the *Griffith Review* was talking about 'emerging writers' and establishing prizes to that affect. There was a great deal of grassroots activity in terms of new writing, the most visible of which was in Melbourne, and the reasons for it could well have been the upsurge in creative writing courses at the universities and colleges. Whether more readers could be found for this new writing would be answered by whether the small magazines survived the decade in whatever format.

16. THE PROBLEM OF POETRY AGAIN

In terms of poetry, John Tranter's response to the upsurge in the late 1990s was to establish *Jacket*, an online literary magazine that is published two or three times a year. According to its website on 20 May 2011, the magazine is

> distributed to every town, city and country in the world via the internet and given away free ... *Jacket* has no advertising, and no source of income. Contributors offer their work free. The staff (of two) work for nothing, and basic internet costs are covered by Australian Literary Management. (n.p.)

Between 1997 and 2010, Tranter and Pam Brown (who joined in 2004 as associate editor) put out forty issues of *Jacket*, containing 7000 pages on the internet and featuring special issues on Polish, Turkish, Mexican and Canadian poetry, among others. There have been co-productions with *Salt* in the UK and *Verse* magazine in the US. The website added, 'The homepage has recorded more than three-quarters of a million visits overall' — a statement replete with a note of glorious relief that poetry, via the internet, was presumably out of its ghetto. But the number of hits does not always tell the full story, as many people surf the net and do not stay for long on any one site.

From anecdotal net evidence, though, *Jacket* appears to have been referred to and quoted on very regularly between 1997 and 2010. Yet despite its presumed internet reach, 'in the thirteen years of its existence, *Jacket* never had a grant from the Literature Board, and was never the subject of a paper presented at an Association for the Study of Australian Literature

Conference' (Tranter, 'The elephant' n.p.). Tranter attributed that to its international focus and the parochialism of arts bureaucrats in Australia. As from the first issue in 2011, *Jacket* was to be published out of the University of Pennsylvania in the US, hosted by the Kelly Writers House and PennSound. Subsequent evidence suggests that since then the amount of original poetry published has declined as 'it needs to fit into the US university system and become a peer-reviewed journal of research and review' (n.p.).

Leaving *Jacket*'s excellence or otherwise aside, an understated question would always be: How are value and hierarchy inscribed and calculated in the literary magazine? Given that writers invest a great deal into their work, would they see online publication as the cheap and lazy option? Certainly, prestige was being calculated over time in the rise of online peer-review academic journals such as *Text: Journal of Writing and Writing Courses*, but it was one of the first of its kind, and time would demonstrate whether this type of magazine would remain scarce and therefore valuable. If anyone could put up an online poetry magazine, who would care?

For argument's sake, the effort invested in hard copy meant, on the surface at least, that publishers cared about the work they had before them. Also, there was the strangest phenomenon of all — that the 'chunky' book-like characteristics of *Heat*, *Southerly* and *Meanjin* contributed significantly to those magazines becoming sites of prestige in a disposable age, a way of discovering status in the publication pile. Support from the Literature Board was another mark of status, in a general crisis over hierarchy. Whether *Southerly*, *Meanjin* and *Heat* had many readers was almost irrelevant. *Jacket*, without paid subscriptions and any payments to its authors, had undercut its own product, and might — like other internet publications over time — wander in cyberspace, become popular and yet by some determinations remain unrecognised. The question was: When would online journals attract status? Were they still seen as easy forms of publication?

Aside from *Island*, another magazine came out of Tasmania between 1987 and 2010. *Famous Reporter*, edited by Ralph Wessman, was a biennial print and online journal 'with a decidedly Tasmanian flavour'. Published by Walleah Press, it also put out the *Currajah* blog, with up-to-date news and information about literary happenings around Australia. The online version was an innovation presumably made to overcome the distribution problems of being away from the mainland for any hard-copy editions, in that, in Australia, it is generally assumed that excellence comes out of Melbourne and Sydney. Despite this, *Famous Reporter* received many good notices and published a variety of authors from outside Tasmania.

As intimated, publishing poetry, in whatever format, is fraught, as it brings with it years of inherited cultural 'baggage', and a peculiar factionalism that is not always useful for the genre. In an earlier chapter, I alluded to the 'poetry wars' that were presumably between Les Murray and John Tranter and his troops, which could be said to have wasted energy when Australian poetry was undergoing continuing marginalisation. Leaving that issue aside, poetry in Australia is a highly subsidised art form. In 2002, the then Poetry Foundation launched a magazine called *Blue Dog: Australian Poetry* to appear biannually under the editorship of Ron Pretty, then at the University of Wollongong. For eight years *Blue Dog* was published in hard copy, the last one in December 2010, and currently it is an online journal, edited from Melbourne by Grant Caldwell. The history of *Blue Dog* shows that a journal devoted entirely to poetry will struggle in Australia unless it receives considerable backing from a host organisation. *Blue Dog* has survived as the *Australian Poetry Journal* but it has not had to negotiate its way to readers, because it has always had an organisation to fall back on — an experience radically dissimilar to most of the newer literary magazines between 1969-2010.

Cordite Poetry Review has proved to be a stayer. Established in 1997 by Adrian Wiggins and Peter Minter, it has been online since 2001, and it describes itself on its website as 'a journal of Australian poetry and poetics'. It is published three times a year and features local and international work. The *Cordite* archives house over a thousand individual poems and a collection of reviews, articles, interviews and audio works. It began as a print journal, and six issues were published in broadsheet form between 1997 and 2000. Contributors to the print versions included Robert Adamson, Judith Beveridge, MTC Cronin, John Kinsella, Anthony Lawrence, John Mateer, Peter Boyle, Gig Ryan and Dorothy Porter. *Cordite* is relatively rare among online journals in that it pays its contributors from a grant from the Australia Council. Over the past ten years it has published thirty-five issues online, and has pursued a themed approach to most issues. In the late 2000s, the birth of a number of online poetry journals, such as *Cordite*, was good for the form as reviews of new books of poetry were very rare in the literary pages of major newspapers, and the established magazines only published three or four poems an issue at the most.

Mascara Literary Review (born in 2007) is a biannual, online publication consisting of poetry and some essays and reviews, published in association with the School of Humanities and Social Sciences at the University of Newcastle. The editors are, at the time of writing, Michelle Cahill and Kim Cheng Boey and its contents are an eclectic mix of well-known poets and some lesser known ones. The publication is evidence of a developing subculture within small-press publishing around poets and the conversations they have about poetry, in that they all seem to know one another. The extent, though, of its influence is unknown as it is with many of the online journals. It, too, is supported by the Australia Council. Subscriptions to the magazine are available (as is the case with *Cordite*), but everything they have published is online, so the model is dependent on taxpayer support as its potential for other forms of income are problematic. Like *Jacket*, it has undercut its own exchange value and is not probably a good model for poets who want to have an income of sorts (the assumption being that poets will always need grants) and who are not employees of universities — in itself, a form of self-imposed marginalisation.

Leaving poetry aside, there were several births late in the decade. *Ampersand*, a quarterly (although it has not, in fact, appeared as regularly as that) from Sydney, has an interdisciplinary basis extending into the visual arts. The editor is Alice Gage, and it clearly sees itself as cutting edge, a specialist in avant-garde conversations, with some of the most challenging artwork in any Australian small magazine. In a paperback size, not dissimilar to paperbacks of the early twentieth century, it is a magazine to watch. From 2011, *Ampersand* was published in association with *Art & Australia*, which will bring with it useful resources. *Ampersand* has all the potential to become a limited-edition type of publication — to become fetishised over time — as it will not be popular in the conventional sense of the word. *Cutwater* made a brief appearance in late 2009, from the New South Wales central coast, edited by Daniel Collins and Sam Twyford-Moore in hard-copy book form with an accompanying blog.

Emerging out of the flurry of online publications (mainly poetry-oriented) in the late 2000s was the realisation that there was, if not an underground of new writers, then a republic of people who on occasion were published in hard-copy (above-ground) journals which were considered established — such as *Overland*, *Meanjin* and the *Griffith Review* — but who were largely unknown except on the web and were pushing for recognition. *Wet Ink*, *Voiceworks*, *Etchings*, *Harvest* and the *Lifted Brow* had been publishing some of these people, confirming the fact that their existence as magazines was partly a respond to the upsurge. The poets — through *Mascara*, *Cordite*, *Jacket* et al. — were having conversations online.

In August 2010, so as to join the fray, a new online journal called *Verity La* came on board with that conversation, publishing mainly short prose. It brought with it the attractions and advantages of online publishing, including flexibility, good design of its site (at least in its own case), the ability to publish almost an unlimited amount of material and minimal production costs. It described itself as

> an online creative arts journal, publishing short fiction and poetry, cultural comment, photo media, interviews and review … [W]e are interested in new voices, different voices, progressive voices … *Verity La* is updated whenever very good writing comes our way. Why 'Verity La'? It's an abbreviation of 'Verity Lane', a hidden back-alley in the small Australian city where the journal was born. (n.p.)

The magazine was co-edited by Nigel Featherstone and Alec Patric. Contributors so far have included a wide range of conceptual artists and writers: Daniel Armstrong, Neil Boyack, Ashley Capes, Shane Jesse Christmass, Nathan Curnow, Christopher Currie, SJ Finn, David Francis, Alice Gage, Tiggy Johnson, Josephine Rowe, Wayne Macauley, Kirk Marshall, Angela Meyer, Pierz Newton-John and Ronnie Scott, among others— most hardly household names, but writers who were writing actively during the late 2000s, some of whom would be picked up by book publishers like Text Publishing and Sleepers in Melbourne.

Verity La gave these writers some visibility, since all content was free online, but people could subscribe to the blog. This made the journal another example of ways in which writers can circumvent traditional gatekeepers yet anxiously undercut their own exchange value in an environment where copyright laws were seriously lagging behind changes to the means of production. *Verity La* was proving the case that blogs can not only be useful promotional tools, but also venues for an electronic extension of discussions between like-minded people. This is reassuring, but could it be potentially insular?

In Queensland, another online journal, *Perilous Adventures*, had also been publishing interesting material for several years under the guidance of Nike Bourke. From Newcastle, New South Wales, *Swamp* (a rather unappealing name) was an online only journal for creative writing postgraduates (with no subscription facility). It was supported by the School of Humanities and Social Sciences at the local university, under the editorship of Samantha Dagg. Even so, despite such online moves, and in a move that reasserted the continuing attraction of hard-copy publication, another magazine appeared in Melbourne despite weak retail conditions in December 2010. *21D* was a not-for-profit literary and art magazine which published fiction, non-fiction, poetry, photography and illustrations. Arising originally out of the Professional Writing & Editing course at the Council of Adult Education in Melbourne, it took its title from the meeting place of its first editorial team — 21 Degraves Street. Of similar size to *Wet Ink*, it was a very attractively designed magazine which integrated artwork with text. It was distributed in Australia by Speedimpex, the distributor of a number of the other small magazines, and received some support from Arts Hub, the creative and arts industry website.

17. A NEW DEMOGRAPHIC?

Informing and seemingly fertilising these developments was a 'republic' of new writers, some published in traditional terms, many of whom only frequented certain writers' festivals. If of a certain demographic, they went to the Emerging Writers' Festival, begun in Melbourne, and the Newcastle-based National Young Writers' Festival. Many of them published zines — small magazines of usually only 10-20 copies at the most, which were distributed among friends and the odd stranger. Zines were retro-moments in effect, and were even less ambitious in terms of preferred circulation than the more peripatetic publications of the late 1960s and early 1970s. Even in a time of reduced and reconfigured idealism, these writers, in terms of the festival in Newcastle, were participating in revitalising public spaces. They clearly realised that much of what was being published was for a middle-class, middle-aged, largely female readership of cultural consumers. Large numbers of them had also been initiated into notions of free cultural products through widespread downloading of musical products (for example, CDs) on the internet. Such free products undermined future income for musicians and creative writers under the guise of the democratisation of culture.

These young writers did not attend mainstream literary festivals on the whole, and were conspicuous by their absence from writers' centres and probably did not read the literary pages of the major newspapers, knowing full well that what they produced would not be noticed in those pages because as a certain kind of writer they (with a few, mainly non-fiction exceptions) had marginal potential for commodification. They participated in events other than the Newcastle Young Writers' Festival, including Fringe Festivals even though the notion of 'the fringe' was increasingly problematic as Fringe events were becoming more mainstream, and in a series of launches/parties. Whether this tendency was a sign of resignation about the fact that the means of literary production were unassailable, or a realisation that there was no need for change (and therefore no need to assemble an audience of readers), would be interesting to watch.

There were some similarities with the 1970s, in that writers will always congregate together, and the decade was noted for its readings. But during the 1970s, performance poetry had an edge to it in that middle-class readers were still able to be shocked, as even the more intellectual fraction of the class was relatively homogeneous. Book censorship was only lifted in Australia in 1972, so 'the new' was crisp, transgressive and unaffected by imitation. Many of the poetry readings by Pi O, for example, were disruptive of the printed word and an affront to linguistic consensus. But by the end of the century, much of that impulse had become blasé.

More to the point, it appeared that more people wanted to become celebrities. If late capitalism was anything at all, it was by the 2000s the living embodiment of libertarian anarchism with governments gesturing linguistically along the margins. What would be edgy and not worn out if political agency was so hard to delineate was a continuing question. If contemporary writing was to regain its quality of transgression, it might have to go slow and become more of a meditative space again, as it has often been in some of the literary magazines.

This group of young writers occupied that fractured post-modern moment where, as I suggested in my introduction, the past is too big and the present too quick. Simultaneously, the writers had tendencies to the pre-industrial and to the blasé consciousness of the post-industrial consumer. If anti-disciplinary tendencies were the main 1960s and 1970s inheritance, then by the end of the first decade of the millennium, as DeKoven has suggested,

> the political has come to be lodged primarily in questions of subjectivity ... [T]he subject is no longer clearly demarcated ... [M]appable space in Jameson's terms, has given way to postmodern hyperspace — mobile, decentred, nomadic, fragmented ... (17)

My qualification is that, apart from the new class of consumers of cultural products (which — facilitated by multimedia platforms — includes this new demographic of young writers), many people are localised in subcultures and workplaces which operate outside decentred space. The question of agency for the new demographic, then, also occupies an intersection that is indistinct, in that the deconstruction of linear stories has wounded even the idea of history. The writers' honest tendency is to be performative in the moment, and to have five minutes of fame, which may explain some of the small-magazine activity of the late 2000s. They also show a lack of plans as to longevity, a concept which could be inconceivable to them given the situation described above, and given the extreme libertarianism of the moment.

Over the forty years of this study, small magazines had generally cultivated an audience of like-minded people and they were sold at launches and events. However, by 2011 this tendency was endemic due to distribution problems in a largely unreceptive marketplace and had become a major alternative source of sales and promotion. The literature of this new republic that the magazines might well have to come to terms with was a much more private experience than that of their predecessors (yet more public in terms of the support for public reading spaces). On one level the new writers were captivated by the virtual world, and its smashing of old industrial restrictions, yet blasé enough about it to eulogise a purer, less complicated past — in the sense that both tendencies were an unacknowledged rejection of commodification. Whether they would be patient enough to relate to the old format (or commodity) of the literary magazine would be interesting to watch, as new models were emerging in the shape of the *Lifted Brow*, and to an extent, *Wet Ink*, through its design and publication of unknown authors.

Several ebb tides were at work in the late 2000s: a significant element of youthful disengagement, which appeared in response to a lowering of publishing expectations during a perceived publishing crisis, and arts administrators who threw money at a generalised 'problem' through supporting festivals, insinuating therefore that there were 'bread and circuses' solutions. Behind all the promotion and the activity, the great majority of the literary magazines remained in crisis to the extent that they were continually under-resourced and reliant on too few committed people because volunteerism appeared to be dwindling.

Back in the world of committed agenda-setting which *Overland* had set for itself through its history, in the late 2000s Jeff Sparrow took over the editorship from Nathan Hollier, the third relatively young editor after Stephen Murray-Smith, Barrett Reid and John McLaren, who had all come from the original group of early supporters. In 2008, *Overland* received $50 000 from the Australia Council and some money from Arts Victoria and in-kind support from Victoria University. Sparrow continued the initiative set in place by Ian Syson of the *Overland* public lecture series and attendance at writers' festivals, which had become essential sites for anyone seriously promoting Australian writing. 'This is how the literary magazine has to function these days. You have to establish a profile through publicity, through putting on forums, lectures, seminars', he said (qtd. in Ommundsen & Jacklin 71). The literary magazine was competing for attention within the expediential expansion of the entertainment industry and the incredible amount of noise on the internet. Most of the print magazines, then, competed for space on the programs of mainstream writers' festivals.

Sparrow also noted changes to the notion of cultural capital attached to literary production, noting that non-fiction was taking over from established literary genres in ways that Mark Davis had suggested in his 'The Decline of the Literary Paradigm in Australian Publishing'. Sparrow stated that,

> as the market demand for non-fiction displaces publication opportunities for literary production, especially in regards to short stories, poetry and literary essays, the work of literary magazines in maintaining support for writers in these genres becomes increasingly important. (Qtd. in Ommundsen & Jacklin 71)

Yet by the late 2000s there was evidence of a general move towards non-fiction (and creative non-fiction) in the pages of most of the magazines, the prime examples being the *Griffith Review* and *Meanjin*. Sparrow was also investing in upping the web profile of *Overland*: 'The question is increasingly that *Overland* is going to have to be more than a print journal' (qtd. in Ommundsen & Jacklin 72) — which was his way of relating to a younger demographic:

> I'd be surprised if there were a great proportion of young people who subscribe to magazines ... [W]hen you compare subscription numbers to literary websites and the huge number of hits they get, well, there is this question: how long will we keep doing the things we have been doing? ... [W]e just need to find the model that works for it. (72)

His observation was strikingly similar to the dilemmas facing all magazines — how to develop a model that is 'groovy' and interactive without compromising the subscription base, which, for better or worse, was a major source of cash flow. *Quadrant* by 2010 had designed a subscription model that would be either/or hard-copy or digital, the *Australian Book Review* instituted a joint subscription in 2011, while *Wet Ink* was resisting the urge by only posting 'sneak peeks' from an issue, in the belief that offering too much online would undercut its growing subscription list.

Sparrow, like other socially aware editors, was also concerned about the perceived predominance of male writers in the literature sector, which was surprising if one closely trawled the new titles of most publishers and considered the dominance of women writers through the 1980s and 1990s. In any case, he saw that *Overland* had been perceived as being 'associated with a blokey kind of culture' (qtd. in Ommundsen & Jacklin 73); it is worth speculating that that came about as a result of its championing of social realism in the 1940s and 1950s. Even so, that was a long time before 2008. Or was it a continuing interest in the world of work which had characterised *Overland*'s para-materialist project over fifty years? For all that, *Overland* during the years between 2005 to 2010 partly revolutionised its layout and look with the introduction of colour inside, including photographic supplements, and half-tones. It had gone a long way from the static, linear, black-on-white columns used throughout most of the magazine's history. The digital desktop had changed all that.

As with all the magazines, *Overland* in 2008 was still not well-resourced. Sparrow complained that funding often came down to designing projects to fit, in the full knowledge that the magazine basically needed more cash for day-to-day operations:

> To put it another way, in order to get money you need in order to function, you are forced to apply for things that will get you the money, even if they are not the things that you'd prefer to do in the ideal world. So, you are driven by their priorities rather than your priorities. (Qtd. in Ommundsen & Jacklin 73)

His remarks were in a way similar to what was characterising the frantic search for funding by many of the writers' centres after 2008: in a desperate battle for validation, opportunism seemed to have become the modus operandi. But, by way of contrast, *Overland* could work its community, as it had identified an ideological base and points of genuine difference other than geography, and was publishing writers, new and old.

In 2008, the *Australian Book Review* had been publishing continuously since 1978, and in April it published its 300th edition (called '300 Not Out'). Broadly, its financial position had stabilised, even without the backing of the National Book Council, which had revived it in 1978. In 2007 it had a paid staff of three — editor Peter Rose (who worked part-time), assistant editor Rebecca Starford (full-time) and the office manager, Lorraine Harding (part-time). This was pretty indicative of the staffing situation of the key magazines — *Meanjin* had two staff members, *Island* one staff member and *Overland* two staff members. Added to the list of paid staff at these magazines were a host of voluntary positions, paid at best through the odd honorarium or gratuity. However, the *Australian Book Review* had to rely on its own marketing resources, unlike *Meanjin*, which could presumably fall back on Melbourne University Publishing for support.

Interviewed in 2007, Peter Rose said that 'priorities for the magazine would be increasing subscriptions, more advertising and higher rates of pay to writers' (qtd. in Ommundsen & Jacklin 87). The *Australian Book Review* was consolidating its position in the 2000s, confident that it had a reviewing niche, unlike the others; but it had not reformed its design and layout all that much, and was seemingly unresponsive to much of the upsurge in small-press publishing, if its review pages were anything to go by. There was a monumentalism inscribed within the magazine which seemed to summarise a policy of being one of the ultimate gatekeepers and arbiters of taste, through 'a fostering of an intelligent readership for good Australian writing' (88). Yet the *Australian Book Review*'s potential role was becoming more relevant on one level at least, according to Peter Rose:

> [T]he *ABR* is fulfilling a role that is increasingly being abrogated in the popular press, in which space for book reviews has often been reduced to 400 to 500 words, and is frequently promotional rather than critical. (88)

By the end of 2007 at least, it was becoming plainly obvious that book reviews in the weekend papers were becoming scarcer and less comprehensive, and when published they were dominated by titles from a few multinationals and favoured independents, such as Text, Scribe and Allen & Unwin.

As with all the magazines, the *Australian Book Review* wanted to increase subscriptions, and did so with some success, rising from 1200 in 2001 to more than 2300 in 2007 (89). The magazine was blessed with a good number of library subscriptions which tended to be automatically renewed each year, providing a base for gaining advertising from publishers — unlike the more creative-writing-based publications. In 2007, the *Australian Book Review* attracted $75 000 in advertising, which gave it a more diversified cash flow than other magazines. Like *Overland*, the magazine could also appeal to long-time supporters for tax-deductible donations, and it set up a Patrons scheme which netted $25 000 (90). Rose suggested that 'cultural philanthropy, which already plays a significant role in the support of the performing arts such as opera and ballet, could have an equally important role in literature ...' (90). The advantage for the magazine was that it had become a respectable institution, and was more likely to attract like-minded sponsors.

As we have seen, *Quadrant* had forged through the 1970s contemptuous of the aesthetics of what it saw as the 'trendy Left'. In the 1980s and 1990s, it foregrounded Keith Windschuttle's contribution to the history wars, where he doubted the authenticity of massacres of Indigenous Australians during the white occupation. The magazine forensically investigated Manning Clark's supposed sympathy for the old Soviet Union, and so forth. In 2006, it turned fifty years old and held a celebratory dinner in Sydney where the then Prime Minister, John Howard, was the keynote speaker — an example of the powerful politicians the magazine was able to mobilise on occasions, in stark contrast to the magazines of the Left, or what remained of the Left. Interestingly, *Quadrant*, apart from a period during the 1970s, had persisted in publishing in its usual saddle-stitch (stapled) format with cheap paper inside and only colour on the covers — a cheap magazine look, resisting the monumentalism that the magazines of the Left had instituted. Pretty well all of them had tried to look bookish and respectable, including the academic quasi-Marxist journal *Arena*, which was presumably attractive to book-buyers in inner-city independent bookshops. *Quadrant* was rarely seen in such places and relied on newsagent sales.

In celebration of its fifty years, there was a flurry of articles in the Murdoch press, and some interviews on radio. On 3 October 2006, Owen Harries and Tom Switzer published pretty much a eulogy, 'Little Magazine Leaves Big Mark' in the *Australian*. Harries was a long-time supporter and contributor to the journal and an early believer in Australian involvement in the Vietnam War during the 1960s; he subsequently left Australia and worked in 2007 for the right-wing United States think-tank, the Centre for Independent Studies. Harries and Switzer argued the typical *Quadrant* line that the magazine had kept the conservative faith against the so-called Leftist onslaught after the 1970s, noting that in their opinion, '*Quadrant* is the most successful and influential magazine of ideas in Australia's history' (6) — a large claim. Yet they were incisive as to the role of all little magazines:

> Little magazines, whatever their political colouration, are — dreaded word! — elitist in character. Who reads them is infinitely more important than how many people do. To ask about their circulation is to ask the wrong question, unless one's object is to embarrass the editor. Their function is to try to set the agenda of public debate and policy. And they do this through what economists call the multiplier effect, by influencing the opinions of a small group who, in turn, influence and mould the opinions of the larger community. (6)

Such a statement amply described *Quadrant*'s agenda, as it had been largely a journal of political commentary rather than one devoted to original creative writing — which, as we have seen, was remarked upon on occasions by the Literature Board during disputation over funding levels. The magazine had often taken up issues — for example, Windschuttle's attack on the 'armband' view of Australian history (and on academics such as Henry Reynolds) — to have them highlighted in the conservative daily press. Harries and Switzer continued their congratulatory tone:

> Soviet communism is in the dustbin of history, the appeal of Marxism-Leninism is lost on all but a few alienated intellectuals in the humanities departments ... yet *Quadrant* remains a lively and substantial monthly. (7)

In passing, they added, 'and, thanks to the work of McAuley, Vivian Smith and Les Murray, the magazine has made a huge contribution to the promotion of Australian poetry'.

There was also a discussion on ABC Radio National in September 2006, where presenter Michael Duffy spoke to the then editor, Paddy McGuiness, Dame Leonie Kramer and Martin Krygier, the son of *Quadrant*'s founder, Richard Krygier. During this discussion, Leonie Kramer also stressed that the magazine was 'on the front line of the development of Australian writing ... ' ('*Quadrant*'s 50th anniversary' 3) — her definition of 'new writing' being AD Hope, Judith Wright, Vincent Buckley and Rosemary Dobson earlier in their writing lives. Both Kramer and McGuiness stressed the magazine's adversarial role in highlighting issues in need of further debate. However, Martin Krygier, retrospectively, was critical of the frame the magazine's supporters had seemingly created for such debate. He commented:

> *Quadrant* people ... actually quite like the role of pariah and being the anti-pack pack. I think that has continued with a vengeance over the Aboriginal issue and many other things in recent years, and it has dismayed me, and it's why I'm not associated with *Quadrant* now. (6)

Quadrant was still, it could be said, publishing largely for the reasons it had been created for in the 1950s, and trading on the advantage of not having to create new spaces and dreams.

On the whole, the other magazines were not consumed with such adversarial agendas; they were gentler in their approach. For example, *Island Magazine* from Hobart renamed itself in 1989 as simply *Island* when Cassandra Pybus took over as editor. She made it into a national space for cultural discussions and even raised its profile internationally despite some local opposition. In 2007, the editor became Gina Mercer, the only paid employee. 'I do everything from admin, to the subscription database, to editing, the whole lot', she said (qtd. in Ommundsen & Jacklin 75). This was pretty typical of the workload of magazines smaller than *Meanjin*, *Overland* and the *Australian Book Review*, such as *Wet Ink*, the *Lifted Brow* and *Kill your Darlings*.

Even so, *Island* has continued to maintain its national coverage of contemporary writing and supporting local Tasmanians while receiving support from Arts Tasmania, the Australia Council and a small subsidy from the University of Tasmania plus office space. Its print run then was approximately 1200 copies, but that had been pretty static for eight years, and as with *Overland*, subscribers were largely in the upper age-bracket. It was developing more of an online presence in an effort to attract students of creative writing courses and younger readers; but, as with some of the other magazines, this was proving to be difficult, as there were questions surrounding whether a subscription culture would continue to exist for much longer. By certain criteria, however, *Island* is an established magazine, but with limited resources. Mercer was quoted as having expansion plans, but as with other magazines, many of those were always compromised by a lack of funding and resources. In terms of her perception that *Island*'s strength was its reliability and quality, she felt that it was a liability in attracting new funding:

> I worry that we might be misconceived as being like the old aunt in the grey cardigan; that we're seen as too reliable, too predictable and therefore not sexy and new. And therefore not worthy of more funding … because *Island* has had a presence in Tasmania since 1979, sponsors don't go, 'Wow, let's support *Island*'. We're just part of the landscape. (Qtd. in Ommundsen & Jacklin 78)

By the late 2000s, it could be argued that culturally in Australia, Mercer's concern had validity because there was still cachet in promotional opportunities in the revolving margins and peripheries, and the centres of cultural representation were still being challenged. Whether because *Island* ostensibly came from Tasmania, rather than from Sydney or Melbourne, and was therefore less important, was a moot point. Geography still mattered, perhaps as a late romantic search for identity, and it worked in contradictory directions if the evidence the magazines provided was any indication. Little magazines were still, to an extent, operating around scenes and circles, sometimes in specific locations such as inner Melbourne, with its plethora of live readings and launches. Such circles could be stimulating and restrictive at the same time.

If, to an extent, the print magazines of the new millennium were pretty much standard in size and ambition, the *Lifted Brow*, which first appeared in early 2007 in Brisbane, edited by Ronnie Scott, was an exception. It was designed to look retro and was launched with the aid of an assortment of musical acts, the emphasis being self-consciously 'indie' in all respects. Privately published by Ronnie Scott, it appeared only intermittently until 2010 when three issues were published, and they were launched in spectacular style at reading nights where many of the sales were made. From 2011, Scott planned to publish six times a year. Most issues have had approximately 300 pages, which supports the theory that it was a magazine 'from the past', with little web presence and literal word of mouth being its marketing device. Contributors have been a mix of well-known authors (with a dash of name-dropping) and an assortment of 'indies' from mainly Brisbane and Melbourne — for example, Chris Sommerville, Christos Tsiolkas, Chris Currie, Krissy Kneen, AS Patric, and Alice Pung.

Scott maintained and promoted himself as independent and the *Lifted Brow* as not being grant-dependent. In response to a question in an interview in *Wet Ink* about avoiding government funding, he said:

> The reason I've never applied to get a grant for the *Brow* is just that we're able to do without one ... [M]ost mags that are grant dependent, which means most magazines could potentially just fall apart if the grants were taken away, and they seem not to have any backups thought through at all. (Qtd. in Paine 30)

From anecdotal evidence at least, the *Lifted Brow* was quite a hit around live performance circuits in those two cities, and sold out (presumably of a small print run). However, that was dependent on a presumption of free labour, as the magazine existed due to the volunteerism of Scott, whereas the established and more frequently published magazines had to pay in some way for people's time. The *Lifted Brow* not only looked like some 1970s publications — such as *Etymspheres*, *Rigmarole of the Hours* and *Magic Sam*, among others — it was a very 1970s aesthetic, assuming that idealism and free labour could survive against everything.

Volunteerism is a vexed notion, as people often have children to look after, and full-time jobs. Ronnie Scott was content to put in the surplus value of unpaid labour on hundreds of submissions from people from all over Australia. However, for all the idealism, such activity is unsustainable in the long term, particularly in Australia, where pragmatism always battles it out with romantic attitudes to the arts. Was the point to establish something for the long term or to further the romantic illusion of a fitful avant-garde? But that made the *Lifted Brow* a fascinating 'avant-garde' bohemian magazine of the moment, attractive from both literary and lifestyle points of view.

This was a type of libertarianism that Frank Moorhouse spoke of in terms of the Sydney Push in the 1960s, and which he chronicled and parodied in his short fiction published in the 1970s and in anthologies such as *Days of Wine and Rage*. The *Lifted Brow* was a blast from a more carefree, seemingly (pre-industrial) past, a small-press move unencumbered by the homogenising markets and governments in jaded post-modern times. It spoke to an audience in the inner cities of at least Brisbane and Melbourne, about themselves and perhaps even about their imaginary independence.

Along that theme, Ilura Press, founded in Melbourne in 2006 by Christopher Lappas and Sabina Hopfer, described itself on its website as an independent boutique publisher:

> Our aim is to provide an avenue for creative work through the publication of quality literature and art. We are run by a dedicated team of writers and artists, and rely on interns and volunteers, supporters, and funding to produce our titles ... [W]e have a select publishing list. (n.p.)

They made a strong point that included in that 'select' list 'is the acclaimed creative journal *Etchings* which showcases new work by emerging and established writers and artists', and there followed a rollcall: JM Coetzee, Robert Dessaix, Antoni Jach, Thomas Shapcott and John Tranter, among others.

Whereas the *Lifted Brow* described itself as an attack journal, *Etchings*, it appeared, desired respectability. Ilura Press published six novels and nine editions of *Etchings* in the period between 2006 and 2011 and these were all notable for their expensively printed, full-colour art reproductions. There was never any evidence that *Etchings* would see itself as a quarterly; in fact, by the available evidence, it was a journal that is both a magazine and a book. One issue was published in 2006, two in 2007, two in 2008, two in 2009, one in 2010 and one in 2011 — figures which support this. The strong promotion of visual artists, photographers, and of essays along that line marked the journal as an attempt to create a desirable limited-edition journal of sorts, which traditionally, in the book trade, achieves commodification through its stylised marginality. This can happen when the artists/writers concerned become famous and sought after, usually over a long period of time, but publishing the work as a magazine/journal compromises the exchange value. For all that, Ilura Press was a remarkably idealistic venture involving the resources of key individuals, and as a boutique publisher, it could eschew notions of success or failure which were continuing stresses on other publishers.

I had prefigured such developments several years before. Speaking of a large part of the small-magazine community and people in the universities, I said, 'Maybe we accept this type of magazine because it reflects the way in which we construct ourselves in the universities: as marginal, substantial, special limited editions' ('Respectable or risqué' n.p). Most writers at the time would not have cared less, as they were happy to be published in any format, and the established authors were supportive of new ventures.

Given the economics of contemporary publishing, squeezed between a crisis in bookselling and difficulties in obtaining publicity, subsidies are essential for this type of operation. In short, commodity fetishism is deeply inscribed in such constructions. Such tendencies have always been present in the small-press movement, depending on ambition and ideology. Yet aristocratic tendencies have at times become shorthand for little magazines that want only 'good' readers, the ambition of promoting new writers and finding new readers seemingly a sideways question.

18. Away from Sydney and Melbourne

Much of the new activity, then, apart from *Wet Ink*, was confined to the eastern seaboard, until *Indigo* journal was born in Perth in 2007 with a policy of deliberately promoting Western Australian authors. Western Australia may have always felt 'out of sight, out of mind' to an extent, even despite the efforts of *Westerly* over at least three decades. It, too, had been publishing less frequently during the 1990s, as the original group of activists such as Bruce Bennett and Peter Cowan had moved on.

The editors of *Indigo* saw the magazine as nurturing local talent by only publishing people who had lived in Western Australia for at least three years. It published six issues between August 2007 and February 2011 (twice a year), publishing a mixture of unknown authors and established names. Irma Gold in a blog on the *Overland* website on 22 July 2010 noted that she was reviewing a magazine that was dying. 'What makes this journal unique — and what ultimately resulted in its downfall — is that it published writing by only West Australian authors' (n.p.). At that time, even though *Indigo* had promoted Western Australian authors to a national audience and had some distribution in the eastern states, the magazine had been advised by the Western Australian Department of Culture and the Arts that it would not continue to fund the magazine.

The managing editor, Donna Ward, said, 'While they considered *Indigo* an important literary project for Western Australia, they felt it was not well known in the Eastern states and should receive submissions from around Australia' (qtd. in Gold, n.p.). *Indigo*, through its supporters, suggested readers write to the papers and petition their members of parliament. As a result, questions were asked in the Legislative Assembly (WA) on 14 October 2010, seeking clarification from the minister responsible, and he (JHD Day) replied that there were already a number of outlets for writers in Western Australia, and that West Australians had access to the literary magazines published in the other states. Without knowing how *Indigo* sold in the eastern states, the market had become more sophisticated in its belief that Australians should be able to compete nationally and internationally. It may therefore have appeared that the editors of *Indigo* were engaging in special pleading, in that they were arguing for a pure local zone, not unlike student anthologies produced by universities to publish their creative writing students. Those types of publications were notoriously hard to sell on an open market.

The paradox was that *Indigo* was a national magazine that only published locals, and whether that limited its quality was an open question. Even so, it was a brutal time for the journal, which was born out of considerable idealism. What was the difference between parochialism and localism for a state that was a long way from the publishing capitals of Sydney and Melbourne? *Wet Ink* had wanted to promote South Australian writers, but under competition from authors all over the country; it had suffered briefly and was seen by some South Australians as not being *local* enough, whilst *Indigo* was penalised for not being *national* enough. When is the local not seen as parochial? Yet it was clear that no literary magazine, wherever it was in Australia, would survive if it was reliant on one major source of income — and that, despite instantaneous communications, distance was always a decisive factor in Australia.

Despite *Indigo*'s problems, another print magazine appeared in Perth in 2009, called *Dotdotdash*, whose managing editor was SJ Finch. It was produced by past and present students of Curtin University and had put out six issues by early 2011. Published triannually, it was graphically spectacular, looked like a magazine in all respects, published the usual genres — along with comics, illustrations, and in the later issues an accompanying CD — and was open to all Australians. It received some initial support from Express Media, and ongoing funding from the Western Australian Department of Culture and the Arts, and sponsorship from Curtin University. It was a demonstration that the literary arts were alive and well in Western Australia, that there was still a commitment to what hard copy can offer.

As I have been suggesting from the evidence of the past three decades (and particularly during the 1970s, when hegemonic challenges to the established magazines surfaced every few years), the little magazine has been and is, more often than not, representative of an evolving search for the establishment of ruling ideas and personalities. Broadly, in Australia until the early 2000s, ideological positions were the foundations on which *Quadrant*, *Overland* and *Meanjin* were built. By the late 2000s, it was clear that such binaries were still evident, but they had been reconfigured by post-modernism in the universities (and as a general social mood), and by the splitting off of the previously democratic public sphere into competing communities of interest and topicality. After the 1980s, market values predominated, and little magazines were increasingly niche publications like never before, not unlike stratification in the broader popular culture. The decades of the 1980s and the 1990s had witnessed the triumph of bourgeois individuality over all other ways of social construction, and there was ample evidence of that in the developing social media, celebrity culture, creative writing courses and in many of the magazines. If there was an ideology, it was decentred and representative of the only Left position remaining — respectable Left/neo-liberalism.

The evidence of this existed in the new magazines of the late 2000s, such as *Kill Your Darlings*, which was named after a line from Chekhov about editing your own work. It was established as a quarterly publication; and its website described itself in 2011 as 'publish[ing] fresh, clever writing that combines intellect with intrigue ... *Kill Your Darlings* is independent, smart and ridiculously good-looking. Just like you' (n.p.). The magazine started publishing in March 2010 and had published six issues by April 2011, qualifying it for Literature Board funding after three issues, of which it printed five hundred copies each time. It was and is essentially a journal of non-fiction essays plus some fiction, interviews and, interestingly, no poetry.

In this way it seems to subscribe to the theory that essays, along with the discourse accompanying them, are a sensible way forward in an environment where fiction is seemingly unmarketable. The size of a paperback book, the covers were generic, with minor cover-illustration changes inside a template, making them identifiable in shops. There is no doubt that the editors, Rebecca Starford and Hannah Kent saw themselves as being cutting edge. The magazine comes with a concerted blogging presence highlighting leading articles and they release a proportion of material on their website. There has been a conscious policy of attracting big names and relatively non-political names to write for it (though its contributors are ostensibly Left/liberal in orientation), including Gideon Haigh and Monica Dux. Fiction writers, who have not been quite as well-known, have included Chris Womersley, Patrick Cullen, Kalinda Ashton, Pierz Newton-John, Karen Hitchcock and Louise Swinn.

There was none of the overt politics of *Overland* in that *Kill Your Darlings* did not wear its heart on its sleeve, as it was and is intelligently reserved and topical, and evidence of a literary magazine that wishes to make its mark on matters of discussion around town, something which some little magazines have always set out to achieve in that they become platforms for their editors. Like *Harvest* and *Etchings*, *Kill Your Darlings* was and is very much a Melbourne product in that it publishes and distributes largely in the inner city, and it wishes to attract like-minded people. It had, at the time of writing, all the potential to survive because it was an indication of a neat hipster moment, an unencumbered 'cool' product in what some might perceive as an otherwise scrubby, cluttered marketplace.

Voiceworks was continuing publication in its accessible, large-magazine format with colour covers and illustrations, twenty-one years after its birth in 1989. In early 2011, Express Media published *The Word We Found*, the best writing from those years in the magazine. The book was edited by Lisa

Dempster, who had been active around Melbourne through various small-press ventures, including the chapbook series Vignette Press. After starting out as a small four-to-six-page, unbound, black and white newsletter, by the early 1990s *Voiceworks* had grown into a journal with glossy covers containing short fiction, articles and opinion. It has had several editors, including Adam Ford, Kelly Chandler, Tom Doig and Ryan Paine, and at the time of writing, Johannes Jakob. It has continued to abide by its charter of promoting young writers, and is in a sense stuck with that given the funding behind Express Media — but, in any case, Dempster claimed that it was 'no longer geared only towards a wholly youth audience'. She made the claim that '*Voiceworks* is now a respected literary journal which belies the youth of its contributors' (qtd. in Place n.p.) By 2011, *Voiceworks* had published for the first time a number of writers who would proceed to book publication. It was notable that the editors and the editorial committee had provided considerable feedback to contributors. *Voiceworks* had become an institution, dependent on the overall finances of Express Media, and established a relatively secure niche for itself.

All this activity in the formation of small presses and little magazines articulated an inflation of desire across a publishing landscape where change was the only constant. Unlike the 1970s, the promotional landscape had been reconfigured away from reviews and retail prominence, a process involving the new spectacle of writers' festivals, which decisively influenced exposure and cultural visibility. The festivals were in essence a form of cultural tourism, which in effect created new levels of hierarchy, along with the heightened influence of literary agents, who also created a middle structure between authors and publishers. In the new millennium it was difficult for little magazines to compete against the bargaining power of multinational publishers and agents, so as to gain exposure at the major writers' festivals. Some magazines would adapt to change and some would go against it in the contradictory small-press tradition of going against the grain. In this context, the role of the literary magazine was even more relevant and urgent than ever.

19. SOME OF THE SAME OLD PROBLEMS

As in the 1970s, associations would develop such as Small Press Underground Networking Community (SPUNC), started in 2006, with remarkably similar aims to the Australasian Small Magazines Association and the Australian Independent Publishers Association during the 1970s. This was evidence that the major problems for literary magazines (and small presses) were different in the 2000s, but with similarities, and further evidence that the 2000s represented a second upsurge of activity. Interestingly, Nathan Hollier, a past editor of *Overland*, was a major driving force behind the formation of SPUNC, suggesting that during difficult times some people have more of a collective consciousness than others.

> In May 2010, the SPUNC website declared:
> SPUNC is committed to building and promoting good relationships with booksellers and maintaining clear channels of information ... [M]any of Australia's favourite authors emerged from the publishing programs of small publishing houses and literary magazines. Yet, due to the difficulties of marketing and distribution for these organisations, many booksellers remain unaware of the wide range of quality publications that small publishers produce. (n.p.)

In 2007 SPUNC commissioned a report, *A Lovely Kind of Madness: Small and Independent Publishing in Australia* (the title based on a quote from Ian Syson, of Vulgar Press and formerly of *Overland*), on the state of small-press publication. The report was written by Kate Freeth, and identified a number of key issues for the sector, including literary magazines. Forty-six presses were surveyed, of which nineteen were members of SPUNC. While acknowledging the diversity and important cultural role played by the presses and the magazines, Freeth identified that members had two major concerns:

> Unsurprisingly, distribution and publicity remain the major difficulties for small and independent publishers. Relatively small print runs, low margins and a large area to cover mean commercial distribution services often don't suit small publishers. (1)

Of the major difficulties identified by those surveyed, unprompted, 39 per cent cited distribution as their major problem, followed by publicity and marketing. Freeth noted that

> the problem of publicity is underlined by a general lack of attention from mainstream media, and low public awareness means less interest from booksellers, low sales and thus low print runs, which further compounds the problem of distribution. (1)

Although the media landscape had changed since the 1970s, one constant was that small presses and literary magazines found it very difficult to get any promotion in major newspapers, and on radio and television. In particular, the book review pages of the dailies had shrunk in size, thus rarely reviewing small-press titles.

Freeth also reported that the majority of small presses 'are in or near Melbourne and Sydney, although all states are represented except the Northern Territory', and that those surveyed 'have an average print run of fewer than 2000 copies (often 1000 or fewer)' (7). SPUNC would go on to attempt a mobilisation and promotion of the independent presses, including many of the small magazines, during the decade. Based in Melbourne, it had the advantage that it was considered by Hamilton as 'a beacon of hope in an industry dominated by global conglomerates' ('Sympathy' 88).

Unlike Book People during the 1970s, SPUNC had no intention of setting up a physical distribution warehouse, and in sending representatives around to the trade, because, with the advent of the impending e-book and the dominance of computerised ordering, much of that would have been a waste of time. Publishers' representatives rarely physically showed retailers new releases anymore, unlike in the 1970s, thus relieving them of the responsibility of choosing stock or considering small-press publications that they otherwise would not have come across. Also, some of the retail distributors were becoming more vulnerable as time went on because of the high value of the Australian dollar, which made local books dearer, and the onslaught of purchasing through the internet rather than through retailers. Magazines and small publishers had responded by creating online facilities, but that might also have weakened the retail trade. For example, given the above, the respondents to the survey said that they sold 37 per cent of their titles through events, closely followed by 33 per cent online via their own websites (Freeth 50). Of the nineteen SPUNC members surveyed, thirteen did not use a distributor (8), probably for the reasons hinted above.

The dynamic of retail book and magazine publishing was changing inexorably, offering opportunities on the one hand and taking away outlets with the other. Of the six journal/magazine publishers surveyed who printed over a thousand copies per issue, four were attached to or supported by universities (34), further suggesting that subsidies to literary magazines were still necessary, as in the 1970s. In broad terms, Freeth's report recommended developing the SPUNC website, creating promotional links with existing organisations and co-operation between members. It discussed the dreaded, perennial problem of distribution, suggesting that 'a publisher-run distribution group like the Australian Book Group has the potential to remove one layer of margin, allowing more profit to flow back to the publisher or into better distribution' (21) — a suggestion similar to those of the small magazine editors conference in Adelaide in 1978.

But in early 2011, the Australian Book Group only represented a handful of the membership of SPUNC, and their catalogue suggested that they were wholesalers (in that they promoted specific titles) rather than providing a list of individual publishers, something desired by small presses. In any case, margins for book and magazine distributors were becoming almost prohibitive and were exacerbated by the sale or return provisions in the retail trade, making it difficult to determine actual sales in any given month. By 2010, several distributors — including Scribo (an amalgamation of Bookwise, Brumby and Tower books, formerly the distributor for Giramondo and *Heat*), then owned by the printer Griffin Press/PMP — were reporting losses, because it was not feasible to take physical delivery of overseas stock (the majority of its trade) due to the price differentials.

For the magazines, then, in 2010, there were only a handful of firms who would take them on: Scribo, Dennis Jones and Speedimpex (formerly Selectair). *Meanjin* was distributed by Pan Macmillan, the *Griffith Review* by Penguin (via Text Publishing), *Quadrant* by Gordon and Gotch into newsagents, *Wet Ink* by Selectair (through which it initially was able to get stock into the Borders chain) and Fairfax (for newsagents), and orders for the new *Kill Your Darlings* by Hardie Grant Books. Whether the larger organisations would be positive about 'small fish' would be interesting to watch, as it was in the 1970s and 1980s when book and magazine retailing went through a different kind of rationalisation as the middle-sized groups separated themselves out from the small groups after the demise of Book People of Australia. At that time, the Book Collective represented the small publishers with potential for growth such as McPhee Gribble and Lonely Planet.

The membership of SPUNC, by 2009, included a range of publishers from Text and Scribe down to miniscule presses who only publish a few books a year, but included pretty well all of the literary magazines, big and small. SPUNC held regular workshops and discussions on industry developments and was active in lobbying on behalf of its 130-odd members (none of whom were exclusively online publishers) to industry bodies; it set up a series of catalogues and acted as a conduit for sales. The general aim was to further promote the sector during a time of resurgence, and it showed that co-operation could be achieved between members, something rare among authors if not publishers. The organisation received some support from the Literature Board and from the Copyright Agency Ltd to employ two part-time staff, a Manager and a Communications Manager from an office at the Wheeler Centre for Books, Writing and Ideas in Melbourne. Evidence was hard to obtain as to tangible results, yet SPUNC became well-known as a place for information.

In terms of the magazines, as we have seen, they were a special problem. There was potential for the duplication of scarce taxpayer dollars being diverted into peak bodies such as SPUNC (and into research projects) at a time when bodies such as the Australia Council were searching for ways to promote the individual publications, and differentiating between them was politically difficult. For example, in 2010, the Literature Board of the Australia Council, which funded ten magazines, including the established publications, formed a marketing arm, Literary Magazines Australia, to promote the magazines through advertisements, bookmarks and screen advertising in some cinemas, the success of which could not be gauged at that time. The promotion also did not at first include a group of newer and arguably more vulnerable magazines such as *Harvest*, *Kill Your Darlings* and *Mascara*, but they were added after several months.

Literary Magazines Australia was another example of the Board's commitment to the magazines, even at a time of intense competition for taxpayer dollars, but it needs to be said that, as in the 1970s, there existed a tendency to create structures around a problem rather than to directly invest in solutions at the level of the individual magazines, whose editors intimately knew of the challenges they faced. An example of this tendency was, as I already suggested, the writers' centres, in that they had been almost bypassed by the grassroots activity of publishing and were largely recycling the heightened level of news and information created, sometimes by the magazines. As Robin Sheehan-Bright has pointed out,

> [f]rom the beginning there was confusion about the purpose of writer's centres, even among those who fought hard to establish them. There was certainly the expectation that centres would operate as a co-ordinating body of some sort, but exactly what they would co-ordinate was not so easily defined. (147)

There appeared to be duplication of services already provided by the Australian Society of Authors, the Australian Writers' Guild and, in terms of author promotion, the increasing role of bookshops with launches.

More to the point, they were consuming considerable amounts of taxpayer arts dollars in salaries and city rents. The problem with writers' centres was that they were creating little value, either commodified or otherwise through their operations. Serious writers want money (and time) to write and publications to support their early efforts, and writers' centres were not attracting them by the close of the 2000s. Memberships were largely over mature age, and as business (and community models) they were spending a great deal of their energy applying for grants. The time taken over grant applications was also a bone of contention for the magazines, yet under new Australia Council guidelines, magazines had to show that they were generating income through other sources.

Although writers' centres had provided valuable meeting places for writers in regional centres who were a long way from established city literary networks, there was evidence by 2010 that they were duplicating existing services. Also, in most cases the income for writers' centres was miniscule apart from government subsidies, as they had little by the way of an actual product (apart from miscellaneous service delivery) to sell. In terms of overall budgets for writers' centres, they had been granted resources far in excess of any of the assistance to magazines. Writers' centres were encouraged by the Literature Board during 2008-09 to become nationally relevant, which was a tough task, but it was something that most of the magazines had always had to strive for.

In 2010 the Literature Board of the Australia Council decided to fund directly only two centres, the Northern Territory Writers' Centre and the Queensland Writers Centre (which had transformed itself as the national centre for digital writing), with the remainder competing for funds under a national organisation called Writing Australia. This was a clear rationalisation that might free funds up for some of the magazines, and perhaps an artful case of cultural engineering.

By 2010 Australia had seen another explosion of small-press activity, primarily in Melbourne, a city that has always seen itself as the intellectual centre of Australia. The City of Melbourne bid for, and was awarded, the title of UNESCO City of the Book; this was soon followed by the establishment of the Wheeler Centre for Books, Writing and Ideas at the State Library of Victoria. If monumentalism in terms of the magazines had been an attempt at status-building and implicit commodification, then the establishment of the Centre was another attempt to replicate the art gallery model, but with public discussions, where bricks and mortar are the ultimate form of commodity. This model is safe in itself and a reliable return on investment, in contrast to the literary magazine, which appears ephemeral and 'messy'.

The literary magazine in Australia has always struggled to attract corporate sponsorship, unlike the opera and the performing arts, which come with such monumental connotations. Even so, in 2010 the *Australian Book Review* would have some success in attracting patronage through promoting itself as an indispensable institution, which separated it from the other magazines — a sign that commodification is all too often predicated on difference and perceived scarcity. Paradoxically, the Wheeler Centre would house a number of the new magazines, thus giving them perceived permanency. It was a paradoxical formalisation of a structure over public space in defence of the marginalised public sphere. It was, in effect, the creation of an ersatz public sphere, not unlike the formalisation of voluntary activity which had occurred under the umbrella of the writers' centres during the previous two decades.

In December 2009 James Bradley published a piece which was a survey of the then current state of the magazines and a discussion of what he saw as the seemingly inevitable move online. In it he suggested that

> one could be forgiven for thinking the future of traditional forums such as the literary magazine is bleak ... yet, counterintuitively, literary magazines are thriving. While readerships are still small, there is evidence they are increasing. (16)

He cited that part of the reason was promotion through readings, events and festival panels. His view was that there were three main groups of magazines by the conclusion of the new decade — 'Griffith Review, Heat, Meanjin and Overland. All have permanent staff, healthy circulations and a degree of recognition outside the relatively narrow confines of the literary world'. Of his second group — Southerly, Westerly, Island and Going Down Swinging — he said, 'these publications seem to cater to smaller audiences ... '. He also identified an

> amorphous group of new or emerging magazines such as Indigo, Wet Ink, Etchings, dotdotdash and Cutwater ... [T]hese journals sometimes aspire to broader long term relevance in the way Etchings or Wet Ink clearly do, but more often speak to narrow audiences or even coteries. (16)

Bradley's analysis (whether accurate or not) in effect summarised a general perception that the status quo prior to the new magazine upsurge in the late 2000s remained intact, and that resources, financial and otherwise, were as central to longevity and promotion as they had been over the forty history of this study. His first group were largely the only magazines reviewed and referred to in the literary pages of the major newspapers. Even so, he was then unaware of developments in 2010 and 2011 in the broader economy, and through online imperatives, that were to come.

Nonetheless, *Meanjin* (in particular) was by then experiencing competition as a prime site of cultural hegemony. It had had a succession of editors over the 1980s and 1990s, reflecting both its tense relationship with the University of Melbourne and its ability to adapt to the new environment, including the internet juggernaut. Ian Britain, editor up to 2007, stepped down when Melbourne University Publishing took over the administration and distribution of the magazine: 'At that time too there were fears the print edition would disappear' (Sullivan, 'The battle' 20). In late 2010, the then editor Sophie Cunningham also resigned and it was reported by Sullivan that 'she feels "frustrated" that she was not included in discussions about the magazine's future'. As to discussions as to the future, Cunningham added, ' ... I was sort of out of the loop then, and I'm certainly out of the loop now' (qtd. in 'The battle' 20). Despite protestations to the contrary by the publisher of *Meanjin*, Melbourne University Publishing, debate raged up until Christmas and into the New Year about what would happen.

Melbourne University Publishing board member Alan Kohler told the press, in respect to the debate about *Meanjin* going exclusively online: 'Not that we think that would necessarily be a good thing ... we really don't understand the frenzied opposition to it ... [I]t is in fact already online and has been for sometime' (n.p.). In any case Sally Heath, a former *Age* journalist, was appointed as the new editor in late December, and Cunningham's last edition was the summer edition of 2010-11. Those events were symptomatic of pressures that had been building for a long time. As I have already suggested, *Meanjin* seemed to be caught between its past and a future that it was struggling to find. In the 1970s, the first editor after Clem Christesen, Jim Davidson, successfully realised he had to modernise due to the cultural changes of that time. Perhaps in a similar spirit, after 2007 Cunningham redesigned the look and layout of the magazine by introducing more colour printing into the body of the magazine, with zany covers which gave it a younger look in the eyes of many. She also broadened the amount of online material, including blogging, because, as she said, 'if you want to broaden the readership, having an extensive online presence is important'. She added, as reported by Sullivan, 'but she would not want to see the magazine exclusively online' (qtd. in 'The battle' 21).

In any case, *Meanjin* published a great deal of its contents online, which may have compromised its subscriber base, in that why would anyone subscribe to the hard-copy edition if they could get most of it for free? As of 2010, no successful business model incorporating print and online was in place, something that media giants such as News Ltd were all too aware of. Also, universities were becoming increasingly wary of subsidising hard-copy academic or literary publications, when online editions were much cheaper. Melbourne University Publishing, formerly Melbourne University Press, was ostensibly running as a potentially profit-making enterprise under its publisher, Louise Adler. The *Griffith Review* seemed to be undercutting *Meanjin*'s title as Australia's pre-eminent magazine of debate and ideas by investing resources into publishing a suite of prominent public intellectuals from around Australia. The magazine also paid very well.

It appeared that *Meanjin* was on the back foot, trying to redesign its mission when nationalism had become unfashionable and potential readers, some of whom were creative writing students, had little or no knowledge of its importance and history. It was confronted, in a small market, by readers with fickle allegiances. Unlike *Quadrant*, with its group of diehards who supported the only magazine of the Right, its constituency was not as stable as it had once been, especially as *Overland* had successfully modernised during the 1980s and 1990s and inherited what was left of an evolving Left. *Meanjin*'s crisis in late 2010 was a point at which the new technology of the internet might contemptuously cast aside, with the aid of some allies, that which had gone before.

20.   A CASE IN POINT — *Heat*

Often new little magazines would start out through a perceived dissatisfaction with existing publications. The establishment of *Heat* in 1996 by Ivor Indyk was a case in point, and its history would demonstrate the pressures I have already alluded to with the established journals and the threat posed by the internet. According to Miriam Cosic, Indyk had been editing *Southerly* and 'was tired of the dry academic tone of the literary magazines of the day, including *Meanjin* and *Overland*' (9). He decided to make a statement: 'I wanted something that was much more engaging and would gain a larger readership. I wanted to take literary writing out into the marketplace' (qtd. in Cosic 9).

Cosic claimed that 'multinational companies were beginning to dominate and they were looking for product: marketable, bestselling novels', and that Indyk wanted to reintroduce the traditional role of the magazine by publishing new work by people before they went on to longer works, in the way that Carey, Moorhouse and Grenville had years before. He was fired up, in that his first editorial described 'the destruction of universities as sites of intellectual and artistic controversy, [and] the devaluation of literary ideals in the marketplace' (9). According to Ommundsen and Jacklin,

> *Heat* was designed from its beginnings to appear more like a book than a periodical, with hopes of breaking into the mainstream market. (The book format and design is a model that other literary magazines in Australia have followed, e.g. *Meanjin* and *Southerly*). (79)

For a brief period the magazine did not publish, but the first series of fifteen issues began in 2001 with two issues a year, increasing to three in 2007, ending in 2011. It had contributors such as Roberto Bolaño, Brian Castro, Helen Garner, Gail Jones, David Malouf, Dorothy Porter, Charles Simic and Susan Sontag. *Heat* became an excellent serious literary magazine, with an emphasis on criticism and the blending of local and international authors, not unlike the ambitious *Scripsi* during the 1980s. *Heat* stood out from other Australian literary journals as it was international in outlook. The magazine certainly concentrated on publishing a number of 'writer's writers', to use the term.

In 2007 its annual budget was approximately $137 000, out of which Ivor Indyk and Fiona Wright received part-time remuneration (Ommundsen & Jacklin 80). Published by Giramondo Publishing and the Universiy of Western Sydney, it was subsidised by both state and federal arts bodies, receiving support from the Australian Council, the New South Wales Arts Ministry and Sydney Grammar School. It is interesting to note that over its publishing history the magazine was supported by regional universities — the University of Newcastle and the University of Western Sydney — rather than any of the Group of Eight institutions. Even so, it established a reputation as a highly sought-after destination for writers, despite its low circulation and the fact that towards the end of its life it appeared only twice a year in contrast to quarterlies such as *Meanjin* and *Overland*.

During its second series, *Heat* often published long contributions, essays, short fiction and also poetry. In 2007, Indyk noted the high level of payments to writers by *Heat*, and that he considered the magazine to be a relatively unpaid clearing house for Literature Board funds: 'In terms of infrastructure, I think we're dispensing the Literature Board's funds for them' (qtd. in Ommundsen & Jacklin 82). He said this raised the issue that, 'while this arrangement fulfils the Board's priority of directing funds to writers, it overlooks the issue of sustainability of the infrastructure upon which the production of literary writing depends'.

In 2007, the subscriptions to the magazine were static at around 1000 — pretty much the same as they had been in 1996. This, according to Indyk, indicated that

> there is a core constituency that reads and supports literary writing, but this core constituency does not grow ... I'm actually resigned to the idea of a minority culture; a very small coterie of readers. The assumption that you have to have a large audience in order to perpetuate or transmit cultural values is wrong. (Qtd. in Ommundsen & Jacklin 84)

In that year he was also aware that the readership was largely in Sydney and Melbourne, with the majority of subscribers coming from New South Wales, and that there could be a readership base among students enrolled in creative writing courses.

Heat, it appears, not only acquired status through the quality of its innovative contributions, but because of its chunky, limited-edition look, which separated it from insinuations of popularism. When *Heat* decided to cease hard-copy publication in early 2011 and only investigate an online version, the incident highlighted both the problematic publishing history of the literary magazine and the contradictions presented by the internet revolution. The obituaries were laudatory, but as with much in the arts in Australia, they bordered on crocodile tears — another example of how we celebrate heroic failure rather than positive continuity. The last issue was in March 2011, and Indyk wrote about the reasons for the decision to cease publication. Intriguingly, *Heat*'s insistence on being expensively produced, so as to make it desirable to potential readers (to make it look like a book) was, he claimed, one of the reasons for its demise:

> Out of respect for the nature of this writing, the literary magazine tends to be bound like a book, to favour the full page rather than the columnar layout of text, and to limit advertising, if it has any at all. It is essentially a magazine in book form, which is why it appears in bookshops rather than newsagents. ('Editorial' 2)

He was speaking, in effect, of the commodification process embarked upon by other publications, particularly *Meanjin* and *Southerly*, and the increased difficulty of setting up a literary magazine after the 1970s. Indyk rightly suggested that 'the market is very small. There might be ten, maybe fifteen booksellers in Australia, who sell literary magazines. The rest probably wouldn't recognise the genre' ('Editorial' 2). He had identified the strange nature of the use value of a book or magazine, which undermines its potential exchange value. He admitted that,

> [j]udging by the discrepancy between the number of copies of *Heat* sold, and the number of readers who claim familiarity with it, the magazine is often passed on, or left in places where visitors are likely to see it ... *Heat*'s reputation has grown, but its sales are the same now as they were for its first issue. (2)

According to Cosic, Indyk 'admitted to being overly idealistic: he thought the circulation of *Heat* would steadily grow and, instead, it has remained at about 1000 copies, feeding the same small, specialised community it did from the start' (9). He acknowledged that he was disappointed that he had confused communal value with commercial value, and that despite the fact that *Heat* was highly subsidised, not enough people were prepared to pay for it throughout the 2000s. He added that an online version made many of the costs disappear — printing, packaging, postage and warehousing — but also much of its income; making the story of *Heat* also the accelerating story of book publishers and small magazines in the early years of the new millennium.

In an intriguing postscript to the *Heat* story, the magazine was given an A-rating in the Australian Research Council (ARC) peer-review ratings in 2009, but in 2010, it fell from the list for reasons as obscure as the editor's refusal to send material out to external reviewers. Despite its perceived prestige, then, *Heat* was in the hands of anonymous assessors, and not always its writers and readers. In June 2011 the assistant editor, Fiona Wright, published pretty much a eulogy and hinted at the possible directions for the magazine. She noted how disappointed some of *Heat*'s readers were at the demise of the hard-copy edition, and that one less print journal is one less outlet for serious and close literary review, for critical discussion of books that don't necessarily have the kind of mass audience that newspapers and their supplements have. (87)

She went on to say that the magazine had played, as she saw it, an important role in not being seduced by topicality; it had promoted the literary essay, poetry and experimental forms. But she evaded several questions as to why the magazine could not achieve a higher circulation and was a publishing failure by some standards. Her evasion was very much evidence of the mystification the magazine had constructed around itself, published only twice a year. Its editors considered it a magazine, (and thus attracted government subsidies for it) when it was, in fact, more an artefact — a gesture at monumentalism. Had it been popular with some writers and some academics 'because it reflects the way in which we construct ourselves in the universities: as marginal, substantial, special limited editions'? (Edmonds, 'Respectable or risqué' n.p.)

Heat had been very heavily subsidised, which may have worked against moves to expand its income base. Interestingly, Wright suggested that its community were writers (and not readers). Noting the subsidisation, she said, 'There is no imperitive for writers to keep journals alive ... [T]he physical form of the literary magazine, then, is not the component that is necessary to its community' (88). She had stated the more often understated assumption of some magazine editors, and many writers, that the taxpayer should and will subsidise their particular obsessions, and that the online alternative that *Heat* was investigating would go ahead dependent on government subsidies (despite its cheaper production methods) — a problematic assumption in times of tight federal budgets. Furthermore, the success or otherwise of online journals can be difficult to assess, as I have discussed elsewhere, as website hits may be scattergun at best.

In 2010 the requirement for sizeable funding support from the Literature Board was still that a magazine would be able to at least raise 40 per cent of its turnover from sources other than its direct subsidy. However, given the realistic lack of any viable business model for digital publishing, online publishing could become the vehicle through which federal and state arts bodies might justify reducing their commitment. In *Heat*'s case, though, editorial standards had been high, and Wright was confident that the poets and others published by *Heat* would continue to be paid:

> We can make sure that our writers are still paid for what they do, even if it's hard to trace just where their words wind up, and we're fortunate that our funding bodies agree. (91)

She spoke of one of the contradictions of the online revolution brought on by digital technology: 'It will soon be feasible and viable to print even a single copy of a customised magazine' (92). This in a sense was a return of the *Heat* aesthetic of cultivating limited groups of good readers. So there is still the possibility of the physical magazine, and 'neither must the publisher pay to print such objects on the speculation that someone will want them'.

Going online, then, could provide further justification for the cultivation of controlled niche audiences. The use of the internet, in this instance, was democratic and anti-intuitive at the same time. Would publishing ever be the same? *Heat* would not have to brave any kind of market ever again, as Wright suggested: 'Continuing publishing subsidies will mean that there's no pressure to make money to survive' (92). The advantages she posited were laudable, but they raised the possibility that a magazine almost totally dependent on one source of income (whether public, private/commercial or otherwise) could never be truly independent — as the history of the literary magazine had already shown. If the magazine lost its subsidy it usually folded. In the 1970s, *Tabloid Story* was the prime example, and most of those that followed throughout the 1980s and 1990s would have been vulnerable with such a plan unless they were within the stable of established magazines.

The demise of *Heat* in hard-copy form was a decisive moment in early 2011, and a distinct loss to the promotion of a diversified Australian literature. The magazine's difficulties occupied the junction of the accelerating online story, and perhaps an admission of defeat in the face of contradictory pressures. Perhaps it meant that a literary magazine that looked like a book was an unsustainable model. Certainly, despite the distress expressed in the literary pages of the major newspapers, *Heat* was never published again in any form after 2011.

21. Anti-democratic tendencies

As you will have seen by now, all too often any history of small magazines in Australia is partly a story of revolving crises mediated by particular circumstances. 2010 also saw the culmination of the collection of the Excellence in Research Australia (ERA) data on publications in academic-ranked peer-review journals by the Australian Research Council—potentially yet another crisis to affect literary magazines. For several years, the Australian Research Council had been conducting this research. As had become the status quo in the sciences (where theories required evaluation by academic peers), peer reviewing had crept into the humanities. The process became central to research funding through the Australian Research Council, and despite protestations in the press and in private, academics were dutifully buckling down to the new guidelines. Results were to be posted early in 2011.

During 2008 and 2009, preliminary lists were published listing some of the established literary journals such as *Meanjin*, *Overland*, *Southerly* and *Heat* as either A, B, or C journals. Initially introduced in the sciences, this categorisation meant that humanities journals, whether specialist academic, or more generally literary, were coming under the spotlight. Dennis Tourish, a British academic, was, like some of his Australian colleagues, particularly scathing about the potential impacts of the process. He argued that academics were being steered towards publishing in preferred journals and 'lambasted for their inadequacy if they do not' (qtd. in Rowbotham, 'Journal

Rankings' 37). This presented the possibility that academics would only submit to top publications.

The issue had implications for broader literary publications, in that it had the potential to make some academics less community-focused, less like public intellectuals, if, for promotion, they had to largely publish in peer-reviewed journals. Under the guidelines, no research points were allocated for essays/articles or book reviews in the popular press or non-academic journals — raising the implication that academics who engaged with the public sphere would be effectively penalised for speaking to broad audiences. Also, no research points were allocated to editors of any journals, whether academic or non- academic. These developments were taking place in a landscape where academics in Australia (who have only ever partially supported the literary magazines) are, by all the evidence, becoming increasingly cultural spectators rather than critical participants. Broadly, an indirect form of self-censorship could be the result from the stringent new guidelines.

For less specialised magazines such as *Overland* it might mean 'clambering over obscure prose' (Sparrow, 'Interview with the author'), the reviewing process itself taking up precious time for under-resourced publications. For the creative writing industry in the universities, which were fighting tooth and nail internally to validate creative practice as research in its own right, it could prove especially dangerous, as postgraduates might come to see their futures only tied up in hierarchical terms (peer-reviewed publications) and therefore disregard the desire to find readers outside the specialised academy. Within this framework, *Wet Ink*'s unofficial position of resisting the urge to validate itself through scholarly articles was a statement that creative writing was and is research in its own terms, within an overall brief of attempting to establish a new, relatively populist model for the literary magazine. In broader terms, the issue had the potential to divert resources away from community initiatives, (such as general literary magazines) and further marginalise already endangered genres such as poetry and the short story into even tighter enclaves. In terms of funding, a comparison is timely here. As a rough estimate, most literary magazines would receive around $50 000 a year from the Australia Council, when in 2010, the average postgraduate scholarship for a PhD candidate in creative writing was $23 000.

Throughout Australia at that time there were at least seventy PhD creative writing candidates, indicating that there is a serious disjunction between production, on the one hand, and publication and distribution on the other. In other words, the literary magazines were extremely vulnerable, and were subsidising the creative writing industry in the universities during the very time when peer reviewing would potentially further stretch their resources. The mere fact that the magazines existed gave the impression to hundreds of creative writing students that there were outlets for their work, when many universities appeared to ignore the work the magazines were performing. Although *Wet Ink* was an independent structure, it had received some advertising from the University of Adelaide over the first five years of its life. But on 10 May 2011, it was told in an email from the university's marketing department that the advertising had been withdrawn because the marketing department was, in the wording of the email,

> looking for targeted and trackable advertising and communication opportunities to promote the Faculty's various offerings. It was felt that we don't have evidence of a clear return on investment from the *Wet Ink* sponsorship ... (Edge n.p.)

This was a clear indication that notions of commodification, as expressed by the new 'science' of marketing, were resulting in the homogenisation and encroaching corporatisation of cultural structures despite all the talk of difference and choice. Creative writing courses at universities were being aggressively marketed through writers' festivals, daily newspapers and writers' centre newsletters, using the idea of attracting people who saw themselves as would-be authors. Did universities have any responsibility to disseminate outputs from their courses? In any case, the irony was that the possible further institutionalisation of little magazines could result in some of them succumbing to the pressure of becoming more academic and obscure, thus putting pressure on the nature of the creative writing PhD itself by making it also more theoretical.

For years in the United States criticism had signalled out peer-reviewed journals of creative writing. Critics argued that such journals served largely institutionalised interests only, during a period of intense commodification of creative writing courses in United States colleges (Healey 30). The irony, two decades later, was that the ERA process in Australia likewise had the potential to be a sword in the heart of democratised creativity after the advances of the 1970s and 1980s. The ERA process was an unacknowledged realisation that much of the voluntary activity involving new writers in the decades preceding its development was being institutionalised in universities alongside the belated acceptance of the teaching of creative writing in the academy. Would this mean a dissipation of bold creativity? If the ERA process weakened existing literary magazines, which could no longer attract high-profile contributors because of a lack of peer-reviewing profile, would that result in an increasingly narrow range of publications? Would the only writers who could afford to write have to be associated in some way with a university?

In 2011, the contradictions of the process were becoming relatively absurd, in that online publishers (particularly in the United States) were starting to charge exorbitant amounts for subscriptions. Indeed Toby Miller claimed that an apocalyptic future 'will see all journals paid for by authors rather than subscribers' (40). Furthermore, Peter Shergold of Macquarie University — in a piece entitled 'Seen but not Heard' — discussed the widening disjuncture between academic research and the public sphere. While citing the reviewing process for several Australian journals, he came to the conclusion that

> [i]t is scarcely surprising that a direct contribution to public policy is generally not viewed highly by most academics or the universities in which they work. Nor is the task of spending valuable time translating research to the broader public. (4)

On a broader level the ranking of peer-review journals in the humanities (and of some literary magazines) had the potential to reify hierarchy and maintain the status quo.

> It was put another way by Tim Soutphommasane in the *Australian*:
> [F]ew scholars these days dare to think big ... [T]he much safer option is to concentrate one's energies on small, specialised areas of study. The path to promotion lies in generating a steady output of journal articles, written for a handful of other academic specialists in one's field. (12)

Raimond Gaita also commented, 'Universities have retreated from the public institutions of culture ... [E]ven interdisciplinary work within universities ... is now discouraged because publications in disciplines other than one's own earn no points for one's department'. He added, 'In many universities even academics in the humanities are discouraged from writing books rather than for A-grade journals' (79).

Would the 'cultural cringe' then snuggle through the cracks of a journal-ranking system that privileged international journals at the expense of local journals that published research and original creative writing directly relevant to Australian issues and experience? All of these issues were debated in universities and in the press, until finally, on 31 May 2011, the then Federal Minister for Innovation, Senator Kim Carr, announced that he was directing changes to the ERA process, which included dropping the rankings of peer-review publications. This was met with general approval from the sector. Senator Carr said that his decision was partly based on the fact that ranking journals had meant that 'their existence was focusing ill-informed, undesirable behaviour in the management of research' (Rowbotham, 'Carr bows' 25).

The period of the ranking of peer-review journals was a sad episode which had only further dramatised the powerlessness and individualised ambition of the intellectual class. It had come to this: the once politically engaged academics (or public intellectuals) of the 1960s, 1970s and 1980s were reduced to scrambling for research points in A-grade journals, and those who taught creative writing were also implicated because many of them had spent years attempting to validate their methodology by engaging in similar hierarchical games. Beneath the manoeuvring for positions, there was an undeclared war between practitioners and critics in the universities.

The post-modern university was a long way from the theories of difference and respect for marginality upon which it was supposedly built. But the multifarious story of the literary magazine in Australia shows that people will try to institute change at certain points. The advent of peer ranking of journals was an anti-democratic move against the very genesis of that part of the story, at least.

The changes in the means of production, which I have been discussing on the micro-level of magazines as commodities, were therefore part of a larger crisis in Western education in the new millennium. They were, a move towards increased specialisation and a breaking-up of possible connections between disciplines. Threats to the viability of the hard-copy small magazine desirous of a readership outside friends and relatives were coming from everywhere, it seemed, by early 2011. Although a different product to the printed book, the magazine, as I have discussed, is in some hands a book and in others a relatively portable commodity. But the contents of the literary magazine are radically different from other magazines, which appear more frequently — sometimes weekly, sometimes monthly. The very essence of the literary magazine (even in its current hard-copy and online versions) is that it publishes material that is less topical than more regular periodicals. As Geordie Williamson has suggested, by making a comparison with the updating online possibilities of textbooks, dictionaries, travel guides and instruction manuals,

> other forms are more stubbornly wedded to their physical form; content and medium cannot be severed without doing violence to what remains. Novels, poetry, short stories, writings on metaphysics: anything that demands contemplative immersion and is resistant to improvement by regular updating should, ideally, remain as it is. ('Kindling' 23)

In other words, the use value of most of the small magazines discussed here is in being 'other' to the discontinuity and pace of much of contemporary Western society. For all this, many of the new magazines astutely realised that the internet had opened up promotional opportunities for hard-copy editions, through the use of e-commerce websites (such as Paypal) for the payment of subscriptions, and through Facebook, Twitter and blogging for the generation of online chat about the contents of the latest issues. Expediential change was such that the new social media were continually creating new platforms, and commodification had clogged up one of the earliest sites, Myspace, which after a few years become full of advertisements by individuals and businesses. In any case, all the magazines listed in Literary Magazines Australia in 2010 were engaged in promotion on the internet.

The paradox was such that the internet was providing the promotional possibility that perhaps it was possible to break the 'glass ceiling' of distribution through social media, yet further raising false expectations of free content — thus potentially eroding the very product being promoted. An example of this in May 2011 were the subscription policies that *Quadrant* and the *Australian Book Review* were offering. In *Quadrant*'s case, the magazine offered separate online and print subscriptions, plus the option of a joint subscription, but the online price was much cheaper than the print edition. The *Australian Book Review* offered separate online and print subscriptions that were similarly priced, raising the scenario that print subscriptions might become a thing of the past, putting further pressure on the viability of the print edition. Universities, local councils and some school libraries had long been a reliable subscription base for literary magazines, but with the onset of cheaper online subscriptions, would they continue to subscribe, whether to the online edition or the hard-copy edition? *Overland* and *Meanjin* had print subscriptions only, but there was a great deal of each new edition published free immediately online. Ironically and by chance, the internet had provided the perfect excuse for cost-cutting in education and for government agencies.

Other questions included: Would the chat on social media expand the market (whether hard-copy or online) or become another manifestation of a narcissistic cultural climate — in other words, a stylised shorthand for discourse between like-minded people, a reproduction of the kind of circular discussions which had characterised many of the little magazines of the 1970s? In saying that, such a concern, probably, would not be a concern for some of the new magazines, as their criterion was clearly to preach to the converted, as that, I have argued, seemed to be partly the reason for their existence.

Anyway, the availability and exposure of old hard-copy products was an issue in early 2011 in Britain, the United States and Australia, where retail changes to bookselling reached crisis levels. Normally, magazine publishers are not concerned with bookshops as sales sites, but — as small magazines cannot, on the whole, reach other outlets such as newsagents — what happens in bookshops will still affect their small sales. In Australia in mid-February, private-equity-backed REDgroup Retail (which owned two large chains, Borders and Angus and Robertson) was placed in receivership. The group employed 2500 staff across 169 Angus and Robertson stores and 26 Borders stores across Australia, as well as 60 stores in NZ. It blamed a high Australian dollar (in 2010 and 2011 particularly), which made imports much cheaper, and the onset of online shopping for its demise. Other booksellers also spoke of a decline in sales over 2010 (Coronel 3).

Normally, this would not have been concerning to the small magazines, as the majority of their sales were in a handful of independent bookshops such as Readings in Melbourne, Gleebooks in Sydney, Avid Reader in Brisbane and Imprints in Adelaide, but reports suggested that the fall in sales was across the sector and not confined to the chains. Also, Borders was a large seller of niche publications of all kinds such as *Dumbo Feather*, *Frankie* and art and music industry publications. Their corporate model had been to stock wide ranges of products and publications. Ironically, after years of trying, some of the little magazines were stocked by the chain, such as *Wet Ink* around Australia. This was because the magazine did not consider its readers to be purely frequenters of inner suburban independent bookshops. Sales of literary magazines are small fry by publishing standards, but were essential to the individual magazines concerned.

A general debate ensued in the press both as to the demise of the book and of small independent bookshops, and in broader terms, the price of books in a globalised and increasingly internet-oriented marketplace. In a piece on prices, Matthia Dempsey, the editor of the *Bookseller & Publisher*, championed local, community-based booksellers, while acknowledging that imports were cheaper, likening the booming online retailer Book Depository to the mass-market model of IKEA. But it should be added that online sites such as Book Depository were also establishing ways around the gatekeeping role of all booksellers, who have always played a large role in making or breaking any book by mentioning a chosen few in their newsletters, and by prominently displaying others in their windows or next to cash registers. The role of Readings in Melbourne in promoting the novelist Alex Miller is a good example. Booksellers, of whatever persuasion, have never stocked every new title, and their motives are never entirely altruistic; and they have, in the case of Borders and the Angus and Robertson chain, made bestsellers of authors such as Bryce Courtney through discount (loss leader) pricing and window displays. The poor cousin, that is the literary magazine, did not have a chance if stocked spine-out in any store. Eliminating the middle man was a contradictory, if non-hierarchical, moment.

Backing the crisis was a continuing debate about the challenge of e-books. Characterising the printed book as old-fashioned technology, Sherman Young in 2010 argued for a democratic opening-out, stating that 'books as physical objects are easily controlled — they need to be printed, sold and shipped. And the entire book industry is based on that premise of control, extracting revenue at key gateways'. He further suggested that 'resistance to the introduction of e-books is as much about the struggle for business survival as any romantic notions of ink and paper' (19). In comparison, Dempsey's piece was also a call to the local if not quite the national for book buyers. The question, for little magazines, was: How committed would people be to pay the necessary price? In broader terms, Enzensberger's claim over three decades ago that 'even today, the predominance of the book has an episodic air' is chilling to those brought up with it, suggesting that the book had usurped and formalised oral traditions of the past, and 'was a stand-in for future methods which make it possible for everyone to become a producer' (Enzensberger 47).

Phillip Edmonds

For all that, the advent of digital printing has meant that small magazines with short print runs are probably more viable than ever. Unit costs are not factors in abandoning print altogether, but the old problem of lack of distribution remains. In 2011, proponents of the printed word could well have been wondering whether they were latter-day Luddites resisting another revolution in the means of production.

22. An unreliable commodity

In his essay *The Work of Art in the Age of Mechanical Reproduction* Walter Benjamin prefigured some of the current contradictions. He quotes from Paul Valery as an epigram. At the conclusion of the quote, Valery suggests that

> we must expect great innovations to transform the entire technique of the arts, thereby affecting artistic invention itself and perhaps even bringing about an amazing change in our very notion of art. (Qtd. in Benjamin 217)

Benjamin suggested that future changes to the means of production would result in more intensive exploitation of the proletariat and 'ultimately ... create conditions which would make it possible to abolish capitalism altogether' (217). This is useful with regards to Marx's prescription of ongoing crises in surplus value resulting in a declining rate of profit as specific points in the trade cycle. One such point was reached by the conclusion of the 1990s, in that the internet had exposed a crisis of profitability in the production of most books, and in the case of magazines, of sustainability.

At the conclusion of the twentieth century, Eric Hobsbawn summarised the contradiction inscribed within the changes. He noted, as I hope I have demonstrated, that the arts are not inseparable 'from their contemporary context, as a branch or type of human activity subject to its own rules, and capable of being judged accordingly'. He added that

> even this ancient and convenient principle of structuring a historical survey becomes increasingly unreal. Not only because the boundary

> between what is and is not classifiable as 'art', 'creation', or artifice became increasingly hazy, or even disappeared altogether ... Technology revolutionised the arts most obviously by making them omnipresent. (500)

Put another way, cultural works are no longer purely superstructural expressions. On the contrary, they are among the basic processes in the formation of the economic substructure itself. The internet is an example of this, but the deconstruction of the binary between high and popular that was convenient to representations in less complex times is only a part of the story. Technological change had also created a fracturing of the public sphere and instigated narrow communities of interest, and a frantic, repressed desire for hierarchical distinction — the literary magazines of Australia were partial evidence of that. At the level of the printed word, marketing genres proliferated, niche audiences were targeted, authors were privileged over their work and bookselling was, it seemed, cracking under the strain of internet buying, wedged between e-books and a stratified marketplace, resulting in unemployment.

Returning to Benjamin, the question of whether traditional notions of commodification would be abolished is a moot point, in that late capitalism had already shown how adaptable it was in commodifying and reconfiguring the anti-disciplinary initiatives of the 1960s. However, with the advent of e-publishing in its varied guises, the book and the magazine as twentieth-century constructions and commodities, were being deconstructed by an open-ended, 'democratic' informational network which for years had published and republished information (and cultural artefacts) for free, raising entitlement expectations in perhaps an entire generation. The internet had opened up the possibility that it was possible to publish around the traditional gatekeepers in publishing houses and magazines; and in that sense it was at least superficially revolutionary. For the literary/small magazine around the years of 2009 and 2010, the onset of e-publishing meant that print publishing in an age of celebrity took too much time. Online publishing, and its attendant social media sites, were also a massive, narcissistic temptation in an environment where, as Justin EH Smith has suggested:

> The internet has concentrated once widely dispersed aspects of a human life into one and the same little machine: work, friendship, commerce, creativity, eros … This is, in short, an exceptional moment in history, next to which 19th century anxieties about the railroad or the automated loom seem frivolous. Looms and cotton gins and similar apparatuses each only did one thing: the internet does everything. (Qtd. in Williamson, 'Kindling' 10)

I take his point, but the internet still is unable to dig holes and perform manual labour, even if it can direct such things. We are looking at the fifth 50-year wave in the history of capitalism, to use Ernest Mandel's thesis in *Late Capitalism* (qtd. in Windschuttle 19). From 1940 to 1990, there developed the generalised control of machines by electronic devices; and now, post-1990, we are going through a wave where further advances in devices have had profound social impacts. As changes to superstructural levels are currently both preceding and informing the industrial substructure, it is necessary to engage with the contrary nature of the new media formations in terms of what could be in store for the literary magazine, in ways that Enzensberger has prefigured:

> The new media are orientated towards action, not contemplation; towards the present not tradition. Their attitude to time is completely opposed to that of bourgeois culture, which aspires to possession … [T]he media produce no objects that can be hoarded or auctioned. They do away completely with 'intellectual property' and liquidate the 'heritage', that is to say, the class-specific handing-on of nonmaterial capital. (31)

A contemporary postscript could be that the modern bourgeoisie (or the intellectual fraction of it) in Australia at least (post-1970s) regards itself as classless in the traditional sense, non-specific, mobile and part of an international class with few cloying loyalties. Within this framework, there are dangers for magazines of any format, in that readers now appear to be increasingly fickle with their enthusiasms. In terms of the strict commodity, magazines that are, to all intents and purposes, books could be more vulnerable than serial publications, which have at least the advantage of periodic publication.

So as to not be too ephemeral, from 2000, the most spectacular results in changes to the means of production have been occurring as new production sites have been established. Such changes have permeated throughout all other industries. In Australia we are at the point where the rate of profit is declining in traditional sectors, thus leading to a search for surplus value in new product creation. Given the pace of change, the very exchange value of these new products is being instantly deconstructed, posing a threat to existing profit-takers and producers and raising the prospect of ongoing deflation — a situation which is only underpinned by credit and the shaky prospect of inexhaustible natural resources.

In the area under discussion, the production of print editions involved more (and different) work and was far more expensive, which was a contributing factor in the threat to a number of the print publications. Even so, at the time of writing, things were changing so fast that an overall perspective on the full extent of the changes is hard to reach. Furthermore, even if the internet revolution has led to declining profitability in previously traditional sectors, and made informational dissemination much cheaper, a swing over time was resulting in increased labour and costs being incurred in continuous website maintenance and content delivery, so the cost of e-publishing would eventually increase.

As noted, at the end of 2010, the then editor of *Meanjin*, Sophie Cunningham, resigned for reasons that remained unclear but were rumoured to include a desire by the publisher, Melbourne University Press, to go entirely online. There were protests about such moves from traditionalists such as the former editor Jim Davidson:

> [T]o go entirely online would be a form of suicide — certainly it would corral it into ineffectuality. Ten years ago *Eureka Street* was riding high ... but [now] the wider audience of the magazine, appearing only on the net, is negligible. Many former readers are unaware of its continued existence.
> ('A cork' 131)

In Cunningham's desire to update *Meanjin* from its (perceived) dour, nationalistic past, a lot of the content had been put online — maybe too much? Given that in 2011 no successful business media model had been set in place for online content, Davidson's comment also raised the issue of how to remain dominant and visible over time in all the internet clutter and traffic.

The internet as a new form of technocratic, indeed post-industrial, reproduction was also showing up the contradictory tendencies of mass communication/the public and the private as tendentious constructions — the symptoms of late capitalism's search for new markets throughout the previously designated margins rather than from a static centre. Ironically, the internet and e-technology, while freeing up masses of people from the strictures of industrial labour, created a new class of workers who slave before its latest demands, and are industrially organised in their workplaces.

As Caroline Hamilton has pointed out, '[I]t is important to keep in mind that creative enterprises facilitated by the internet are no more independent from capitalist processes than their traditional counterparts are'. Speaking of online working environments, she added that the internet

> has meant that workloads but not budgets have increased, just as traditional revenue streams (especially advertising) have dried up … [C]ontent is routinely produced free of charge by the audiences that also consume it. ('The exposure' 89)

In a desire for exposure, many writers have become further proletarianised: 'The exposure economy sustains the notion that writers need the imprimatur of others to legitimise their labours' (94). All of this is predicated (according to Benjamin Laird) on the ways in which information technology, despite its perceived lack of ideology, is increasingly living off cheap labour in India and China to produce new products ('CEOS' 83). Even so, small-press publishers and magazine editors, according to Hamilton, are optimistic (almost utopian) as to the refigured landscape. One publisher told her: 'The internet has split the market into niches … [I]t's easier … for a small publication [now], we can find our readers and our writers anywhere in the world … so much that sales aren't even a pressure' ('The exposure' 90).

Such contradictions were evidence of other forces, for if the history of the late twentieth century suggests anything, it is that a crisis of hierarchy was evident in most social formations, especially the corporatised universities. The crisis would not go away, if evidence of the growth of peer-review journals — many of which were only published electronically on the internet — is anything to go by. To paraphrase, an increasingly complex society, especially in terms of its representations, was, in the universities, desperately searching for hierarchical validation and cultural commodification. Indeed, society was searching for a new language away from the masses, which were constructed as 'the other'. The universities had always been about inculcating students in specialist languages as a mark of success, yet by the new millennium, such a quest had become chronic even despite democratic and inclusive promotions.

Outside the anxious universities, readers were desperately searching for hierarchies of reading, because established canons were slipping from memory, and static notions of high and popular culture were all but disappearing. This, perversely, could have been informing the rationale behind the formation of some of the new magazines. New multicultural and feminist canons had been created during the 1980s to satisfy the socially aware aspirations of the 'new class' in the West, but by 2010 they were becoming passé. Writers' festivals, in Australia at least, were attempting to re-establish hierarchies based on topicality, and through an influx of big-name overseas authors to grant hegemony, as the 'cultural cringe' refused to wither in an Australia, still not a republic. Rjurik Davidson has further suggested that festivals may indeed be working against the interests of progressive writers: 'The prevalent liberal answer — fairly common at literary festivals, for example — is that writers should provide a path to truth and beauty. They guide us through questions of taste and appropriate behaviour ... ' ('Political writers' 55). In short, his suggestion was that they could be homogenising structures.

Back into the micro-area of the literary/little magazines, and (despite all the activity in the late 2000s), there was still a lack of confidence among some of the editors of the new magazines, in that they felt they had to be validated by those higher up. For example, when a piece of creative writing they had published was republished in the Black Inc. 'Best of' series each year, their websites waxed about their success — suggesting that, in real terms, a genuine revolution was not taking place, that the need for established Left/liberal structures was still necessary, and/or that the new magazines really did not want to overthrow them. In fact, considerable successes had been achieved through the mere fact of publishing unknown authors in an indifferent environment. More to the point, such publication could insinuate that the formation of the literary magazines' structures was a way of hoping that the establishment might see their work and take them up. Some of the newer magazines were still not at the point where they saw their publications as destinations in their own right.

For example, even 'attack' journals such as the *Lifted Brow* would frequently name-drop, while *Kill Your Darlings* and *Harvest* sounded colonial at times, at least to some ears. The obvious commercial advantage of publishing established authors is a different point. For all the small-press activity (over four decades), a conclusion could be that an insatiable desire for secure structures was the underbelly to the restlessness. Moving forward, it appeared that, despite the so called power of the internet, economic and social powerlessness was evident throughout Australia in 2010. This is not to say that the upsurge in small-press activity was not without its enthusiastic networks; however, it was restrained by the individualistic frame it had assumed for itself as a natural consequence of a post-modern market of separate consumers and publishers. After Mark Davis's doubts over whether people were prepared to support a local publishing industry, the anxiety had not withered away by 2010, raising the inevitable question: 'How can there be mass mobilisation when there is no community?' (Doyle 211)

Where would the new readers come from? Was the upsurge in blogging and social media a manifestation of a privatised dispersal of public space? Had a community of writers and readers been so dispersed that the literary magazines would no longer be able to become mobilisation points, even with the use of the new configurations? For all that, Wenche Ommundsen and Michael Jacklin in their 2008 report to the Australia Council on the Literary

Infrastructure of Australia identified that the magazines were maintaining and developing what they had always done quite well. They were providing a springboard for emerging literary talent, supporting marginalised literary forms, even though fiction had lost ground to non-fiction in the broader marketplace, and offering professional development for young writers and editors (4). But the usual problems remained, such as extremely limited staff levels, the difficulty of gaining more subscribers and regionalism, which last, they said, 'plays a role in limiting the reach of certain magazines' (5). Would digital technologies overcome that problem and suggest a more participatory future, or an illusionary landscape?

Walter Benjamin had commented years before that 'the mass is the matrix from which all traditional behaviour toward works of art issues today in a new form. Quantity has been subsumed into quality' (239). Granted, but aesthetic consumers have, over the history of the capitalist mode of production, demonstrated a desire to differentiate because the concept of distinction is central, for better or for worse, to relationships mediated by class, and thereby, in broad terms, through image creation as marketing. This tendency would continue to work its way through the story of the literary magazine.

We require measures of distinction to differentiate products, irrespective of inherent quality — such as, for example, the 'Best Of' series published by Black Inc., which has attempted to monumentalise some of the small-press upsurge. As suggested by Jeff Sparrow of *Overland*, a subscription culture among the younger demographic currently looks problematic, something also noticed by teachers of creative writing courses. Paradoxically, entries to short story competitions run by the magazines in this period attracted scores of entries. In 2010, approximately 600 were received by *Wet Ink* for a small entry fee. The *Australian Book Review* initiated its own prize in 2011 — a clear indication that it could be another revenue stream and a useful promotional device. In other words, a prize that anoints winners promotes (or 'consecrates', in effect) the desire for hierarchy — in contrast to taking out a subscription, which, although it is a purchase of a specific commodity (a magazine), invokes notions of support and community and to an extent anonymity. In the face of the internet challenge, and such a crisis of hierarchy, the book trade would then presumably have to change its mode of production, becoming more diversified and canny in its constructions.

As we have seen, the hierarchical crisis the magazines had been working through, particularly in the 1980s and 1990s, was a tendency that pushed towards book formats. Cost pressures and problems of publishing at least four times a year had also persuaded some magazine editors such as the editors of *Heat* to go biannual, which presumably lowered their visibility and subscription potential, which is based on regularity and frequency. Thus in a sense economics has always informed whether good ideas can be pursued and what a magazine really is. At the time of writing, the future is uncertain, as it is with any technological advance. Even so, the overwhelming popularity of e-commerce as a marketing tool has already demonstrated that increased profitability (for some media) can be achieved by pruning back on the shopkeeper. Booksellers and other retail outlets which sell the printed word came under increasing pressure to limit their range of stock, which is a no-win position that further undermines their viability. It is the case that niche publications such as small magazines have increasingly marketed via the web because the internet, as it stands, is the world's largest shopping mall — a privatised space that is replacing face-to-face chatter and gossip.

Originally a social and educational networking site, the internet is commodified, not so much in linear ways (as is the case with the traditional print media) but rather as a militant lateral expansion of marketing opportunities. For all of the above, would people pay a price for the experience of reading magazines, so that there would be some independence from the state, no matter how benign? In turn, authors, traditionally unable to demand a price for their work, had to work within a framework asking them to perform for next to nothing. The age of celebrity had formalised the romantic image of the artist into the informational workplace.

In a sense, then, is the question not that late capitalism, as a lively, evolving social system, is working out new ways to ditch inefficient means of production, distribution and exchange, through further proletarianisation (and more specifically casualisation)? Concurrently, it would be naïve to assume that with the death of specific commodities, multinational corporations will vacate the field, especially as some of the larger corporations produce the replacement commodities (iPads, etc.). What is concerning is that the authors as producers are stymied by consumer expectations for free products and by an almost total lack of bargaining power in the new decentred workplace. Margaret Simons, in a piece in *Crikey*, noted how it is becoming almost impossible for freelance writers to get paid in Australia (qtd. in Hamilton, 'The exposure' 88) and *Publishers Weekly* in the United States recently reported that the most serious challenge facing people writing in the digital age is 'the fact it's become very hard for writers to get paid' (qtd. in 'The exposure' 89). Writers, then, outside of those on academic salaries who can afford to write for next to nothing for peer-review journals, could be wedged out of a shrinking market where very little intellectual labour is actually paid for.

Within the creative writing industry in the universities, what will happen to ambitious postgraduates? Will they consider it realistic to only write for peer-review journals and eschew the desire to find as many readers as possible so as to gain employment as teachers of creative writing? Concurrent with these developments has been the almost total commodification of creative writing courses in United States colleges and universities, evidenced by even the most cursory reading of the *Writers Chronicle*, the journal of the US Association of Writers and Writing Programs, where residencies and courses are advertised for very expensive fees, thus effectively excluding working- and lower middle class students. Further to gathering commodification in the first instance, I would argue that as the creative writing industry has established itself in the universities, fetishisation of the discipline is appearing in what is at times over-theorisation of the writing process — a reification of what is essentially a craft-based practice. So while there was a resurgence of literary magazines during the mid- to late 2000s in Australia, countervailing tendencies were at work.

As I have argued, the increase in the number of small magazines was largely a democratic move; but the commodification of creative writing in the universities was proving to be counterintuitive, making creative writing a broad commodity — a brand name. Furthermore, creative writing was becoming fetishised at the higher-degree level (with positive and negative aspects), so as to gain academic respectability. The aftermath of the post-structuralist ascendancy meant that many academics not only ditched the possibility of 'a public', but also that their discourses were overwhelmingly bureaucratic.

In a piece discussing broader concerns in academia, Peter van Onselen has made the point that the drive to secure research grants from the ARC is warping productivity and possible conceptual models in the sector:

> Publish or perish. That's the adage often used to describe the challenges within academe. However, increasingly grants matter more than research publications ... Filling out grant applications takes time and the funds are often used for a wide range of self-justifying endeavours ... [T]here are many academics who spend their time on a merry-go-round to nowhere, instead of improving their publishing outputs. (24)

This illustrates an interesting parallel with many activities within the literary arts, and particularly with the activities of writers' centres, which have to negotiate annual funding rounds with state and federal governments.

By way of contrast, magazine publishing was and is 'value adding' in the broadest sense — adding value to one's Curriculum Vita, and providing credits for scholarship and job applications. In its broadest sense, as I suggested in Chapter Three, literary magazines each provide a positive externality that benefits the broader society. Seemingly utopian activities were then set against a backdrop where a coupling of corporate, bureaucratic and academic language and activity had occurred, a tendency that is relatively typical of our current formations. We see a search for a form of commodification predicated on preciousness and perceived scarcity after branding has been successful, and on the micro-level, an appearance of economic and cultural production.

I have already alluded to the increasing role of writers' festivals in the promotion of certain writers, and by implication, publishers. Over the period of this study, the number of festivals has grown from the solitary Writers' Week at the Adelaide Festival in the 1960s to Writers' Festivals in every major capital city in the country and a growing band of much smaller regional festivals. On one level they have demonstrated growing community participation in literary activities; at the same time, they have been marked by increasing commodification through the need for corporate sponsors to finance the overseas writers invited. Sponsors have included state and federal arts bodies and, in the case of the Byron Bay Writers Festival, local businesses.

However, by 2011, commodification expressed as specific market branding reached a new level when Writers' Week in Adelaide accepted sponsorship from the University of South Australia (for the 2012 festival) which precluded any branding from other organisations and included the stipulation that invited writers could not speak outside official Writers' Week functions. Such an anti-democratic tendency is contrary to the somewhat heterogeneous nature of much literary activity — in particular, the historical role of the literary/small magazine, which, as an unreliable commodity, fertilises ideas of difference. Even when a particular magazine gains hegemonic status and marketing potential, it is often a participatory conversation sideways to paternal structures.

Despite rhetoric to the contrary, as to the breaking-down of the boundary between high and popular culture, such specialisation was ripping at the very notion of readers and writers. With universities in particular in mind, Drusilla Modjeska prefigured much of this in 2006. Speaking of the disjuncture between intellectuals and the public, she suggested that 'the question that concerns those of us working in this area is how to reverse the disconnection and open a space of creative and intellectual potential' (40-7). Given that supporting any type of literary magazine has always been a chore for the universities, supporting magazines that were largely creative writing magazines in 2011 (apart from discreet student anthologies) would then be working against such a contradiction, arising out of the commodification of creative writing. In other words, popularising original creative writing at a more grassroots level would make the brand, paradoxically, too popular, and not high-cultural enough. Thus the appeal of supporting ranked peer-review journals in the years between 2008 and 2010 was not merely a way of attracting research money; it was also a flight from a fractured, public sphere.

The moment, then, after the Global Financial Crisis of 2009, has been increasingly one of disjuncture between theory and practice in the means of production and the subsequent formation of commodities, facilitated and allied to technological advances. That contradiction inevitably builds up and fractures as it did in 2009, and will probably do so again, as debt issues remain unresolved in the global economy.

My point here is that the commodification process is ruled by a tendency that requires that only some products can ever be popular; and that the 'popular' and 'the esoteric' construct one another. The irony in all of this, in terms of the magazines, is that a few of the journals that only published one or two issues, such as *Polar Bear* and *Manic*, started to appear on antiquarian bookseller websites; and other magazines (from the 1970s) appeared on eBay in 2011 advertised at considerable prices. Here was evidence yet again of the often imperfect nature of commodification, at times predicated on scarcity. It is also evidence that the value of the small magazine (and at times the value of books) is often not expressed over time in useful terms; it can manifest itself in its own performative failures. The bohemian moment of the small magazine, then, can be challenging, and a time of recreational grieving — an amusing entertainment if it refuses to challenge cultural power structures.

Creative writing in the universities, therefore, became successfully commodified — sold as a discrete educational option (with specific branding). Yet if there is one thing that also shows how the literary magazine is an unreliable commodity, it is the difficulty of magazines to attract advertising. Over the years, the magazines have carried little advertising apart from 'swap' advertisements between journals because, on the whole, advertisers are suspicious of their low circulation, and of the fact that they target neither core, niche constituencies with considerable income nor readers like local newspapers. *Meanjin* and *Australian Letters* carried paid advertisements from some businesses, but they were largely sponsorship agreements. *Wet Ink* carried some advertisements as a result of aggressive selling, and the *Australian Book Review* carries advertising from some publishers due to its circulation into libraries. But the literary magazine, in general, is still considered ephemeral and marginal, and the literary arts not of crucial interest to cultural consumers, unlike the more highly visible and more thoroughly commodified forms such as ballet, theatre and opera.

So many questions come from the history of recent literary magazines because of the very nature of their contradictory relationship with the means of cultural production. Socially and culturally, the small magazine has traditionally been (as we have seen) a canary in the coal mine, a precursor to what can follow, an irritant, and a site of guilt for the intellectual class when they fail — often a romantic construction, in effect, depending on the nature of the perceptible discourse at any one time.

In writing of the period from the late 1960s I have observed that the nature of the literary magazine as a relatively limited publication meant that it could (to varying degrees) indulge itself in eccentric and even expensive productions by popular standards, as it meandered between the magazine format and book-like constructions. Some journals, such as *New Poetry* and *Rigmarole of the Hours* in the 1970s, and *Harvest* and *Wet Ink* in the 2000s, were quite beautiful tactile productions predicated on the primacy of print. With the internet, and the flight online in the years after 2009, the idea of the magazine was deconstructing. Would, then, online become a site of representation which would lead to homogenisation, in that it was a formalisation of a move away from the tactile? Perhaps there is also an even more overriding observation to be made as to problems of visibility for little magazines (hard-copy or online) in the age of information explosion. During the 1970s especially, little magazines had the advantage and power to shock and be transgressive, whereas today, it seems, nothing shocks: 'Modernist artists are no longer significant in society ... [T]hey have won. They have transformed culture, or at least played a major part in its transformation, and there is nothing left for them to do' (Gare 148). And, currently, the previously designated margins are moving in and out of a revolving centre in a desperate search for new marketing opportunities.

Another consideration is that literary magazines in 2010 were publishing in a society dominated by spectacle and accelerated self-promotion. Despite and because of the so-called connective nature of social media sites, participation in community events appeared to be trailing off in comparison to the 1970s, when the little magazines, for all their faults, were types of interactive, participatory communities. Over the latter period of this study, according to a bleak view from Michael Wilding, (which belies a nostalgic view of the 1970s), there has been a

> remorseless imposition of control and monopolisation ... [V]oluntary organisations, small presses, little magazines and learned societies are gradually being squeezed out of existence. The amateur and the voluntary are being replaced by the professional, the global, the corporate. ('Wild & Woolley' 89)

It appeared that the small magazines of the new millennium were trying to buck the trend, in some cases having to work within an environment where their initiatives were being formalised in writers' centres and in the universities. Whether social media is a co-operative or privatising phenomenon is another open question at the time of writing.

23. Complications and Conclusions

The 'bourgeois public sphere' that Habermas defined and discussed has been further eroded during the period of this study, even if his definition was dependent upon a relatively radical and questioning intellectual class of writers and readers desirous of conversation in relatively close proximity. Yet there is some evidence of the remnants of a public sphere, if only in the support that the *Griffith Review* has maintained for its type of discursive essays on contemporary issues.

Australia, though, may only be capable of supporting one such journal. The bourgeois public sphere is now, if anything, decentred, asymmetrical in terms of potential communities of interest and basically pragmatic rather than idealistic — and radically different from Habermas's organic idea. As Stuart Glover has pointed out, 'the contemporary public sphere is very different from the free public sphere Jurgen Habermas imagined about eighteenth century London'. Glover suggested that 'by the nineteenth century this idealised free literary sphere gave way to a quasi-literary public sphere wherein corporate and state interests predominated' ('No Magazine' 24). Even so, he has argued that small magazines represent, apart from geography, a second sphere defined by 'diversity and independence' where news and media are dominated by corporate voices (23).

Overland has retained and refertilised its constituency through its own brand of Leftism. The *Australian Book Review* has deliberately promoted itself as respectable and authoritative, and is still in search of respectability, whereas *Meanjin* is attempting to refind its feet. Of the other magazines I have discussed, most were creative writing journals, some of which were exclusively oriented towards poetry. It is a moot point as to whether the more anarchistic and less commercially oriented magazines were evidence of transgression in this stage of late capitalism. Yet lack of recognition and market coverage can go hand-in-hand, so it can be construed that they were incompatible with useful bourgeois norms, which are sometimes expressed in commodified terms. In any case, publishing unknown authors, as was the brief of several of the magazines, is transgressive (whether or not conceived in ideological terms) and counter to the dynamics of commodification in a culture dominated by celebrity as market branding.

In contemporary Australia, it is no longer necessary to have censorship and surveillance by the intelligence agencies of writers and magazines, as it was when Stephen Murray-Smith first published *Overland* in the 1950s, or when Clem Christesen battled with recalcitrant elements in and out of the University of Melbourne to keep *Meanjin* afloat. To ignore new cultural developments, either through a lack of reviewing or more simply through an overall absence of recognition, is sufficient. There will be the odd alternative exemption, examples of which I have posited, as they are sites, in a totalising landscape (which plays with 'difference') of an ethical other. In other words, for all the changes in the means of production, there are always countervailing, 'retro' moves.

In broader terms, would the massive change to the informational means of production lead (in real terms) to a more diversified media, or would it provide the apparatus for further homogenisation, given the indiscriminate nature of internet traffic and the flat and, in aesthetic terms, relatively one-dimensional nature of the very technology? Is the internet a vehicle for representational shorthand rather than 'new worlds'? As Geordie Williamson has suggested when writing of the demise of *Heat* in early 2011:

> [T]here is a tension here. The web dissolves the boundaries between sound, image, text; it allows endless recombination of writings drawn

> from different times and places. It is not clear how journals, which have so far survived on the basis of their physical and editorial distinctness — will continue to stand out among an endless crowd. Those who migrate online should be wary of the border between miscellany and total disorder. ('Journal' 20)

He is referring to (and lamenting from a liberal democratic stance) the fact that the spectral aspect of capitalist development is now actualised across social formations in ways that have fetishised and dematerialised money in cyberspace, as a retreat from cognitive mapping and the actuality of work. As Zizek suggests, 'the human being [the worker] comes to relate more as a watchman and regulator to the production process itself' (*In defence* 355). Quoting Marx, Zizek suggests that

> no longer does the worker insert a modified natural thing ... he inserts the process of nature, transformed into an industrial process, as a means between himself and inorganic nature, mastering it. He steps to the side of the production process instead of being its chief actor. (355)

Williamson is, it appears, defending a pre-post-industrial idea of the magazine (and that of the worker and traditional notions of work). A further question could well be that his notion of print is a type of 'thick' description rather suspicious of a discontinuous series of 'thin' moments. So, then, would a remorseless move to online publishing accelerate the production of pastiche in literary terms through the discontinuous demands of the technology, as Fredric Jameson had suggested of much of post-modern writing and architecture during the 1990s? And apart from the structural changes to the informational means of production allowing for cheaper production, to what extent would online publishing destroy the anticipation-effect that had always underpinned much of print publishing and author promotion during the twentieth century?

On the local level, Williamson also had fears for *Meanjin* — fears that could not be assuaged by events when he quoted the editorial for Volume 70, no 2, in June 2011: '*Meanjin* cannot be a publicly funded exercise aimed at bringing private pleasure to a fortunate few' (qtd. in '*Meanjin*'s place' 20).

Clearly, his concerns hinged on a preference for distinction over mass representation, which has been one of the literary magazine's reasons for being, alongside countervailing moves towards cultural democratisation, particularly in the 1970s. Its contrary forms have determined, to an extent, its content.

Contributing to the debate in 2011, Richard King accused defenders of the printed artefact such as Williamson, and, particularly, opponents of *Meanjin*'s threatened exodus online (like Peter Craven and Jim Davidson), of an elitism: of an attempt to hold back the tide of cultural participation. Citing the story of the *Spectator* (published between 1711-12) in Britain as an attempt at popularism, which he likened to the internet's current potential, he quoted the historian Jenny Uglow on the eighteenth-century publishing boom: '[T]he danger as some saw it, was that culture itself was going to be defined by the new, "vulgar" public' (qtd. in R King 17). In a swipe at the traditional media, including his view of the role of the literary magazine, King further noted that the *Spectator* 'was thus not only widely available but also peculiarly accessible; without talking down, it managed to bring the man in the street (or in the coffee house) into the cultural conversation'.

There is some truth in his view of the frame that some of the literary magazines in Australia have fashioned for themselves; even so, the exception has often been a major part of the story, as I hope I have demonstrated. *Wet Ink* set itself apart from the special project of *Heat* and from journals desirous of academic status. *Overland*'s ideological agenda and format largely contrasted with *Meanjin*'s monumentalism (notwithstanding its online innovations). *Voiceworks*, for better or worse, is continuing a populist agenda due to its younger constituency. In other words, the small magazine in Australia has more often than not been without the resources to 'talk down to' anyone.

Given its formatting in the history to date, the literary magazine by its very nature has been, and still is, a contemplative space in the discontinuous space of our contemporary batch of simulacra. But further questions are: To what extent will it retain readers who see themselves as interactive subjects in their own history? To what extent would there be countervailing tendencies back towards the traditional book or magazine, or would they be left to flounder as outworn commodities, only to achieve their traditional path of achieving late, imperfect commodification as limited-edition artefacts? Would the little magazine survive in new forms, or even in its traditional shapes, as an alternative to an increasingly depthless and homogenising mass media? Overreaching all of these considerations, questions of political economy were the ghost in the machine.

In early to mid-2011, Australia had survived the first global economic crisis of 2008/2009, but debt problems in Europe and a high local dollar meant that retail trade was very flat and impacting on many of the magazines, especially those that were not highly subsidised. In an afterword to the collapse of REDgroup, Rosemary Neill reported that 'one of the country's largest book distributors, Scribo, was shut down in June. Its managers blamed this on factors including competition from on-line sellers offshore and "the closure of key retail outlets"' ('Paging' 5). Scribo had been one of the very few distributors of magazines to the retail book trade of magazines such as *Overland* and *Heat*.

In another development on 17 August 2011, *Meanjin* announced that it was going to publish all content free online. As reported in the *Bookseller & Publisher*, the deputy editor, Zora Sanders, told the *Weekly Book Newsletter* that 'the idea is to expand what *Meanjin* does, rather than altering or reducing it' (n.p.). She went on: 'As a publication that is largely funded by public money, we have an obligation to provide *Meanjin* to whomever wants to read it … [W]e'll be publishing a new piece every weekday on the website'. Of the concerns raised in 2010 as to whether the magazine was to become only an online publication, she said, 'We certainly have no intention of ceasing publication of the hard copy journal … [W]e also want to cater to people who are increasingly at ease with reading online and on digital devices'. She explained that they were hoping to create a high-quality daily online literary magazine — the first of its kind in Australia. *Meanjin* would launch its new website in early September with submissions being considered in both formats. Concurrent to developments within specific magazines, RMIT Publishing in Melbourne established a digital download service aimed at libraries called Informit in early 2011, through which magazines would receive royalties. Its success or otherwise is unknown at the time of writing.

Such news was almost a postscript to all the trends that had been building for the past forty years. It was evidence that, although there existed fundamental changes to the informational means of production, much of the change was not unlike the jittery nature of the share-market in August 2011, skittish and reactive. It was also an extended evangelical moment as much as it was a rationalisation of the cost base of the means of production — a fractured moment that ran the risk of imploding, in that professions of faith in 2011 seemed to be inverted traumatic gestures suggesting democracy while masking a sense of powerless. Despite this, in an almost anti-intuitive move, *Wet Ink* negotiated with Fairfax Media for distribution into 400 selected newsagents throughout Australia, the first time a literary magazine had achieved such coverage since *Australian Short Stories* in the 1980s and since *Quadrant*. This demonstrated, naïvely perhaps, that *Wet Ink* saw itself as occupying a third space between the monumentalism of *Heat* and *Southerly* and the segmenting spaces of popular culture by looking and acting like a magazine.

Meanjin's decision seemed to be an effective deconstruction of the very value of the literary magazine as a commodity at a time when online representations were struggling to establish platforms that could be commodified. By offering free online content it had abandoned placing a price for its writers, and this may result in the death of its subscription base and retail sales. There was an assumption, as with *Heat*, behind its decision, that government funding was self-evident, something problematic in a precarious economic environment, in that by largely ditching alternative sources of income, it would remain more dependent on subsidies. It was a sad move after many years in which a range of magazines had fought to expand their independence and readerships. Whether regular online content would mean that *Meanjin* gained more readers, only time would tell; and its desire to establish a version as, in effect, a continuous blog might change the very idea of the literary magazine in Australia.

In effect, the website became the product and the hard copy a sideline, and either of them would have to give way. With so much material on the worldwide web, much of it what many people would consider pure rubbish, would anyone really care if *Meanjin* added to the traffic? Would the magazine pay for its periodic online contributions, and if not, would a two-tier hierarchy develop? In any case, it would possibly destroy the anticipation value of publishing a hard-copy quarterly (indeed a quarterly online version) — and, by implication, the prestige and value of *Meanjin* as a publishing destination. Even so, the Australia Council could not be seen to abandon the magazine. It could be interpreted that *Meanjin* was wedged between the *Griffith Review* and *Overland*, and the challenges from the new magazines that were established between 2004 and 2011.

Panic had set in with the rush to provide material online. In Tasmania, for example, *Island* had set up *Islet*, a digital alternative, in a move to presumably maximise circulation and visibility. But on 31 August 2011, the Hobart *Mercury* reported that the Premier and Arts Minister, Lara Giddings, had announced extensive funding cuts to the arts including the Tasmanian Theatre Company and *Island Magazine* for 2012. In 2011, *Island* received a subsidy of $68 744. Giddings was quoted as saying that the cut in funding to *Island* 'was based on a trend towards online rather than hardcopy publications for literature' (qtd. in 'Tasmanian government cuts all funding for *Island* magazine' n.p.). Coincidentally, the Tasmanian Writers' Centre was allocated $100 000 per year in funding for the years 2011 to 2013, but as is sometimes the way in arts policy, the Literature Board of the Australia Council stepped into the breach in October and provided *Island* with 'a one-off grant of $60 000 to keep *Island* above water next year, buying it time to develop a new business model' (Romei 27). This decision further demonstrated the vulnerability of dependence on taxpayer support.

There was quite a community flurry as to the perceived harshness of the decision. *Island*'s editor, Sarah Kanowski, noted that the decision also involved reasons from Arts Tasmania such as 'there was limited benefit to the Tasmanian audience of maintaining a magazine just because it is published in Tasmania'. She likened that kind of thinking to an acceptance of monetary values and commodification and a resurgent 'cultural cringe' (6). The Chairman of the Board, Dennis Haskell, was quoted as saying, 'We do not want to see this important magazine slip from view' (qtd. in Romei 27). Despite this decision, as of November 2011, the future of the magazine was still in doubt, in that it had ceased selling subscriptions pending a meeting of the *Island* Board. In December 2011 *Island* had decided to continue publishing into 2012.

Issues and contradictions were crashing in on one another. *Island*, which had pioneered the local to a national audience, was being squeezed by its own government at a time of fiscal restraint. It was a case of arts administrators (if all reports are accurate) wondering whether money should subsidise cheaper online alternatives. By undercutting the market value of its own unreliable product, the magazine appeared to have compromised its very existence — a trend, as we have seen with *Meanjin*, that had been accelerating towards the later years of this study. Also, despite the perceived fiscal constraints, the Tasmanian Writers' Centre, along with some other writers' centres around Australia, continued to be supported, as gestures towards local and national literatures.

Further changes to the shapes and sizes of the magazines were pretty much inevitable given the evidence above. By its eleventh issue in September 2011, the *Lifted Brow* had abandoned its chunky book-like appearance, and had, in its desire to become a bi-monthly publication, published in a forty-four page newspaper format, which was certainly much cheaper to print. Would this be a new model for the literary magazine? Retailing for $9, it was publishing in a space between the commercial formats of the daily press while leaving behind the magazines that looked like books such as *Kill Your Darlings*, *Southerly* and *Island*.

It was, in a sense, a revisiting of the newsprint formats of the 1970s after the revolution of offset printing. It was extremely close to the appearance of the *Digger*, *Nation Review* and *Lot's Wife*, with the major difference that they were intensely political, whereas the *Lifted Brow* had inherited the deconstructive tendencies of the subsequent decades, and was 'cool' and quite hipsterish. Whether it would sell at $9 retail when newsprint dailies sold for $3 at the most would be interesting to watch, given the free-entitlement expectations of younger generations, and the wedging between free online content and hard copy underway at that time. There was no online component on evidence, suggesting that they then evidently saw little potential in such a format. The contents were largely the ironic journalism of Generation X and Y — almost exclusively a type of lifestyle non-fiction with, in this case, very little fiction, some cartoons, and an eye on popular culture and alternative celebrities, all of which incorporated 'retro' tendencies.

Meanwhile, zine-style publications persistently floated about in a subeconomic sphere, such as the *Mozzie* out of Brisbane, which was into its twentieth volume. Co edited by Ron Heard and Bill Henderson, it was a stapled publication without even card covers, publishing a range of known and unknown poets including Bruce Dawe and Thomas Shapcott. It was very much a throwback to the uncommodified publications of the 1960s — unprofessional to look at, containing the work of a lot of relatively unknown poets within an unstylised layout. In Melbourne, *Higher Arc* was a more ambitious zine in terms of layout and production standards, with a clear predilection for visual art and colour reproduction. Such moments perhaps, represented a realisation that by 2011 the upsurge in small-press activity, after 2005, was if anything a late romantic, bohemian moment (rather than any revolutionary fracture) eventually coinciding with the dispersive activity of the internet.

In September, news had come through that the *Australian Literary Review*, which had been a free book-reviewing fixture once a month in the *Australian*, was finally ceasing publication after a number of years. The later editions were entirely subsidised by the Group of Eight universities, who withdrew funding, after previous assistance from the Australia Council. Its ultimate closure was evidence that any journal (of whatever shape or size) was vulnerable to funding cuts, particularly when it had no other form of income or business model, something prefigured in this study with the demise of *Tabloid Story* in the early 1980s.

Ali Alizadeh, writing in the *Overland* blog 'Meanland' on 22 September 2011, effectively summed up much of the debate and the developing urgencies. Citing *Island*'s loss of funding from the Tasmanian state government, he noted that conditions were becoming 'brutal'. Even so, he claimed that *Overland* was one journal that was 'an example of how a print magazine can use the internet to attract new readers, new contributors and even — to the best of my understanding — new subscribers' (n.p.). He suggested that hybrid forms were possible future models. He was aware that all the foment for change was raising the question as to what the literary journal was and might be: 'Suffice to say that one could see the literary journal as an elitist project possessing what Walter Benjamin has termed "aura"', he said.

This is a claim both right and wrong in the Australian context in that, as I have argued, some of the journals have strived for an elitist aura, and others, particularly in the 1960s and 1970s, were produced in cheap formats for reasons including the need to organise around monopolistic print and publishing structures. It is impossible, then, to homogenise all journals into the category of an elitist aura. But Alizadeh's evangelism was a type of post-modern utopianism which assumed that the economic privileges of Western economies would remain. Furthermore, he cited the online poetry publication *Cordite* as a cheaper alternative, even though the magazine has no business model for subscriptions or other income:

> Ten years on and having recently released its 35th issue, *Cordite* has succeeded in not only surviving as such but also attracting ongoing financial support from the Australia Council for the Arts ... (n.p.)

His evangelical fervour also belied the ongoing assumption of state support.

Overarching all of these discussions were serious questions as to whether magazines would be able to gain any meaningful exposure on the internet (whether hard-copy or otherwise), given that information on the web had reached saturation levels at a time when it had provided some new writers with the conceit that they could achieve instant celebrity status.

By November 2011, *Voiceworks* had established a concurrent online alternative to its hard-copy version, selling for half the price. In Brisbane, and later in Hobart, Matthew Lamb set up *Review of Australian Fiction* as an online journal without any pretensions to a hard-copy alternative. *Meanjin*, as mentioned, had put all content free online by the end of 2011, but only offered hard-copy subscriptions, which was making their online excursion more dependent on government grants. It, like some of the other magazines, was being seduced by the conceit of popularity that could not be tested without hard evidence of retail and subscription sales. Data collection mechanisms such as Google diagnostics may well have been in place to identify time taken on specific pages, yet in any case, conclusions were speculative. As Glover pointed out at the close of 2011,

> so far, the internet hasn't created a viable literary magazine model. Literary magazines have multiplied on the internet, but mostly ... they are edited by the unpaid with varying levels of skill. Expertise is costly and is crowded out. (24)

In December 2011, reviewing the changes in the period since 2003, Benjamin Laird discussed the social media applications and the online technology employed by the most visible of the magazines in an article notable for its lack of commentary on the quality or otherwise of published content. He correctly summed up the main change. In 2003, he said, 'the publisher's attitude to the online space was that it was essentially a placeholder for the print journal' ('Australian Literary Journals' n.p.), and magazines were using Facebook and Twitter, some also embracing smartphones and tablet readers. He concluded that in his terms, there was another imperative, since

> with these additional demands, running a quarterly literary journal in 2011 means doing everything you did twenty years ago, plus updating Facebook regularly, tweeting constantly, creating or sourcing blog

content, building websites that support multiple devices ... writing a regular e-newsletter. (n.p.)

He ended with a conclusion as to how the technological changes were working in contradictory ways:

> That is not to say print is dead. With print-on-demand expanding, traditional journals have a cheaper way to sell overseas, printing directly in that country, and can have flexible print runs by printing only what's needed ... [L]astly, it will be interesting to see where social media will be in four years ... [I]n the short history of social sites, however, popularity can dissipate as quickly as it grows.

This warning came amidst a relative sense of optimism, according to Hamilton:

> [A]s the large corporate publishing companies continue to worry about revenues and annual growth, small publishers are doing their best to meet the market on the middle ground somewhere between commerce and community. ('Sympathy' 93)

Meanwhile, by 2011, the Australia Council had adopted the new buzz word 'digital' to inform its policy decisions, and presumably, future directions. Jason Nelson from Griffith University had been appointed to the Literature Board as someone with IT expertise. The *Australian Book Review*, the magazine which received the highest level of assistance (in the vicinity of $100 000 per annum), had adhered to pressure to digitise many of its operations and therefore increase its circulation.

By the conclusion of 2011, *Wet Ink* was still resisting the trend to convert to the digital while publishing the largest array of new authors in the country. *Kill Your Darlings* was still largely unknown outside Victoria but had enlarged its online options with approximately 50 per cent of its content free online while offering a choice of subscription options — print or online, or print *and* online, a choice that was undercut by the free content. Like *Meanjin*, its hard copy was looking chunky, evidence that the advent of online was making the print alternative, in some eyes, more of a high-cultural, limited-edition artefact in terms of commodification. *Kill Your Darlings* was largely a non-fiction journal of essays, with little fiction, no poetry; in effect, it was positioning itself to become another layer of the soft Left/liberal Melbourne literary establishment. In terms of its non-fiction and fiction it was relatively unadventurous, despite a cool online presence, due to its search for well-known authors and cultural agendas. Interestingly, *Quadrant* finally partially modernised its design in early 2012 by revamping its layout (if not its typeface) and printing a perfect-bound magazine, well suited for newsagent distribution, after almost forty years of saddle-stitch, stapled editions; and, despite earlier fears of death on the internet, *Meanjin* was still publishing chunky hard-copy editions.

Several strands were becoming very clear. The literary magazine was reverting (as I mentioned above) to a high-cultural commodity in print form despite attempts to democratise it as a print phenomenon (such as *Tabloid Story* in the 1970s as a supplement in newspapers and popular magazines, *Australian Short Stories* in the 1980s, and *Wet Ink* after 2005). And coincidentally, with the online moves of *Meanjin*, some were morphing into continuous blogs. In December 2011, Bethanie Blanchard on the Crikey website noted how *Meanjin* and *Kill Your Darlings* were moving to multiplatform publishing and preached of the ways 'in which the two forms can co-exist' (n.p.). By 2012, *Southerly* had also developed a two-tiered publishing strategy with blogs and online subscription facilities alongside its normal chunky print edition. SPUNC (the Small Press Underground Network), which represented most small publishers in Australia, had decided to work assiduously to develop online platforms and applications for mobile phones and other reading devices as a recognition that physical book and magazine distribution appeared futile in the brave new world of publishing. This was in contrast to the nervous concerns of the Australian Small Press Association and Book People of Australia in the 1970s and 1980s over market marginality.

Overarching all of the above, it appeared that the literary magazines were becoming more dependent on government assistance in Australia, despite the efforts of the individuals and publications detailed in the forty years of this study. Could it be said that after reviewing forty years of pugnacious effort and at times hopeless idealism, a case can be made that many of the magazines (despite persistent under-resourcing) have been and are currently secure in their subsidised, marginal and special status? *Overland*'s desire to popularise its Leftist agenda over the years may have been an exception.

Many of the magazines, especially the *Griffith Review*, *Meanjin*, *Overland*, *Quadrant*, *Kill Your Darlings* and *Island*, were also of the view that non-fiction was a priority, and this accelerated a trend during the 2000s in the broader book trade away from fiction. The *Griffith Review* was particularly successful in interpreting the zeitgeist through their themed issues. Generally, it appeared that the rise of online options was providing some writers with the conceit that the path to fame and respect could be shortened and less frustrating as vanity e-publishing sites were proliferating across the internet and self-promotion via the net became endemic.

Coincidentally, the institutionalisation of peer reviewing of some of the magazines was establishing a competitive (and thereby privatised) environment in which the publications were being forced to operate. Writers who were associated with universities were largely being encouraged to only submit to peer-review magazines as such writing brought research money through the ERA rankings to institutions. Paradoxically, under the guidelines, no editor of a magazine (either peer-review or otherwise) gained research points for their efforts — destroying much of the incentive to engage in bringing together differing voices and opinions. In essence, the building of community and democracy was, as we have seen, the traditional function of the literary magazine in Australia over the past forty years.

On the micro-level of the magazines (despite the online initiatives), Zizek's pronouncement at the Occupy Wall Street rally in New York during October of 2011 that 'the marriage between democracy and capitalism is over' (*Raw story* n.p.) appears (in Australia, at least) as the consummation of percussive tendencies over the period of this study. That is, it could be argued that the magazines, as marginal moments of democracy, had been battling against homogenisation caused by economic realities.

In any case, any marriage between democracy and capitalism has always been a stormy, discontinuous and partial union even during the best of times. By late 2011, it could be argued that due to the bureaucratic tendencies detailed in a previous chapter, anti-democratic moves were being naturalised through education into the broader society in more covert ways than the censorship necessary in previous decades. Had the democratic moment around 2005 (when a number of new magazines were created) expired, partly due to the pressures of the Global Financial Crisis? What incentive would there be for people to start up new, unprofitable ventures when validation was seemingly measured by peer-reviewed status and perceptions of prestige, rather than by risk-taking and creativity initiatives? Even so, as I have demonstrated, the market had always mediated against freewheeling democracy in societies such as Australia (as opposed to state censorship in other societies such as the former Soviet Union), creating a form of commercial censorship — evidenced again by the weakening market conditions of 2011/12. In broad terms, there was little discussion as to whether the internet was a device that transferred social and economic value while continually undercutting the price of labour.

So it was hardly surprising that in such an uncertain economic and cultural environment there was some nervousness as to future directions and survival strategies. Early 2012 brought an announcement from *Overland* that '*Overland* relies on its subscribers for survival. For that reason, the editors prioritise submissions by subscribers. While all work will be read, we cannot guarantee response times to submissions from non-subscribers'. Laurie Steed commented that,

> like many Australian literary journals, [*Overland*] works with limited staff numbers and pressing deadlines, so it isn't surprising that the magazine has implemented a system to ensure subscriber submissions are read and replied to in a timely manner. (46)

He was generally sympathetic to the idea, and quoted editor Jeff Sparrow: '[T]he distinction was made to remind writers that *Overland* depends on their support'. But it was a risky strategy, even if it articulated the commonly held belief that writers in Australia (and creative writing students particularly) had not been supporting the industry they wanted to perhaps support them. New issues of *Overland*, however, were available largely for free online at the same time as it was vigorously trying to pursue only hard-copy subscriptions. Interestingly, the edition of *Overland* published in March 2012 dropped much of its free online content. Coincidentally, Dale Campisi from *Island* announced in May 2012 that, in its then current form, 'there is a real chance that *Island* will not see beyond 2012'. He explained that 'subscriptions and readership have declined' in its hard-copy format, and that 'digital, online; the internet represents *Island*'s best chance for survival' ('Attack' 7). Meanwhile, the *Lifted Brow* was unable to sustain its hard-copy bi-monthly appearances and was not being published in the first half of 2012; Ronnie Scott left in the latter half of the year.

So, then, could it even be suggested by early 2012 that the digital rush could have been leading to the encroaching homogenisation of cultural products (and less choice of platform options), despite the professed democratisation brought forward by the internet? Grassroots art forms such as crafts (which were not applicable to digitalisation) were losing government support, and for what it was worth, the hard-copy literary magazine was having its business model eroded in the rush. The move online seemed to be accelerating a trend towards the reading of particular items rather than the concept of a magazine as a collection of diverse elements in the first instance.

These developments were further evidence that the economy was again negotiating with idealism, which was playing out in the history of the magazines. Would Australia be able to support a diverse range of publications and glimpse a future? Would some of the small magazines continue to showcase and advocate the local (let alone the national) as an urgent concern, even though much of the local had fallen from favour and was 'uncool' in intellectual circles, irrespective of their published formats? Would literary magazines participate in addressing what Hassall identified as the 'unprecedented disconnect between schools and universities and the broader reading public' (19), and in some way become more widely known?

Or would such concerns continue to be seen as the anxieties of a small, isolated intellectual subclass which engaged in special pleading to taxpayers when required? Would it be, then, a minor scuffle over next to nothing in a pragmatic culture? Other general observations could also be made. Literary magazines that were not overly academic in their direction represented some of the things many of the universities seemed to be losing: independence, creativity and links to the broader community. The magazines would continue to find it hard to gain support despite enrolments in the creative arts.

Conferences had always been a way of showcasing research for the universities, and their growing predominance, at a time when the notion of the magazine as a series of conversations was under threat, was perhaps an attempt to occupy small corners of the hitherto endangered public sphere at an institutional level. Conferences were perhaps an ersatz public sphere, and indeed a pleasant admission of defeat that an audience may not exist outside the academy. Were such gestures becoming circular and insular — a gesturing towards, rather than a consummation of, activity — even if it could be argued that social media was reconfiguring the notion that the public sphere involved actual face-to-face communication?

Another conclusion could also be suggested. The relatively under-resourced magazines (particularly in the period after 2005) provided avenues for the production houses of the creative writing industry in the universities; more to the point, they created a type of unheralded and unpaid surplus value, through a perception that serious publishing in Australia was more diverse than it actually was. While the creative writing industry was flourishing in state-supported educational institutions, the magazines had to weather the fractious post-GFC economic climate largely on the back of voluntary labour, a constant factor through the course of this study. At the very end of 2011, with the onset of a second wave of global financial pressures, the situation for many book and magazine publishers was becoming difficult due to a subdued retail environment rather than the challenge from e-books. In Australia the high dollar was making local products overly costly, and whether that would affect the already precarious sales of the magazines would be interesting to watch. Bookseller Tim Coronel commented that 'book sales have fallen off a cliff ... early indications for 2012 show that revenue across the trade has dropped as much as 20%' (18).

And, as in most economic crises, narratives of class were appearing as demonstrations against budget cuts in Europe. In the United States, the 'occupy movement' with all manner of grievances was raising questions as to the misappropriation and concentration of global wealth. More specifically, the movement appeared as a symbolic, utopian move towards taking back public space (not unlike the performative gestures of the anti-war/anti-imperialistic movements in the 1960s). In effect, there was a realisation that, despite the connective nature, and information dispersal, of the internet and social media, discourse and democracy were dominated by interests that were not those of working people.

Even so, as Hamilton suggested, the new technologies became 'deeply transformative. During the space of a decade, "the network" has become the dominant social logic. And the way we do business' ('The new networking' 73). But she further acknowledged that the digital networks underpinning the expansion were operating off futuristic business models — in the case of Facebook, stock market speculation — which 'haven't yet achieved the usual standard of success known as "profitability"'. Despite this, Lisa Dempster (who was by then noted for a desire to overthrow her idea of the literary establishment) idealistically called for an evangelical shift towards interactivity for literary organisations across the board (129).

In effect, the ownership of the means of production (as opposed to the mechanics of publication) had not really changed despite its online representations. Rather, it was being dispersed and disguised across differing platforms and implicated in credit-based assumptions. The question posed earlier as to whether the digital formats would expand what had been argued as a diminishing public sphere was still open. Perhaps it was a case of an increase in mobile private promotional spheres. Ironically, another contradiction has surfaced: the privileging of peer-review journals by the universities had created a perverse form of commodification based on scarcity, despite the conceit of online accessibility.

For all of the above, a constant factor over the forty years of this study is that government subsidies of one variety or another were a necessity — for the magazines and for the organisations promoted by Dempster, such as the Queensland Writers Centre, and for other festivals that were dependent on taxpayer support, in lieu of other viable business models. During 2012, the internet was alive with chatter about crowd funding, something which became appealing to arts bureaucracies, as it offered possible ways in which funding pressures might subside. The idea was very useful for start-up businesses because people were asked to subscribe ahead for particular products, which could be handy for a handful of new magazines in the first instance, but problematic for magazines that were already publishing. The pre-subscription idea might be ideal for individual books, as it had been during the nineteenth century.

Another broad observation is pertinent: from the available evidence, the magazines, despite the online innovations, were still largely publishing, it appeared, for inner city readers in Sydney and Melbourne, and to an extent in Brisbane — inhabiting in effect the limited space they had always catered for, even though on occasions, some of the publishing participants were wishing for more exposure.

In October 2012, sorely affected by a weak retail climate, difficulty in attracting advertising and an absence of support by educational institutions, *Wet Ink* stopped publishing without reverting to publishing online. Its experiment of creating a magazine relatively independent of institutional support failed in the long term, although it published for seven years. The value of institutional support is crucial in this study — at times in editorial salaries and office space, and in incremental support such as host universities paying for postage, as has been the case with *Heat*, *Southerly*, the *Griffith Review*, *Westerly* and *Meanjin* at different times. In any case, David Sornig made the case that *Wet Ink* played a serious innovative role over its seven years in a broad argument where he stressed that innovation 'doesn't come out freshly hatched. It begins outside the market, in a place where it can gestate ... [T]his is probably the most important function literary journals serve' (37).

With its demise, the number of new short stories published in Australia in the immediate future would drop considerably. *Wet Ink* published around eleven stories each issue, or forty-four a year, compared to the established magazines which usually published three to four an issue. Yet the future for short fiction was not necessarily bleak, in that 'indie' publishers such as *Spineless Wonders* were publishing across digital, audio and print formats in 2012. *Westerly* was publishing again after an absence of several years, the *Lifted Brow* was making a comeback under Sam Cooney, and the print and online future of *Island* seemed more positive after the restoration of funding from Arts Tasmania and a commitment to regionalism from the Australia Council (Campisi, 'More than a magazine' 7). Yet, despite the apparent optimism, *Island* was still finding subscriptions hard to come by, as was the case with other journals — so much so, its co-editor, Rachel Edwards, was to announce:

> [W]e call on all writers to support ... literary magazines by subscribing so we can go on providing these opportunities. We have introduced, as has *Overland*, a prioritised submissions system, whereby we prioritise subscribers' work ... (34)

In broad terms, was the demise of *Wet Ink* a partial fracturing of the utopian/democratic moment that was 2005? (Edmonds, 'A democratic moment' 59) Was the demise of *Famous Reporter* in late 2012 another symptom?

Stuart Glover realistically pointed out that compared to the United States and the United Kingdom, where *McSweeney's* and *Granta* have over 10 000 subscribers, even *Meanjin*, the *Griffith Review* and *Overland* exist on between 500 and 2000 subscriptions, and that, 'despite decades of funding the reader base for little magazines hasn't grown much' ('Little magazines' n.p.). Even as the number of new titles had proliferated in the preceding decade, the established group of magazines were allocated the majority of Literature Board funds — in fact *Meanjin*, the *Griffith Review* and *Overland* were regarded as organisations of national importance and funded at a higher level. They also gained other sponsorship, making it difficult for newer journals to establish and market themselves. Glover's view of the future was equally cautious: '[S]maller journals ... will, I expect, never have enough readers to offer [their] editors full-time paying jobs'.

As we have seen, despite flurries of periodic small-press activity over the forty years of this study, the question was always whether Australia could or would support more than a stable of half a dozen print magazines on a permanent basis.

So has the 'cultural cringe', in terms of the magazines, been reduced over the forty years of this study? Five or six magazines have survived, but there are many obituaries which confirm some of AA Phillips's diagnosis in the 1950s as to the estrangement of the Australian intellectual. Despite evidence of high book sales among the population, Phillips had said of the 'cultural cringe' in the 1950s:

> The crust feels thinner because, in a small community, there is not enough of it to provide the individual with a protective insulation ... [H]e feels a sense of exposure. This is made much worse by that deadly habit of English comparison. (*The Australian tradition* 114)

The question remained pertinent in 2012.

Postscript

If evidence of the social mood of 2011 and 2012 was anything to go by, the new tech-savvy demographic seemed too mobile and hyper-political to display loyalty to any particular site or publication, unlike the allegiances originally developed by *Meanjin*, *Overland* and *Quadrant* during and after the Cold War. It was also becoming clearer that the traditional oppositional role of the magazines — developed firstly in the Cold War, and later during the 'alternative' 1970s — was fading and harder to differentiate, because it appeared (to some) that battles had been won. Evidence of this could be seen in the changing of SPUNC to the *Small Press Network* — the 'underground' reference disappearing. Another major observation is that the magazines which had survived across the decades had predominately published non-fiction, memoir, interpretative journalism and cultural commentary, as opposed to short fiction and poetry, which the universities were still promoting and preserving. It appeared that the *Griffith Review* was the most stable journal, heavily subsidised and promoted by its publishing partners (Griffith University and Text Publishing) with high-profile themed issues such as 'Tasmania — The Tipping Point'.

In 2012, while print subscriptions seemed to be stalling, online was on the rise, and Glover argued that there was a future in the digital, 'bringing citizen-journalists to the screen' ('Little magazines' n.p.) and, 'as little magazines begin to do this they are not really issue-bound and time-bound little magazines anymore; instead they are high-end literary commentary sites' (see *Meanjin* blog and *Overland* Online).

With the advent of free online material offered by many of the magazines, readers could catch up with preferred articles and stories without having to subscribe or buy the whole publication. But such developments were contrary to what had distinguished the little magazine over its history — the desire to reflect on events rather than report them, as was the traditional function of the newspaper. The social media experiments, then, seemed counterintuitive to the anticipation aspect of less frequent publication, and possibly a threat to considered quality of depth and context. There is a fine line between social media promotion of the main product and the evaporation of the anticipation factor. Sornig, in turn, likened this digital obsession with self-promotion to advertising in its crudest form (36).

In any case, Glover was of the view that, 'like music, like DVDs, and like television shows — little magazines are on the cusp of their greatest change … since the early nineteenth century' ('Little magazines' n.p.). He concluded that there would be a 'Promethean transformation' for the magazines as they wrestled with form. As a case in point, in 2013 the wrestling over form — digital or otherwise — was probably coming to an end at *Meanjin*, when Zora Sanders replaced Sally Heath as editor. At its November 2012 meeting, the Literature Board of the Australia Council, in deciding on grants to less established magazines, clearly tagged 'online' as the preferred outcome.

Over time, the printed literary magazine might paradoxically consolidate its position in the way the printed book achieved in slower times with the proviso that it had to find a form that was a third space between the limited-edition book and its online 'other' — an acceleration, then, of its boutique aspects. Given that the Saturday editions of the major newspapers were being starved of resources to devote to investigative and quality journalism (due to the online assault), the literary magazine might even be seen as having a more vital cultural role than ever before. In another way, it could well recover its anticipation aspect as a tendency towards scarcity and the retro 'other' in late capitalism, making a comeback in the way that Indyk has suggested of its printed cousin, the book:

> Both of these uses of the physical book — the book as gift, the book as the expression of a community — have reciprocity as their common property. It is this reciprocity, this embodiment or anticipation of recognition, which gives them their life. ('The book' 89)

By 2012, there was clear evidence that the magazines were particularly vulnerable to the e-revolution because of their regularity and topicality, something which books did not have to contend with. In terms of print publishing the direction might well be towards very small circulation, limited-edition, zine-style publications — cheap to print and having the characteristics of many of the magazines of the 1970s. In 2012, the *Canary Press (Story magazine)* appeared out of Melbourne, stapled, with adventurous artwork and an avant-garde feel, plus a paid online access facility. A number of the stories were from the United States, but it included locals Tony Birch and Josephine Rowe. Several issues of *Unusual Work* (Collective Effort Press), edited by Pi O, a deliberately uncommodified zine, also appeared out of Melbourne.

In any event, the future of the magazines would need to involve conversations around content and ideology over and above any of the technological imperatives and/or choices. In an age of instant access to published material, who would be the editors? Would new e-publications begin which had reputable quality control? Would there be some that acquired such quality over time? How many of the new publications would be able to create an ongoing organisational structure to sustain them as had *Meanjin, Overland, Quadrant*, the *Australian Book Review* and the *Griffith Review* over the course of this study?

On available evidence, *Meanjin, Kill Your Darlings*, the *Lifted Brow* and *Overland* and others were confidently using multimedia platforms, but it remained difficult to determine, from the outside, real circulation levels and reliable indications of their success, given the inflated nature of self-promotion in and around contemporary culture. They had survived, though, even if vulnerable to their own free content on the internet. The net was a neater fit with the new reviewing venture the *Sydney Review of Books* (supported by the Australia Council and the University of Western Sydney), which was inspired by the diminishing number of reviews in the major newspapers. The magazine had the advantage of commenting on writing in existing publications without the stress of publishing new creative work.

In any case, the established journals would continue to be supported by the Australia Council for the Arts, given budgetary considerations which were not looking healthy at the end of 2012 due to talk of government deficits. In any case, to entirely withdraw support would undermine the remaining edifice. Without some magazines, the literary culture of Australia would not look diverse and encouraging, and whether that would be considered important only time would tell. Assistance to magazines from the Australia Council (as we have seen) is largely to pay contributors, and without the further support garnered by the established magazines, new ventures have (and will) find it extremely difficult to pay their editors. Broadly, cuts to government expenditure in the arts and education could work against idealistic initiatives, the likes of which we saw over the forty years of this study. On the other hand, cuts might force writers into creating new publishing structures.

The literary magazine, as I have described it over the past forty years, was a product of print. The e-changes challenged that format to the extent that the conventional notion of the magazine I have discussed, between the years 1968-2012, may not exist in the future. Whatever form it morphs into, it appeared at the time of writing that it was even more dependent on government and private subsidies than ever before if it desired longevity. History moves in cycles.

Works Cited

Alizadeh, Ali. 'Meanland: The internet — friend or foe to the small magazine.' *Overland [Online]*. Posted 22 September 2011: n. pag. Web. Accessed 22 September 2011. <http://web.overland.org.au>

Annear, Robyn. 'Puzzling the purpose of Australian literary magazines: Unripe fruit. *The Monthly* (October 2013): n. pag. Web. Accessed 16 December 2013. <http://www.themonthly.com.au/issue/2013/october>

Bell, Daniel. *The cultural contradictions of capitalism*. London: Heinemann, 1979. Print.

Benjamin, Walter. 'The work of art in the age of mechanical reproduction.' *Illuminations: Essays and reflections*. Ed. Hannah Arendt. Trans. Harry Zohn. New York: Schocken Books, 1969. Print.

Bennett, Bruce. *Cross currents: Magazines and newspapers in Australian literature*. Melbourne: Longman Cheshire, 1981. Print.

Bennett, Bruce, and Peter Cowan. 'Westerly.' *Cross currents: Magazines and newspapers in Australian literature*. Ed. Bruce Bennett. Melbourne: Longman Cheshire, 1981. 202-10. Print.

Billeter, Walter. 'Etymspheres.' *New writing in Australia*. Spec. issue of *Australian Literary Studies* 8.2 (1977): 219-21. Print.

Blanchard, Bethanie. 'The medium & the message: Australian literary journals move to multi-platform.' *Crikey: Independent media, independent minds* (23 December 2011): n. pag. Web. Accessed 2 February 2012. <http://blogs.crikey.com.au/liticism>

Bolton, Ken. 'Magic Sam.' *New writing in Australia*. Spec. issue of *Australian Literary Studies* 8.2 (1977): 216-17. Print.

Bourdieu, Pierre. *Distinction: A social critique of the judgement of taste.* Trans. Richard Nile. Harvard: Harvard University Press, 1984. Print.

———. *The fields of cultural production: Essays on art and literature.* Cambridge: Polity Press, 1993. Print.

———. *The rule of art: Genesis and structure of the literary field.* Trans. Susan Emanuel. Cambridge: Polity Press, 1996. Print.

Bradley, James. 'Growing content.' *Review, The Weekend Australian* 2 December 2009: 16-17. Print.

Brett, Judith. 'Literature and politics.' *The temperament of generations: Fifty years of writing in Meanjin.* Ed. Jenny Lee, Philip Mead and Gerald Murnane. Carlton: Melbourne University Press, 1990. 320-2. Print.

Brophy, Kevin. 'In memory of Richard Tokatlian, and the early days of GDS.' *The Victorian Writer* (May 2013): 20-1. Print.

Burns, Shannon. Letter to the author. December 2012.

Campisi, Dale. 'Attack of the killer internets.' *Island* 128 (Autumn 2012): 7-9. Print.

———. 'More than a magazine.' *Island* 131 (Summer 2012): 7-9. Print.

Capp, Fiona. *Writers defiled.* Ringwood: McPhee Gribble, 1993. Print.

Carter, David. 'Boom, bust or business as usual? Literary fiction publishing.' *Making books: Contemporary Australian publishing.* Ed. David Carter and Anne Galligan. St Lucia: University of Queensland Press, 2007. 231-46. Print.

———. 'Capturing the liberal sphere: Overland's first decade.' *Outside the book: Contemporary essays on literary periodicals.* Ed. David Carter. Sydney: Local Consumption Publications, 1991. 177-91. Print.

———. 'Critics, writers, intellectuals: Australian literature and its criticism.' *The Cambridge companion to Australian literature.* Ed. Elizabeth Webby. Cambridge: Cambridge University Press, 2000. 258-85. Print.

———. 'Magazine culture: Notes towards a history of Australian periodical publication 1920-1970.' *Australian literature and the public sphere.* Eds. Alison Bartlett, Robert Dixon and Christopher Lee. Toowoomba: Association for the Study of Australian Literature, 1999. 69-79. Print.

Carter, David, and Roger Osborne. 'Case-study: Periodicals.' *Paper empires: A history of the book in Australia, 1946-2005*. Ed. Craig Munro and Robyn Sheahan-Bright. St Lucia: University of Queensland Press, 2006. 239-56. Print.

Castro, Brian. 'Slow boat to culture.' *The Australian Literary Review* 5 October 2011: 20. Print.

Clancy, Laurie. 'Editor's statements.' *The contemporary Australian short story*. Spec. issue of *Australian Literary Studies* 10.2 (1981): 245-8. Print.

Clunies-Ross, Bruce. 'Some developments in short fiction, 1969-1980.' *Australian Literary Studies* 10.2 (1981): 165-80. Print.

Cornes, Richard, and Todd Sandler. *The theory of externalities, public goods and club goods*. Cambridge: Cambridge University Press, 1986. Print.

Coronel, Tim. 'Book sales have fallen off a cliff: What next for the publishing industry?' *Island* 128 (2012): 18-26. Print.

Cosic, Miriam. 'Incandescent Indyk turns down the heat.' *Inquirer, The Weekend Australian*, 5-6 March. Print.

Davidson, Jim. 'A cork in the ocean: *Meanjin* and the changing context 1940-2010.' *Meanjin* 70.1 (2011): 126-31. Print.

———. 'Editor's statements.' *The contemporary Australian short story*. Spec. issue of *Australian Literary Studies* 10.2 (1981): 249-52. Print.

———. 'Making *Meanjin* survive.' *The temperament of generations: Fifty years of writing in Meanjin*. Eds. Jenny Lee, Philip Mead and Gerald Murnane. Carlton: Melbourne University Press, 1990. 228-35. Print.

Davidson, Rjurik. 'Liberated zone or pure commodification.' *Overland* 200 (2010): 103-9. Print.

———. 'Political writers in the neoliberal age.' *Overland* 209 (2012): 54-8. Print.

Davis, Mark. 'The decline of the literary paradigm in Australia.' *Making books: Contemporary Australian publishing*. Ed. David Carter and Anne Galligan. St Lucia: University of Queensland Press, 2007. 116-31. Print.

Debray, Regis. *Teachers, writers, celebrities: The intellectuals of modern France*. Trans. David Macey. London: Verso, 1981. Print.

DeKoven, Marianne. *Utopia limited: The Sixties and the emergence of the postmodern*. Durham and London: Duke University Press, 2004. Print.

Dempster, Lisa. 'Literary participation at the digital frontier.' *Island* 128 (2012): 116-29. Print.

Denholm, Michael. *Small press publishing in Australia*. Sydney: Second Back Row Press, 1979. Print.

———. *Small press publishing in Australia. Volume II. The late 1970s to the mid to late 1980s*. Footscray: Footprint, 1991 Print.

Desmond Jones, Rae. 'Your friendly fascist.' *New writing in Australia*. Spec. issue of *Australian Literary Studies* 8.2 (1977): 212-14. Print.

Dixon, Robert. 'Deregulating the critical economy: Theory and Australian literary criticism in the 1980s.' *Australian literature and the public sphere*. Ed. Alison Bartlett, Robert Dixon and Christopher Lee. Toowoomba: Association for the Study of Australian Literature, 1999. 194-201. Print.

Doyle, Timothy. 'Playing postmodern games: The politics of resilience.' *Green Power: The environment movement in Australia*. Sydney: University of New South Wales Press, 2000. 196-215. Print.

Dugan, Michael. 'A selective checklist of "little" magazines.' *New writing in Australia*. Spec. issue of *Australian Literary Studies* 8.2 (1977): 222-5. Print.

During, Simon. 'Professing the popular.' *The temperament of generations: Fifty years of writing in* Meanjin. Ed. Jenny Lee, Philip Mead and Gerald Murnane. Carlton: Melbourne University Press, 1990. 374-83. Print.

Edgar, Ray, and Stuart Geddes. 'Peripheral visionaries: Australia's independent publishing tradition.' *Meanjin* 69.4 (Summer 2010): 18-49. Print.

Edge, John. Email to author. 10 May 2011.

Edmonds, Phillip. 'A democratic moment: Or more of the same?' *By the book: Contemporary publishing in Australia*. Ed. Emmett Stinson. Clayton: Monash University Publishing, 2013. 59-66. Print.

———. 'Interrogating creative writing outcomes: *Wet Ink* as a new model.' *TEXT, Journal of the AAWP* 11.1 (2007): n. pag. Web. <http://www.textjournal.com.au>

———. *More than a mere story: Social and political markers in Australian* short fiction of the 1980s. PhD thesis, Deakin University, 1996. Web. <edmonds-morethanamere-1997.pdf>

———. '*Overland* is twenty-one: Interview with Stephen Murray-Smith.' *Australasian Small Press Review* 4 (1976): 1-6. Print.

———. 'Respectable or risqué: Creative Writing programs in the marketplace.' *TEXT, Journal of the AAWP* 8.1 (2004): n. pag. Web. <http://www.textjournal.com.au>

Edmonds, Phillip, and Dominique Wilson. 'Editorial.' *Wet Ink* 1 (2005). Print.

Edwards, Rachel. '*Island*'s near-death experience.' *The Victorian Writer* May (2013): 34. Print.

Enzensberger, Hans Magnus. *Raids and re-constructions: Essays in politics, crime and culture.* London: Pluto Press, 1976. Print.

Flanagan, Richard. 'Colonies of the mind: Republic of dreams, Australian publishing past and present.' *Making books: Contemporary Australian publishing*. Ed. David Carter and Anne Galligan. St Lucia: University of Queensland Press, 2007. 132-48. Print.

Florida, Richard. *The rise of the creative class: And how it is transforming work, leisure, community and everyday life.* Melbourne: Pluto Press, 2002. Print.

Foucault, Michel. *The history of sexuality, Volume One: An Introduction.* New York: Pantheon, 1978. Print.

Freeman, John. 'Small treasures: Literary journals are an antidote to these straightened times.' *Review, The Weekend Australian* (18-19 July 2009): 18. Print.

Freeth, Kate, and Small Press Underground Networking Community. *A lovely kind of madness: Small and independent publishing in Australia.* Melbourne: Small Press Underground Networking Community, 2007: 1-69. Web. Accessed 15 June 2011. <http://spunc.com.au>

Frow, John. *Cultural studies and cultural value.* Oxford: Clarendon Press, 1995. Print.

Gaita, Raimond. 'To civilise the city.' *Meanjin* 71.1 (2012): 64-82. Print.

Galligan, Anne. 'Build the author, sell the book: Marketing the Australian author in the 1990s.' *Australian literature and the public sphere*. Ed. Alison

Bartlett, Robert Dixon and Christopher Lee. Toowoomba: Association for the Study of Australian Literature, 1999. 151-9. Print.

Gare, Arran. 'Globalization, postmodernity and the environmental crisis.' *Arena Journal* 4 (1994/9): 137-60. Print.

Geertz, Clifford. 'Thick description: Toward an Interpretative theory of culture.' *The interpretation of culture: Selected essays*. New York: Basic Books, 1973: 3-30. Print.

Gelder, Ken, and Paul Salzman. *The new diversity: Australian fiction 1970-88*. Melbourne: McPhee Gribble, 1989. Print.

Glover, Stuart. 'Little magazines, McSweeney's, Jordan Bass, and the Future.' *Stuart Glover: Helped by monkeys blog*. Posted 16 October 2012: n. pag. Web. Accessed 18 October 2012. <http://www.stuartglover.com.au>

——. 'No magazine is an island: Government and little magazines.' *Island* 127 (2011): 21-4. Print.

Gold, Irma. 'Journal review — *indigo*, vol 5.' *Overland blog*. 22 July 2010: n. pag. Web. Accessed 14 May 2011. <http: web.overland.org.au/2010/07/journal-review-indigo-vol-5>

Gruber, Fiona. 'Words matter here.' *Review, The Weekend Australian* 11-12 October 2008: 13. Print.

Habermas, Jürgen. *The structural transformation of the public sphere: An inquiry into a category of bourgeois society*. Trans. Thomas Burger. Cambridge: Polity Press, 1962. Print.

Hamilton, Caroline. 'The exposure economy.' *Overland* 202 (2011): 88-94. Print.

——. 'The new networking.' *Island* 128 (Autumn 2012): 71-80. Print.

——. 'Sympathy for the devil.' *Overland* 205 (Summer 2011): 88-93. Print.

Harries, Owen, and Tom Switzer. 'Little magazine leaves a big mark.' *The Australian* 3 October 2006: 6. Print.

Hart, Jim. 'New wave Seventies.' *Paper empires: A history of the book in Australia, 1946-2005*. Ed. Craig Munro and Robyn Sheahan-Bright.

St Lucia: University of Queensland Press, 2006. 53-7. Print.

Harvey, David. *The condition of postmodernity*. Oxford: Blackwell, 1989. Print.

Hassall, Tony. 'It's academe.' *Review, The Weekend Australian* 24-25 September 2011: 18-19. Print.

Healey, Steve. 'The rise of creative writing and the new value of creativity.' *The Writer's Chronicle* 41.4 (2009): 30-9. Print.

Hemensley, Kris. 'The wild assertion of vitality.' *New writing in Australia*. Spec. issue of *Australian Literary Studies* 8.2 (1977): 226-39 Print.

Hobsbawn, Eric. *Age of extremes: The short twentieth century 1914-1991*. New York: Abacus, 1994. Print.

Hollier, Nathan. 'Diagnosing the death of literature.' *Wet Ink* 6 (2007): 11-15. Print.

———. 'Overland plan.' Report to O.L. Society, Footscray, 2003. Unpublished paper. Print.

———. 'What can we hope to achieve.' Editorial report for O.L. Society, Footscray, 5 December 2002. Unpublished paper. Print.

Howarth, R.G. 'Foreword by the editor.' *Southerly* 1.1 (1939): 3-4. Print.

Hurley, Michael. 'Writing, the body positive.' *Meanjin* 51.1 (1992): 199-219. Print.

Indyk, Ivor. 'The book and its time.' *Meanjin* 20.4 (2011): 84-90. Print.

———. 'Editorial.' *Heat* 24 (2011). 2-3. Print.

Jameson, Fredric. *Postmodernism, or the cultural logic of late capitalism*. Durham: Duke University Press, 1991. Print.

Jennings, Kate, ed. *Mother I'm rooted: An anthology of Australian women poets*. Fitzroy: Outback Press, 1975. Print.

Jones, Richard. *Report to literary magazine editors' seminar*. Ed. Elaine Lindsay, Department of Continuing Education, Adelaide University, 1978. Print.

Kanowski, Sarah. 'For what it's worth.' *Island* 127 (2011): 6-11. Print.

Kelly, Paul. *The end of certainty: The story of the 1980s*. Sydney: Allen & Unwin, 1992. Print.

Kenny, Robert. 'Living, sulking and fighting in the Seventies.' *New writing in Australia*. Spec. issue of *Australian Literary Studies* 8.2 (1977): 202-7. Print.

King, Malcolm. 'Sold on a creative impulse.' *The Australian* 21 October 2009: 27. Print.

King, Richard. 'Written revolutions.' *The Australian Literary Review* August 2011: 17. Print.

Kirkpatrick, Peter. 'The strange death of Australian literature.' *Australian Author* 4 (2007): 20-3. Print.

Kohler, Alan. 'Kohler: On why Cunningham quit *Meanjin*: Online strategy.' Media Diary, *The Australian*, 9 November 2010: n. pag. Web. Accessed 23 May 2011. <http://blogs.theaustralian.news.com.au/mediadiary>

Krauth, Nigel. 'Editor's statements.' *The contemporary Australian short story*. Spec. issue of *Australian Literary Studies* 10.2 (1981): 259-60. Print.

———. Interview with the author, 10 May 2011.

Kropotkin, Peter. *Mutual aid: A factor of evolution*. London: Heinemann, 1915. Print.

Laurenson, Diana. 'The writer in the present century.' *The sociology of literature*. Ed. Diana Laurenson and Alan Swingewood. London: Paladin, 1972. 140-69. Print.

Laird, Benjamin. 'Australian literary journals: Virtual and social.' *Cordite Poetry Review* 1 December 2011: n. pag. Web. Accessed 4 December 2011. <http:/cordite.org.au/features/australian-literary-journals-virtual-and-social>

———. 'CEOS, authors and white collar work.' *Overland* 206 (2012): 78-83. Print.

Lee, Jenny, Philip Mead, and Gerald Murnane, eds. *The temperament of generations: Fifty years of* Meanjin. Carlton: Melbourne University Press, 1990. Print.

Lindsay, Elaine, ed. *Literary magazine editors' seminar*. 22-24 February 1978, Department of Continuing Education, University of Adelaide. Adelaide: The Literature Board of the Australia Council. Print.

Linnell, Ken. 'Dresden to Doomsday, with humour but scant hope ... ' *The Melbourne Times* 14 September 1983: 9. Print.

Lysenko, Myron. 'The formative years.' *Going down swinging: The blue corner.* Posted 11 June 2012: n. pag. Web. Accessed 14 June 2012. <http://goingdownswinging.org.au/site/author/the-blue-corner>

McGann, Jerome. *The romantic ideology: A critical investigation.* Chicago: Chicago University Press, 1983. Print.

McKernan, Susan. 'The question of literary independence: *Quadrant* and Australian writing.' *Outside the book: Contemporary essays on literary periodicals.* Ed. David Carter. Sydney: Local Consumption Publications, 1991. 165-76. Print.

McLaren, John. *Writing in hope and fear.* Melbourne: Cambridge University Press, 1996. Print.

McMahon, Elizabeth. 'Editorial.' *Southerly* 69.2 (2009): 1-14. Print.

McPhee, Hilary. 'Timid minds.' *Meanjin* 69.4 (2010): 56-62. Print.

McQueen, Humphrey. *Australia's media monopolies.* Camberwell: Widescope International, 1978. Print.

Martin, Sam. 'Publish or perish? Re-Imagining the university press.' *M/C Journal* 13.1 (2010): n. pag. Web. Accessed 27 February 2011. <http://journal.media-culture.org.au>

Marx, Karl. *Capital, Volume 1: A critique of political economy.* Trans. Ben Fowkes. London: Penguin, 1992. Print.

Miller, Toby. 'Worldwide jitters over publishing.' *The Australian* 4 May 2011: 40. Print.

Modjeska, Drusilla. 'Our future thinkers: The search for the next generation of public intellectuals.' *The Monthly* July 2006: 43-5. Print.

Moorhouse, Frank. *The Americans, baby.* Sydney: Angus and Robertson, 1972. Print.

——. *Days of wine and rage.* Ringwood: Penguin, 1980. Print.

——. *Futility and other animals.* Sydney: Gareth Powell Associates, 1969. Print.

——. 'What happened to the short story.' *New writing in Australia.* Spec.

issue of *Australian Literary Studies* 8.2 (1977): 179-82. Print.

Murray-Smith, Stephen. 'Editor's statements.' *The Contemporary Australian short story.* Spec. issue of *Australian Literary Studies* 10.2 (1981): 266-7. Print.

——. '*Overland* is twenty-one: Interview with Phillip Edmonds.' *Australasian Small Press Review* 4 (1976): 1-6. Print.

Mycak, Sonia. 'Case-study: Multicultural literature.' *Paper empires: A history of the book in Australia 1946-2005.* Ed. Craig Munro and Robyn Sheahan-Bright. St Lucia: University of Queensland Press, 2006. 268-78. Print.

Neill, Rosemary. 'Lost for words.' *Review, The Weekend Australian* 2-3 December 2006: 4-6. Print.

——. 'Paging all authors.' *Review, The Weekend Australian* 13-14 August 2011: 5-7. Print.

Nelson, Anitra, and Frans Timmerman. 'Non-market socialism today.' *Overland* 207 (2012): 76-81. Print.

Nile, Richard. *The making of the Australian literary imagination.* St Lucia: University of Queensland Press, 2002. Print.

Ommundsen, Wenche, and Michael Jacklin. *Mapping literary infrastructure of Australia: A report to the Australia Council for the Arts' Literature Board.* July 2008: 1-155. Web. Accessed 18 August 2011. <http://ro.uow.edu.au>

van Onselen, Peter. 'Secure grants or you're likely to publish and perish.' *The Australian* 14 September 2011: 24. Print.

Paine, Ryan. 'The interview: Ronnie Scott.' *Wet Ink* 21 (2010): 25-31. Print.

Phillips, AA *The Australian tradition: Studies in a colonial culture.* Melbourne: Cheshire-Lansdowne, 1958. Print.

——. 'The cultural cringe.' *Meanjin* 4 (1950): 299-302. Print.

Pierce, Peter. 'Little magazines in the 1970s.' *Cross currents: Magazines and newspapers in Australian literature.* Ed. Bruce Bennett. Melbourne: Longman Cheshire, 1981. 219-26. Print.

Place, Belle. 'The words we found.' *The Blackmail.* December 2011: n. pag. Web. Accessed 19 June 2012. <www.theblackmail.com.au>

'*Quadrant's* 50th anniversary.' *Counterpoint.* Australian Broadcasting

Corporation. ABC Radio National, Sydney. 18 September 2006. Radio transcript.

Reid, Ian. *Fiction and the Great Depression: Australia and New Zealand, 1930-1950*. Melbourne: Edward Arnold, 1979. Print.

Romei, Stephen. 'A pair of ragged claws.' *Review, The Weekend Australian* 15-16 October 2011: 27. Print.

Rowbotham, Jill. 'Carr bows to rank rebellion.' *The Australian* 1 June 2011: 25. Print.

———. 'Journal rankings a sword over unis.' *The Australian* 2 March 2011: 37. Print.

Ruthven, Ken. 'The an-ethical imperitive.' *Wet Ink* 3 (2006): 31-3. Print.

Sanders, Zora. '*Meanjin* to make all content free on-line.' *Books + Publishing* 16 August 2011: n. pag. Web. Accessed 18 August 2011. <www.booksellerandpublisher.com.au>

Sayers, Stuart. 'A home for a quarterly.' *The Age* 24 May 1986: 15. Print.

———. 'Stories in search of readers.' *The Age* 18 December 1982: 14. Print.

Shapcott, Thomas. *The Literature Board: A brief history*. St Lucia: University of Queensland Press, 1988. Print.

———. 'Poetry — Mainly Melbourne.' *Overland* 60 (1975): 77-80. Print.

Sheehan-Bright, Robyn. 'Case-study — Writers centres.' *Paper empires: A history of the book in Australia*. Ed. Craig Munro and Robyn Sheahan-Bright. St Lucia: University of Queensland Press, 2006. 146-50. Print.

Shergold, Peter. 'Seen but not heard.' *The Australian Literary Review* 4 May 2011: 3-4. Print.

Simons, Margaret. 'What are freelancers paid?' *Crikey: The wrap* 8 February 2010: n. pag. Web. Accessed 23 February 2010. <http://blogs.crikey.com.au/contentmakers>

Sornig, David. 'The demise of *Wet Ink* and the future of short fiction.' *Island* 131 (2012): 34-7. Print.

Soutphommasane, Tim. 'Visionary of the big picture: Ask the philosopher.' *The Weekend Australian* 9-10 July 2011: 26 Print.

Sparrow, Jeff. Interview with the author. 21 March 2011.

Speedy, Blair, and Stephen Romei. 'Dark chapter for booksellers.' *The Australian* 18 February 2011: 3. Print.

Steed, Laurie. 'Ever decreasing circles: *Overland* and the modern submissions model.' *Kill Your Darlings* 23 February 2012: n. pag. Web. Accessed 24 February 2012. <http://www.killyourdarlingsjournal.com>

Stephens, Julie. *Anti-disciplinary protest: 60s radicalism and postmodernism.* Melbourne: Cambridge University Press, 1997. Print.

Strahan, Lynne. *Just city and the mirrors: Meanjin Quarterly and the intellectual front, 1940-1965.* Melbourne: Oxford University Press, 1984. Print.

Sullivan, Jane. 'The battle for *Meanjin*.' *Weekend Review, The Age* 27 November 2010: 20-1. Print.

——. 'Bright spots in the publishing gloom.' *Weekend Review, The Age* 24 March 2007: 30. Print.

Syson, Ian. 'Editing *Overland*.' Report to the O.L. Society, Footscray, 2003. Unpublished paper. Print.

——. Letter to the author. 27 May 2011.

'Tasmanian government cuts all funding for *Island* magazine.' *Bookseller & Publisher Online.* August 2011: n. pag. Web. Accessed 2 September 2011. <www.booksellerand publisher.com.au/articles>

Tipping, Richard, and Rob Tillett. 'Mok.' *New writing in Australia.* Spec. issue of *Australian Literary Studies* 8.2 (1977): 208-9. Print.

Toy, Mary Anne. '*Quadrant* cites political bias for $15,000 funding cut.' *The Sydney Morning Herald* 22 December 2009: 5. Print.

Tregenza, John. *Australian little magazines (1923-1934).* Adelaide: Libraries Board of South Australia, 1964. Print.

Tranter, John. 'The elephant has left the room: *Jacket* magazine and the internet.' *Journal of the Association for the Study of Australian Literature* [Online] 12.1 (28 June 2012): n. pag. Web. Accessed 5 September 2012. <http://www.nla.gov.au/openpublish/index.php>

——. 'Growing old gracefully: The generation of '68.' *The temperament of generations: Fifty years of writing in Meanjin.* Ed. Jenny Lee, Philip Mead and Gerald Murnane. Carlton: Melbourne University Press, 1990.

268-78. Print.

———. 'Poems from the heart of the favoured few: Review of "The *Quadrant* Book of Poetry 2000-2010".' Review, *The Weekend Australian* 13-14 October 2012: 27. Print.

University of Adelaide, Department of Adult Education and Unesco Seminar for Literary Magazine Editors. *Australian literary magazines in the 1970s : Report on the Unesco Seminar for literary magazine editors, Writers' Week — Adelaide, 4th-5th March, 1976*. Print.

Wakeling, Corey. 'Pam Brown's Sydney poetry in the 70s: In conversation with Corey Wakeling.' *Cordite Poetry Review* 1 May 2012: n. pag. Web. Accessed 5 May 2012. <http://cordite.org.au>

Ward, Peter. 'An open letter to Rob Tillett.' *Mok* 5 (1969): 3. Print.

Webster, Michael. 'Into the global era.' *Paper empires: A history of the book in Australia, 1946-2005*. Ed. Craig Munro and Robyn Sheahan-Bright. St Lucia: University of Queensland Press, 2006. 81-5. Print.

Wilding, Michael. 'Australian literary studies and Laurie Hergenhan.' *Overland* 168 (2002): 75-6. Print.

———. 'History of scholarly journals writ large.' *The Australian* 20 November 2013: 33. Print.

———. Letter to the author. 24 September 2011.

———. 'A random house: The parlous state of Australian publishing.' *Meanjin*, 34.1 (1975): 106-11. Print.

———. 'A survey.' *New writing in Australia*. Spec. issue of *Australian Literary Studies* 8.2 (1977): 115-26. Print.

———. 'The *Tabloid Story* story.' *The Tabloid Story pocket book*. Sydney, Wild & Woolley, 1978. Print.

———. *Wild & Woolley: A publishing memoir*. Artarmon: Giramondo, 2011. Print.

Williams, Raymond. *Marxism and literature*. Oxford: Oxford University Press, 1977. Print.

Williamson, Geordie. 'Journal of accord.' Review, *The Weekend Australian* 19-20 February 2011: 20. Print.

——. 'Kindling for postmodern pagans.' *The Australian Literary Review* 2 March 2011: 8-10. Print.

——. '*Meanjin*'s place in the local web of life.' *Review, The Weekend Australian* 11-12 June 2011: 20. Print.

——. 'Worth their weight: The future of Australia's "little magazines" is no small matter.' *Review, The Weekend Australian* 18-19 December 2010: 18. Print.

Windschuttle, Keith. *Unemployment: A social and political analysis of the economic crisis in Australia*. Ringwood: Penguin, 1979. Print.

Wright, Fiona. 'Readers' feast.' *Overland* 203 (2011): 87-92. Print.

Young, Sherman. 'It's not the reader.' *Meanjin* 69.2 (2010): 19. Print.

Zizek, Slavoj. 'Marriage between democracy and capitalism is over.' *Raw Story* 10 October 2011: n. pag. Web. Accessed 2 June 2012. <http://www.rawstory.com>

——. *In defence of lost causes*. London and New York: Verso, 2008. Print.

This book is available as a free fully-searchable ebook from
www.adelaide.edu.au/press

www.ingramcontent.com/pod-product-compliance
Lightning Source LLC
Chambersburg PA
CBHW080023110526
44587CB00021BA/3828